The Bathers

SPONSORED BY

John Leighton
Richard Thomson

WITH
David Bomford
Jo Kirby
Ashok Roy

Seurat and The Bathers

NATIONAL GALLERY PUBLICATIONS,
LONDON

DISTRIBUTED BY
YALE UNIVERSITY PRESS

This book was published to accompany an exhibition at:

THE NATIONAL GALLERY, LONDON
2 July–28 September 1997

© NATIONAL GALLERY PUBLICATIONS LIMITED 1997

First published in Great Britain in 1997 by
NATIONAL GALLERY PUBLICATIONS LIMITED
5/6 Pall Mall East, London SW1Y 5BA

ISBN 1 85709 175 2 hardback
525229

ISBN 1 85709 174 4 paperback
525228

British Library Cataloguing-in-Publication Data.
A catalogue record is available from the British Library.
Library of Congress Catalog Card Number: 97-67662

Editors
Felicity Luard and Celia Jones

Art Director
Andrew Gossett

Design and typesetting in Walbaum
Studio Gossett, London

Printed and bound in Great Britain by
Butler and Tanner, Frome and London

Cover illustration and frontispiece:
Georges-Pierre Seurat, *Bathers at Asnières* (Plate 178)

Acknowledgements

*The authors would like to express their thanks for their advice
and assistance to Marie-Madeleine Aubrun, Julian Barran,
Timothy Bathurst, Heinz Berggruen, Olivier Berggruen,
Michael Bliss, Peter Bower, Helen Braham, Christian Briend,
Françoise Cachin, Dennis Cate, Simon Chase, Michael Clarke,
David Daniels, Pascal Deroche, Ingmre Desaix, John Dick,
Barbara Divver, Douglas Druick, Robert Emery, Inge Fiedler,
Robert Bruce Gardiner, George Goldner, Anthony Griffiths,
Michael Hall, Vivien Hamilton, Robert L. Herbert, Sarah
Herring, Ragnar von Holten, Richard Kendall, the late Mary
Jane Kirk, Aidan Weston Lewis, Henri Loyrette, Suzanne
McCullagh, Véronique Moreau, Joachim Pissarro, Aimée Brown
Price, Rebecca Rabinow, Theodore Reff, William Robinson,
Joe Rock, Cora Rosevear, David Scrase, Paul Smith, Susan
Alyson Stein, Harriet Stratis, Gary Tinterow, Belinda Thomson,
Kirk Varnedoe, Jean-Claude Virmaux, Roger Ward.*

*Richard Thomson would like to express his gratitude to the
Leverhulme Trust for the Research Fellowship, 1995–6,
during which his contribution was written.*

Contents

Sponsor's Preface

It gives me considerable pleasure both as Chairman of Pearson and of the Trustees of the Tate Gallery to be associated with the exhibition 'Seurat and The Bathers'. Under Neil MacGregor's leadership, the National Gallery has become one of the supreme institutions in the visual arts world. This exhibition is yet another example of the series of imaginative and beautiful exhibitions that he and his colleagues have created. On this occasion they have been assisted, I am glad to say, by the recently agreed exchange of loans between the Tate and the National Gallery, as well as by the exceptional generosity of Heinz Berggruen through his recent gift of Seurat oil sketches to the nation.

Pearson believes in backing excellence in its sponsorship as much as in promoting it in our business. We have every intention of using this sponsorship to the advantage of our customers and our shareholders. However, we very much hope and believe that the exhibition will bring the same enjoyment and excitement to its many thousands of visitors, both British and non-British, as it does to us.

DENNIS STEVENSON, CBE
CHAIRMAN
PEARSON PLC

Foreword

The passage of time has a mellowing effect on most works of art. Since its purchase in 1924 and during its years of exposure at the Tate Gallery and, since 1961, at the National Gallery, Seurat's *Bathers at Asnières* has become one of the most famous and familiar images in Western Art. A monumental canvas, it magisterially dominates the room where it hangs, attracting the attention of visitors of all ages and nationalities. It breathes a sense of order and serenity, bringing to an everyday subject an aura of timeless beauty. Yet we know that it has not always been so. For reasons that can only be guessed at, the Jury of the 1884 Paris Salon refused to accept it, and when it was shown later that year with the Groupe des Artistes Indépendants it was relegated to the beer hall. Those who noticed it at all were clearly not sure what to make of it. Paul Alexis, naturalist writer and friend of Zola and Cézanne, wrote: 'it's a fake Puvis de Chavannes. What funny bathing men and women! But it's so committed that it's almost touching and I don't dare joke any more.'

The *Bathers* was Seurat's first large-scale canvas, painted when he was only twenty-four. In it he announces his concern with the ordering of elements in a composition, and with the rigorous application of colour and brushwork which were to preoccupy him during the remainder of his short career and which he was soon to develop along much more radical lines. The critics were baffled because they had not seen modern art like it before. For us to begin to understand how they felt and why the picture seemed so strange to them, we have to see it in the context of the artistic currents of the late nineteenth century when artists of all persuasions were looking for new ways to represent the modern, and when the idea of a single orthodoxy had all but vanished. By bringing together so many of Seurat's early paintings and drawings – including virtually all the preparatory studies for the *Bathers* – and examples of the work of artists who influenced or worked alongside Seurat, the organisers of this exhibition, John Leighton and Richard Thomson, help us to recapture some of the 'shock of the new' that Seurat's contemporaries must have felt in front of the picture. They suggest levels of complexity and meaning which inevitably escape us today and which can but deepen our enjoyment of this great painting.

Such an enterprise would have been impossible without the willing co-operation of the many lenders who have so generously given up their works so that they could be included in the show. We are indebted to them and also to the sponsor of the exhibition, Pearson plc, who have offered not only much needed financial support but also unstinting enthusiasm and encouragement. This is Pearson's fourteenth exhibition sponsorship, but their first with the National Gallery, and we are grateful to them for such enlightened support.

NEIL MACGREGOR
DIRECTOR

Introduction

Our book, like the exhibition it accompanies, is about a single painting, Georges Seurat's *Bathers at Asnières*. This large canvas was Seurat's masterpiece, in the precise sense of the word; it was the work he intended to demonstrate his mastery of the craft of picture-making and the independence of his voice as an artist. In 1884, when the twenty-four-year-old painter exhibited his canvas as *Une baignade (Asnières)*, both his abilities and creative identity were called into question. Forty years later the painting, owned by Seurat's family after his early death in 1891 and then by his supporter, the critic Félix Fénéon, was purchased for the British national collections using the Courtauld Fund.[1] In 1924 it entered the Tate Gallery, and since 1961 its magisterial presence and radiant calm have reigned over other late nineteenth-century pictures in the National Gallery. That dominant identity on the final walls of such a treasury of Western pictorial culture, in which it seems to stand as an emblem of both finality and continuity, has given Seurat's painting a status in the history of art and the appreciation of millions that he could never have anticipated.

In this volume that single painting is explored from various directions. All the writers are concerned with different aspects of the *Bathers'* history, and the starting-point is always the painting itself. The *Bathers* was a key work in Seurat's career. It was a beginning, and art historians enjoy beginnings because they allow us both to trace the past – to guage the weight of influence, to measure the force of tradition – and to plot the future – to project development, to estimate significance – both with our advantage of hindsight.

One of the objectives is to give close attention to how Seurat made the *Bathers*. It is important to reckon the effect that his training in the conservative and academic climate of the Ecole des Beaux-Arts in Paris had upon his artistic practice and temperament. To understand his masterpiece we need to pull together various aspects of Seurat's creative identity. Among these are the ways in which his imagination and vision had been framed by the aesthetic values in which he had been trained, and also the very business of his craft: how he drew and painted, mixed colours and set them down on canvas. This raises interesting points. There is a persistent myth – which dates back to critics in Seurat's lifetime who found his paintings difficult to understand – that as an artist he was something of an automaton, one who proceeded by theory and pre-planned practice to produce work that is intellectual and lacking in both sensuality and spontaneity. Inadvertently Seurat contributed to this myth, telling his friend the fellow-painter Charles Angrand, 'People see poetry in what I do. No, I apply my method and that's all.'[2] But this is a remark that might better be interpreted as an expression of confidence in his own powers as a painter to conjure up his chosen effects of luminosity and atmosphere without recourse to contrivance or sentiment. The spectator's response to his works did not necessarily trouble Seurat, who believed that his own efforts in the making made the work all it needed to be. Those efforts were often considerable, as detailed analysis of the *Bathers* proves, and involved rigour and rethinking in the conception and the execution of his work. By looking very closely at how Seurat planned the *Bathers*, how and where and in which order he made his oil sketches, by questioning the functions of his drawings, by scrupulously determining the material structure of his masterpiece, we can see that the *Bathers* was not painted by an automaton. It was the work of a young artist who changed his mind, made mistakes, covered his tracks, made sacrifices – all in the course of producing a picture that has an independence and grandeur which mesmerises us today as much as it troubled his contemporaries. Just as the recently discovered evidence that Seurat's contemporary Van Gogh prepared his chromatic harmonies with balls of coloured wool dismisses the fiction that his work is simply spontaneous expressiveness, so our analysis of the *Bathers'* 'making' reveals an artist of doubt and confidence, control and verve.

This analysis of Seurat's methods is complemented by a more conceptual and contextual approach to the *Bathers*. The young Seurat was educated as an artist under a particular discipline, a particular aesthetic. At the Ecole des Beaux-Arts he would have been trained to value the classical tradition, in which ordered forms convey lucid ideas, and to submit the sensuality of colour to the discipline of drawing. To what extent did these notions mark Seurat, and how much, and by what means? Did he react against them, or mould them with other possibilities to suit his own purposes? For the *Bathers* was in many senses a melting pot in which the constituents of Seurat the artist – his own taciturn temperament, his training, his search for order, his willingness to experiment, his eye for the modern – were mixed to achieve a concrete and ambitious result. What is presented in considerable detail here is not only the trajectory of the young Seurat but also the choices that were open to him as he matured as an artist. These form the warp and the weft of *Seurat and The Bathers*. On the one hand the progress of his work, and the ideas which informed it, are traced from his period as an art student to the *Bathers* and beyond. On the other, we investigate the work his contemporaries were doing, the ways they painted and the subjects they adopted. In this way we can come to terms with the possibilities that were available to this young painter, what he knew, what he admired, what he rejected, what he had to measure his work against. This means setting Seurat's work against his Impressionist contemporaries, whose art is well known to us today but in the early 1880s was still treated with suspicion or disdain. It also necessitates comparison with artists less familiar now but in Seurat's day figures whose examples a young painter had to gauge, and might emulate: Puvis de Chavannes, for instance, or Cazin. Only by making the effort to recreate what Seurat opted not to do, as well as understanding what he did, and the context in which he made those choices, do we come closer to the complex character of the *Bathers*.

Finally, the book places the *Bathers* in the wider context. There are, for example, continuities in Seurat's career that require consideration. The *Bathers* grew out of the drawings and oil sketches Seurat had made in the Parisian suburbs, but his interest in such motifs did not stop there. His next major canvas, *A Sunday on the Grande Jatte (1884)*, also took a suburban subject, and with these two major independent paintings Seurat set examples to which other young painters in the 1880s felt the need to respond. There are consistencies too, above all Seurat's almost instinctive feel for the classical and ordered. Instilled during his training, that characteristic is to the fore in the *Bathers*. His masterpiece was to some extent shaped by his admiration for a specific painting by Poussin that he would have known from the Louvre, and his classicism endured after 1884, resurfacing several years later in the *Models*, executed at the height of his avant-garde reputation.

The *Bathers* is a painting of great resonance: in the galleries of Trafalgar Square, in the history of art and the history of taste. Although the work of a young artist, it holds its own in distinguished company because – painted by an admirer of classical sculpture, Poussin and Ingres – it is an extension of tradition. Yet with hindsight we know that the *Bathers* stands at the beginnings of a challenge to that tradition. Seurat's later paintings were much more radically experimental, even more than many in the avant garde of the 1880s could easily tolerate. His work was greatly admired by later avant gardes,

and we know that at the height of his Cubist experimentation Georges Braque had a reproduction of Seurat's *Chahut* pinned to his studio wall. The appearance of the *Bathers* in the Tate Gallery in 1924 must have had a considerable impact on British painters of the mid-war years, and we find its echoes in the frozen realism of Meredith Frampton and the serene balance of Ben Nicholson's abstract reliefs. Part of the fascination of the *Bathers* is that it holds in delicate balance Seurat the traditionalist and Seurat the innovator. Well does the painting deserve to preside, with Cézanne's *Bathers*, over the last rooms in the National Gallery.

1. London 1994, p. 14.
2. Coquiot 1924, p. 41.

Works illustrated are by Georges-Pierre Seurat unless otherwise stated.

A fold-out illustration of Bathers at Asnières *is opposite p. 168.*

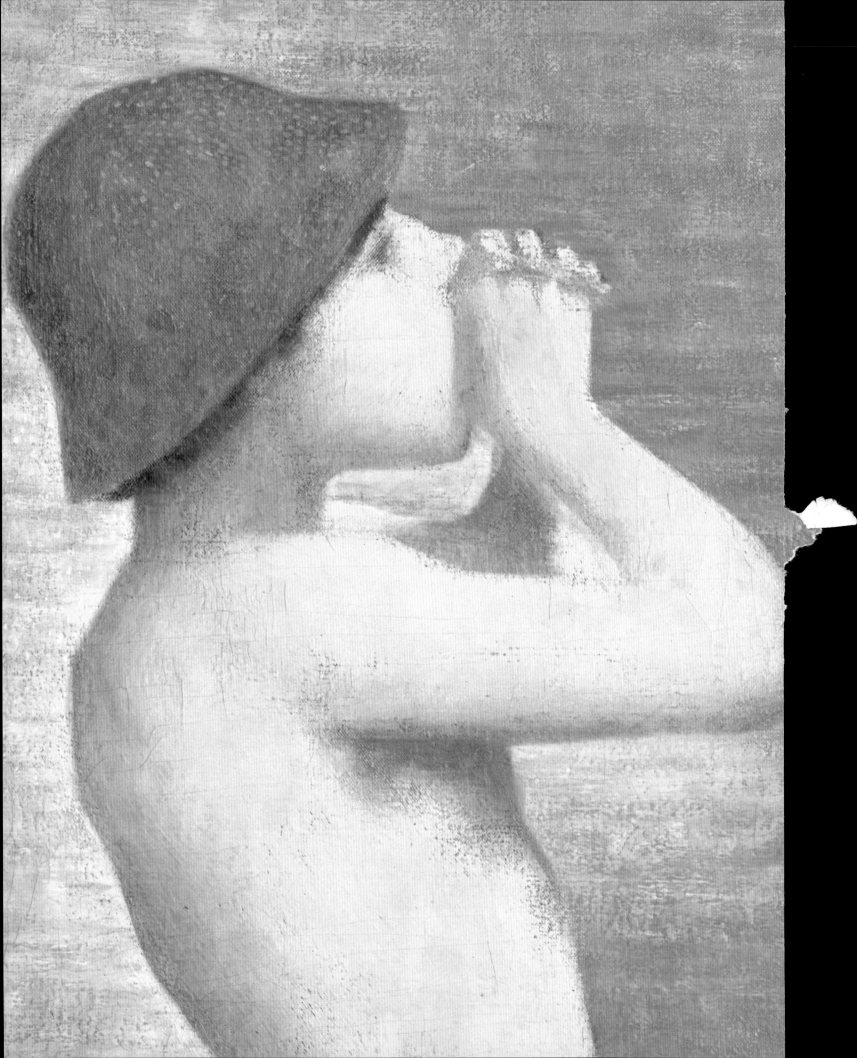

1 Seurat: The Early Years

When the *Bathers* is set against the background of Seurat's early career it seems like an astonishing debut. With its conspicuously modern subject rendered in luminous and insistent colours this vast canvas seems calculated to draw attention to its maker. The *Bathers* may not have been widely noticed when it was first shown in 1884 but, as one of Seurat's early biographers noted, 'the effort was huge'.[1] The numerous drawings and oil studies that relate directly to the painting testify to this 'effort' as he plotted the composition of his first major work. But the *Bathers* was more than the result of a single summer campaign of sketching on the banks of the Seine and a winter of labour in the studio. It stands at the end of several years of intense study and research as a picture which, in effect, announced the completion of his training. In this sense the *Bathers* may be viewed as Seurat's 'masterpiece', a public demonstration of skill and accomplishment and a declaration of artistic emancipation.

Seurat's education as an artist was unusual. It included not only the relatively brief period that he spent within the academic system but also the years leading up to the *Bathers*, when he followed what might be described as his own course of self-directed study in collaboration with other former students. The drawings and paintings that date from this period in the early 1880s reveal Seurat's attempts to master new techniques and chart his emergence as a robust and singular artistic personality. There is evidence of his openness to a wide range of stimuli, including literature and scientific theory as well as the work of artists past and present. We find an artist who is alert to his surroundings in modern Paris but also deeply sensitive to tradition. There may be signs of rebellion against accepted conventions in his early work but, as Robert Herbert has described it, this was the revolt of 'an intelligent and ambitious young artist eager to assert himself . . .'[2]

The scant biographical details that we have of Seurat's early years offer few signs of rebellion or melodrama. He faced neither parental opposition nor hardship, but instead enjoyed the financial backing of his wealthy middle-class family who allowed him to pursue his independent researches regardless of any need to sell his work or to seek commissions. Seurat's father was a self-made man who had acquired his wealth first through his activities as a bailiff and then through speculation in property. The behaviour of Seurat *père* might have betrayed certain endearing eccentricities but he seems to have been a remote and dispassionate character.[3] Seurat was probably closer

1. *Woman reading, c.*1883
Conté crayon on paper, 30.7 x 23.3 cm
Private Collection, California (CAT. 28)

to his mother and, even after he had left the family home, he returned to dine with her on most evenings. Yet the homely figure who appears in several of the artist's drawings (Plate 1) is also said to have been strict and demure. The young artist seems to have inherited this middle-class reserve. Most descriptions of him record a bourgeois respectability and formality in combination with an inscrutable character. According to Signac, he was 'very discreet, very reserved. He "hid" his life.'[4] Gustave Kahn recalled that Seurat remained silent in a crowd, but, 'among a few close friends he would talk at length about his art, its aims and methods'.[5]

From 1862 the Seurat family occupied a large apartment on the Boulevard Magenta in the tenth *arrondissement* of Paris. Seurat began his formal artistic training nearby when, in 1876, he enrolled at the municipal drawing school run by the sculptor Justin Lequien *fils*. The teaching at this school was intended primarily for apprentices in the industrial arts. Students were encouraged to draw using soft media such as chalk and charcoal on rough-textured paper and, with a view to adapting their work to the applied arts, they were taught to simplify and schematise forms rather than to accumulate detail.[6]

Seurat had already acquired considerable experience as a draughtsman before he entered the Ecole des Beaux-Arts. He took the entrance examinations for the Ecole in February 1878 and shortly afterwards enrolled in the studio of Henri Lehmann. This German-born artist was one of Ingres's most loyal pupils and he had a reputation as a strict disciplinarian. According to Seurat's fellow student Aman-Jean, Lehmann was one of Ingres's 'pawns' who 'never said anything that opened up a vista or gave young people a leg up'.[7] For Seurat, however, this immersion in the academic programme was an extension of the training that he had already received under Lequien. He made copies from plaster casts of antique sculpture (Plate 2), worked from the life model (Plate 3) and made drawings after a range of revered artists from Holbein to Poussin. His drawings are accomplished and, although his placings in the competitions at the Ecole were far from spectacular, he appears to have been a reasonably diligent student.

In November 1879 Seurat had to leave Paris for his military service based in Brest in Brittany. When he was discharged a year later he did not return to the Ecole des Beaux-Arts. This break in what was to date a conventional academic career is usually seen as an act of defiance, but we can only guess at Seurat's motives for striking out on his own. It is likely that he had already heard siren voices calling from outside the confines of the Academy. According to Aman-Jean, Ingres was Seurat's idol during this period, but he had probably begun to take note of other major artists such as Delacroix and Millet.[8] He may also have had his first encounters with more recent, innovative trends. One report has Seurat and his friends from

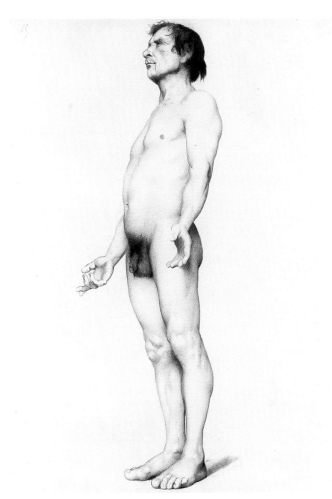

2. *Warrior with a Helmet: Copy after the Borghese 'Ares'*,
*c.*1877–8. Conté crayon on paper, 64.5 x 49.0 cm
Collection of Margo and Irwin Winkler (CAT. 62)

3. *Standing Man, Hands Outstretched, c.*1877–8
Charcoal on paper, 73.7 x 48.3 cm
New York, Private Collection (CAT. 63)

the Ecole des Beaux-Arts visiting the fourth Impressionist
Exhibition in 1879 where they received an 'unexpected and
profound shock'.[9] The sketches that Seurat made while on
military service in Brest may have confirmed his interest in
an art based on everyday life rather than on the imitation of
classical exemplars. Most of all, however, Seurat probably felt
that the Ecole des Beaux-Arts had nothing more to offer him.
To the poet Emile Verhaeren he described his period under
Lehmann's tutelage as, 'a whole chapter of efforts trapped by
routine and dreary practices'.[10] With his private means Seurat
did not need to compete for academic honours and, having
acquired the basic skills of draughtsmanship, he was ready to
find his own way.

4. Ernest-Joseph Laurent,
Georges Seurat: Study for 'Scene at the Brook', 1883
Black chalk on paper, 39 x 29 cm
Paris, Musée du Louvre (CAT. 38)

The period between his return from Brest and the exhibition of the *Bathers* in 1884 was a productive one for Seurat. However, besides the evidence provided by his work, we have relatively few details of the young artist's daily life. His friendships and the pattern of his work suggest a degree of continuity with his days of formal studentship. After his military service, he continued to share a studio with Aman-Jean in the rue de l'Arbalète, an area of the fifth *arrondissement* inhabited by workers, students and artists. From 1882, he rented a small studio in the rue Chabrol close to his family's home, where shortly afterwards he would paint the *Bathers*. He remained in contact with other friends from his days at the Ecole des Beaux-Arts, including Alphonse Osbert, Alexandre Séon and Ernest Laurent, who drew Seurat's likeness for inclusion in one of his compositions (Plate 4).

The winters were probably dominated by work in the studio while the months of better weather would have been punctuated by frequent trips to the suburbs and to the villages that lay beyond the city boundaries. This pattern of work would have been familiar to Seurat from his days at the Ecole des Beaux-Arts, where masters often encouraged their students to go on sketching expeditions. Seurat visited some familiar artistic haunts such as the Auberge Ganne in Barbizon, once a meeting place for the avant garde, but by the 1880s overrun by students from the academic ateliers.[11] There were some suburban areas of Paris that would have been familiar to the artist from an early age. Several members of his family owned property in the suburbs as well as apartments in the city itself. His uncle, Paul Haumonte, had a villa at Chatou and his brother-in-law, Léon Appert had a family home nearby at Croissy-sur-Seine, opposite Bougival, all areas which the Impressionists had frequented in the 1870s (see Plate 129). Seurat's father owned a villa at Le Raincy in north-east Paris and the artist probably made many of his early studies there.[12] Seurat did travel further afield. In 1881 he spent two months in Burgundy with Aman-Jean and several works have been linked to this visit. More tantalising are the indications in a recently discovered notebook of a trip to the north, probably in 1877–8, to the Low Countries and along the Rhine, Seurat's only known journey outside France.[13]

Although Seurat had turned his back on the formal programme of the Ecole, he continued his own programme of research. His earliest biographers describe frequent visits to libraries and to the Louvre. According to the critic Jules Christophe, who wrote a brief biographical sketch in 1890, the young painter 'studied the working methods' of artists in the Louvre, but, above all, he returned with Aman-Jean to the Chapelle des Saint-Anges in Saint-Sulpice, 'where they were mesmerised by the spirited frescoes of Delacroix.'[14] Seurat also studied works in the dealers and salerooms. His detailed notes on several works by Delacroix that were for sale in 1881 provide concrete evidence of what was presumably a habitual practice and confirm that the Romantic master now occupied a central position in the young artist's pantheon.[15]

Towards the end of his life Seurat himself gave a brief account of his preoccupations during the early 1880s in a famous letter to his friend, the critic Félix Fénéon.[16] The original context for this letter is important. In 1890 Fénéon had written an article about Signac in which he referred to the new 'optical painting' but made no mention of Seurat and his role as an innovator. Seurat's letter was intended to set the record straight and, in his characteristic, terse style, he recalled the principal phases of his career. The period 1876–84 is associated with what he described as a search for an 'optical formula'. Seurat then gives an account of his successive interests in various artists and texts, ranging from Charles Blanc, Chevreul and Delacroix through to Monet and Pissarro, sometimes assigning precise dates for his discovery of certain ideas or publications. The letter is of course a bowdlerised account of Seurat's early career since it was written to establish his pre-eminence in an avant-garde movement and to account for the emergence of a new method of painting. Some of the details are unreliable also. In one draft Seurat declares that he abandoned earth colours from 1882 to 1884, a claim that is demonstrably false.[17] Nevertheless it is an extremely valuable document, offering confirmation of his interest in establishing a method that could be supported by his favoured theoretical writings and vindicated by the work of certain revered artists.

It is tempting to impose the text of Seurat's letter to Fénéon like a template upon his early years and to search for evidence of his declared interests so that his career develops in the reasoned, logical manner that the artist appears to describe. Yet there is a risk here in censoring the excitement of the artist's most impressionable years. His consistent use of certain formats and his loyalty to carefully selected materials can also disguise the diversity of his explorations. Ultimately, Seurat's art was governed by feeling and instinct as well as intellect. Aman-Jean, who was probably closest to Seurat during this period, evoked this dual aspect to his friend's artistic temperament when he described him as 'sensible and disciplined' in his youth but also noted that 'instinct and talent dominated his whole being'.[18] The work that Seurat produced before the *Bathers* provides ample evidence of an approach that was studied and methodical yet was also intuitive and experimental. The paintings and drawings that are illustrated below are intended to provide an overview of this experimentation and to introduce the years of careful research that preceded the creation of Seurat's first masterpiece.

1. Christophe 1890.
2. Paris, Grand Palais, 1991, p. 13.
3. For Seurat's father and the Seurat family history see Sutter 1964.
4. Coquiot 1924, p. 30.
5. Kahn 1891, p. 107.
6. For Lequien see Boime 1985, pp. 46, 57, esp. p. 51f.
7. Paris, Grand Palais, 1991, p. 377.
8. Coquiot 1924, p. 29.
9. Rosenthal 1911, p. 66.
10. Verhaeren 1927, p. 198.
11. Seurat visited the Auberge Ganne in 1883 with Aman-Jean; Paris, Grand Palais, 1991, p. 401. For the Auberge Ganne see Gassies 1907.
12. Sutter 1964, p. 5; Zimmermann 1991, p. 75.
13. Paris, Grand Palais, 1991, p. 13; Franz and Growe 1983–4, pp. 54–5, 90.
14. Christophe 1890.
15. Fénéon 1922; the notes are reproduced in Paris, Grand Palais, 1991, pp. 394–6.
16. The letter exists in several versions; see Paris, Grand Palais, 1991, p. 384, where they are discussed in detail.
17. Several works analysed at the National Gallery include earth colours.
18. Coquiot 1924, p. 26.

The Early Drawings

5. *Two Men walking in a Field*, c.1882–4
Conté crayon on paper, 31.8 x 24.3 cm
Baltimore Museum of Art (CAT. 30)

The critic Gustave Kahn described Seurat as, 'a young man crazy about drawing'.[1] The majority of Seurat's drawings were made before he had painted the *Bathers* and this simple fact alone would seem to justify Kahn's remark. Although it seems unlikely that Seurat concentrated exclusively on drawing in the first years after his return from military service (as Kahn and others have suggested), it was clearly a major preoccupation and it is in his compelling works on paper that the singular character of his art first becomes apparent.[2] As Aman-Jean observed, 'It is drawing, thoroughly understood, that put Seurat on the right path'.[3]

Seurat evolved his mature drawing style in a relatively short period. By 1882, and possibly already in the previous year, he was producing the richly toned drawings in conté crayon that Signac would later describe as the 'most beautiful *dessins de peintre* (painter's drawings) in existence' (Plate 5).[4] For an artist trained in the French academic system, which by tradition favoured the purity and refinement of line, Seurat's rapid development of a style based on broad masses of dark and light might seem all the more remarkable. There were, however, many precedents for these tonal drawings in the art of his precursors and contemporaries, some of which are illustrated and discussed below. There was also some continuity between Seurat's student drawings and his independent, more original drawings of the early 1880s. From his days at Lequien's Academy and the Ecole des Beaux-Arts, Seurat would have been used to working in soft media such as charcoal and crayon. Following the reform of the curriculum of the Ecole des Beaux-Arts in 1863, the use of these drawing materials was actively promoted and, while the traditional medium of pencil was associated with a tightly controlled technique, materials such as charcoal and crayon were valued for encouraging a bolder and more spontaneous approach.[5] Many of Seurat's academic studies after the life model and his copies after antique sculpture were executed in charcoal. The contours of drawings like the *Standing Man* (Plate 3) are firm and continuous, with the modelling concentrated at the edges of the forms, but this is a drawing that depends on subtle nuances of tone rather than line to render the intricacies of the male anatomy.

The successive stages in the development of Seurat's drawing technique have been documented in detail in Robert Herbert's definitive studies of the artist and only a few examples of his earliest sheets are illustrated here.[6] Signs of a conscious search for a distinctive style are apparent in the notebook sketches

6. *Woman seated on a Bench*, c.1880–1
Pencil on paper, 16.0 x 10.5 cm
Norwich, University of East Anglia,
Robert and Lisa Sainsbury Collection (CAT. 24)

7. *The Seamstress: A Painting on the Wall*, c.1881–2
Charcoal on paper, 23.1 x 18.1 cm
Manchester, Whitworth Art Gallery (CAT. 25)

that Seurat produced during his military service at Brest.
He made numerous studies, mainly of his companions in the
barracks, but also of other ordinary subjects in the nearby
town. Working on a small scale, often with the rapidity of
caricature, his technique was energetic and reductive.

This artistic shorthand is still apparent in *Woman seated on
a Bench* (Plate 6) of 1880–1 but here, the graphic scribbles that
animated his other notebook jottings have been hardened into
a more deliberate cross-hatching that spreads across the figure
and into the background. Seurat began by defining the basic
shape of the figure with soft, grey tones. He worked over these

initial layers with darker hatchings and terse, dark outlines,
reducing the complex folds of the woman's costume to a series
of simple, fractured planes. Her compact silhouette is linked to
the patterns of light and dark formed by the bench and the
architecture behind her, so that even in this small notebook
drawing we are aware of a carefully calculated design. A
slightly later drawing of a similar subject (Plate 7) is also
composed with care, although the use of charcoal creates a
softer, more atmospheric effect. It is difficult to judge whether
the drawing is unfinished or whether Seurat opted for judicious
understatement, but the subtle shading and the fluid strokes

8. *The Nanny*, c.1882
Conté crayon on paper, 32 x 25 cm
Private Collection (CAT. 29)

different grades of hardness and were available either as sticks of crayon or encased in wood like a pencil. Although the tonal range of conté crayon might seem similar to other black drawing materials, they have their own distinctive qualities. Whereas charcoal, for example, quickly clogs the surface of textured paper with its splintering, fragmentary particles, the conté crayon is easier to control. Broader areas of tone can be created when the tip is blunt, while the end of the crayon may be sharpened for drawing lines.

In the history of drawing in the nineteenth century, the 1870s and 1880s are usually associated with diversity as artists experimented with an increasingly broad range of traditional and modern drawing materials. However, once Seurat had discovered the potential of his dark crayons he remained loyal to them. Most of his drawings are on a good quality hand-made laid paper made by the company Michallet whose watermark is often visible running along the edge of the sheet (Plate 8). He tended to draw on sheets of similar dimensions. The original, deckle-edge of the paper is sometimes visible but many of the sheets seem to have been cut along two edges so it is likely that Seurat bought larger sheets of one of the standard sizes and then cut these into four quarters to create his preferred format.[8] The Michallet paper had a prominent ridged texture. By varying the pressure of his touch he could create a range of subtle nuanced tones. If Seurat pressed hard on the crayon, the texture of the paper would be flattened in areas of dense, dark tone. But when lightly applied, the particles of crayon would adhere only to the raised peaks of the paper's fibres, leaving the hollows untouched (Plate 10). The speckled greys that result are rich and lustrous and seem to resonate with their own internal light.

The *Sleeping Man* (Plate 9), which probably dates from 1881, illustrates some of the range of effects that Seurat could achieve. He first sketched in a light outline of the figure which he then worked over with the blunt tip of the crayon. The contours of the recumbent man were reinforced with firmer strokes of a sharpened crayon point, which was also used to create the network of wiry marks that animates the foreground and background, evoking the texture of a grassy bank. Seurat seems to exploit effects that many other artists might have regarded as incidental. The grain of his paper, for example, with its regular pattern of laid and chain lines provides a gentle yet insistent geometry that re-enforces the stark horizontal of the lying figure. As usual, he filled the entire sheet with his drawing marks, taking care even to work over the ragged edges of his paper.

The angular outlines apparent in the *Sleeping Man* relate back to the chiselled contours of drawings like the *Woman seated on a Bench* (Plate 6) but in later drawings these lines tend to become submerged within the play of light and dark

that gently pull the figure out from the background anticipate his mature style where detail is evoked rather than defined.

The transient qualities of charcoal may have suited such intimate subjects, but it was the conté crayon with its rich, dark tones that became Seurat's favoured drawing medium. Originally developed in the late eighteenth century as a substitute for pure graphite, conté crayons were widely used throughout the nineteenth century. Named after their inventor, Nicolas-Jacques Conté, they consisted of a mixture of clay and graphite with black pigment combined with a slightly waxy binder and compressed into short sticks.[7] They came in

9. *Sleeping Man, c.*1881–2
Conté crayon on paper, 24.0 x 31.5 cm
Berggruen Collection (CAT. 27)

10. Detail of Plate 9

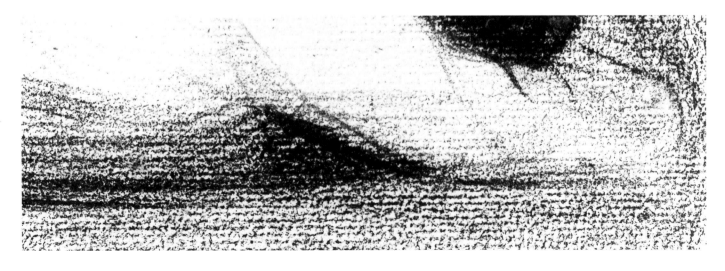

11. *Lying Figure, c.*1883
Black chalk on paper, 31 x 24 cm
Private Collection

12. *Crouching Boy, c.*1882
Conté crayon on paper, 32 x 25 cm
Private Collection (CAT. 26)

across the sheet of paper. A drawing such as *The Nanny*
(Plate 8) shows Seurat's mature style in its most simplified
and elemental form. The patterning of the relationships of
tone is carefully plotted so that the dark edges of the cloak
meet a lighter tone in the background while the white garments
of the child are surrounded by a patch of dark. This pictorial
device, often described as 'irradiation' was sanctioned by several
of the authors that Seurat admired (see below p. 46). Ostensibly,
it was a way of suggesting the illusion of space around solid
objects but, exaggerated by Seurat, it confirms his willingness
to sacrifice naturalism for pictorial effect. Here, the gently
glowing light around the dark shape of the nursemaid's cloak
seems to lend an air of sanctity to the hieratic figure.

Seurat used his tenebrous style to depict a wide range of
subjects. He found much of his material close at hand. From
his surroundings in Paris he drew a whole cast of everyday
characters, from street urchins (Plate 12) to the fashionably
dressed bourgeoisie. In the suburbs and in the countryside he
observed gardeners, rural labourers and stone breakers. He
drew cityscapes and landscapes, sometimes populated but often
empty and even desolate in mood. In his figure studies he
concentrated on the type rather than the individual,
identifying his subjects with a caricaturist's eye for a distinctive
trait, pose or costume; but although these drawings testify to
the young artist's curiosity and to his willingness to engage
with the world around him, they are far removed in spirit

from the journalistic drawings of, say, Daumier or Gavarni. His figures seem serenely detached and even isolated from everyday bustle. Their faces are usually turned away from the spectator or obscured in shadow. Even when he closes in on his subject, as in a drawing which probably depicts his mother (Plate 1), the facial features are hidden in penumbra.

It is difficult to establish whether Seurat made his drawings directly from life or whether he filtered his observations by working from memory or from notes. Robert Herbert has argued convincingly that the subtleties apparent in his drawings can only come from looking and not from recollection.[9] It is true that in a drawing such as *The Nanny* (Plate 8) the carefully judged shifts of tone in the nursemaid's bonnet or the precisely rendered sense of the figure shifting her position to balance the weight of the child suggest close scrutiny and direct observation. Moreover, some of the effects in a modest-sized drawing like this could have been achieved with speed. In parts of the background, for example, the illusion of space and light was created with a single layer of crayon passing in rapid strokes over the rough surface of the paper. Nevertheless, there is a degree of resolution and of completeness in many conté crayon drawings like this one which can only be the result of extensive labour. In combination with broad sweeps of tone there are often repeated layerings of crayon or series of individual marks patiently applied to create dense, velvety darks. There are areas where the paper has been left virtually untouched to stand for highlights and, since conté crayon is difficult to erase, this too suggests a degree of control and planning that seems barely compatible with the spontaneity and directness that is normally associated with drawings made out on the street or in the countryside.

It is possible that many of the figure drawings were worked up from rapid sketches made on the spot. Gustave Coquiot claimed that Seurat made 'constant notes', and he described 'a whole oeuvre that is today lost: little albums that have been dispersed over the years'.[10] Fénéon recorded a mere five notebooks in Seurat's studio inventory and only four other albums have come to light since.[11] But as Coquiot suggested, other notebooks may have been lost or destroyed. Occasionally Seurat made sketches which seem to map out a more developed drawing (Plate 11) and sometimes there are signs of a more spontaneous initial sketch beneath the assured surfaces of a finished sheet. In the end, however, the varying character of Seurat's drawings suggest that his approach was flexible: some may have been drawn entirely from life, others from memory or, most likely, a combination of these approaches. The portrait of Aman-Jean (Plate 20) or the studies of the *Bathers* have a sense of sculptural form and a level of detail that must come from sustained observation, but these were works that could be easily posed in the controlled environment of the studio. By contrast, there are drawings where the forms seem less tangible and where the simplified shapes of figures or architecture dissolve into almost spectral forms. In such pictures it is easier to imagine that Seurat was working from memory. Away from the distractions of the motif he could develop the abstract qualities of his drawing, distilling the essential and the permanent from the diversity of the real world.

The lack of narrative or anecdotal detail and the apparent isolation of the figures in Seurat's drawings have been related to the anonymity of life in a modern city. The 'concealment of the individual' in these works has been described as a reflection of the artist's experience of an industrial metropolis, where, 'human beings remain . . . without reference, as faceless as the factory and suburban landscapes they have created and must inhabit'. [12] Some of his cityscapes are indeed bleak, with views of railway yards, telegraph poles or dark cranes and bridges silhouetted against crepuscular skies. There is, however, a certain affection apparent in these images of the city and its inhabitants. Robert Herbert has drawn parallels between the sentiment of the drawings and the descriptions of Paris and its industrial suburbs that are found in mid-nineteenth century naturalist literature.[13] Works such as the *Locomotive* (Plate 13) could be set alongside numerous passages by the Goncourt brothers, Zola or Huysmans, where trains become giant metal beasts passing through soot-covered landscapes. In *Les Soeurs Vatard* Huysmans describes how an express train thunders by 'in a cloud of steam, pierced by flashes, in a flurry of dust and ash, in a shower of sparks . . . with an appalling roar of rattling iron, of screaming boilers, of moving pistons'.[14] The mood of a drawing depicting a lifting bridge (Plate 14) could be matched by several passages from the novels of the Goncourt brothers, such as this from *René Mauperin* (1864):

> *Above a canal congested with barges, a swing-bridge raised its two black arms into the air. Anglers cast and wound in their lines. Wheels creaked and carts came and went. Haulage ropes grazed the rust-covered towpath – hardened, blackened and stained all sorts of colours by discharged coal, remains of minerals and deposits from various chemicals.*[15]

Seurat's sombre drawings with their encrusted particles of black crayon are a compelling pictorial equivalent for this kind of richly layered prose that evokes both the desolation and the grandeur of the industrial fringes of a modern city. Gustave Kahn said that Seurat always had contemporary novels in his studio.[16] Aman-Jean later recalled that he and Seurat 'read tirelessly' and that 'Goncourt was our god then'. [17]

13. *Locomotive*, c.1882–4
Conté crayon on paper, 24.5 x 31.8 cm
Bern, Collection EWK (CAT. 31)

14. *The Drawbridge*, c.1882–4
Conté crayon on paper, 24.3 x 30.5 cm
New York, The Woodner Collections (CAT. 32)

While literature was an important inspiration for Seurat he also drew on other sources, and in the later 1870s and early 1880s he assembled a folio of prints, reproductions and photographs. The folio has since disappeared, but records of its contents offer some clues to the extent of the young artist's interests.[18] Along with primitive broadsheets and banal prints, extracted from drawing manuals and other sources, the folio contained reproductions of etchings by Rembrandt taken from an 1882 edition of *Le Figaro*. These must have been crude reproductions, but even so the dramatic contrasts of light and shade and the freedom of Rembrandt's graphic style must have been a useful encouragement for Seurat.

Another artist represented in the folio was Jean-François Millet. As an acknowledged master of rural imagery and, more specifically, as an artist associated with tonal drawings, Millet was an important precursor for Seurat. Since his student days, Millet had used conté crayon for drawing, on its own or in combination with other media such as chalk and pastel. He used chalk and crayon for freely handled studies (Plate 15) and to provide the base tones for finished drawings (Plate 16).

In Seurat's youth Millet's drawings were becoming well known. They were reproduced in several publications in the late 1870s and early 1880s and the sale of Emile Gavet's spectacular collection of Millet's pastels which was held in 1875, the year of the artist's death, attracted wide interest. *Watering Horses, Sunset* (Plate 16) is one of the drawings that Millet made for Gavet.[19] The riverside subject immediately strikes a chord with Seurat's oil studies for the *Bathers*, some of which depict horses being watered in the Seine (see Plate 52). Millet returned to this type of subject many times in scenes of washerwomen or animals along the banks of the Seine near Melun, north of Barbizon, but it is the twilight effect with the horses and rider set against the evening sky that offers the most telling comparison with Seurat's work. Millet's landscape is a coloured drawing in which the dark tones of the conté crayon are brightened with pastel to evoke the lurid tints of sunset. Yet in works like this Millet showed how a web of crayon strokes could be spread across the paper surface, defining the forms with sinewy, nervous lines but also creating nebulous shadows that suggest the retreat of daylight. The mood of quiet resignation that permeates this work would surely have appealed to Seurat whose own drawings are often suffused with a gentle melancholy. Both artists were fond of effects of half light. Millet is reported to have said that the dim lights of dawn and dusk had been his 'best teacher'.[20]

Seurat's debt to Millet is conspicuous, yet the drawings of both artists should be seen in the wider context of the increasing popularity of tonal drawing in the second half of the nineteenth century. Many of Millet's contemporaries, including the Barbizon landscapists, made extensive use of

15. Jean-François Millet, *The Tired Haymaker*, c.1850
Black chalk on paper, 27.0 x 20.6 cm
Cambridge, Fitzwilliam Museum (CAT. 34)

black drawing media, exploiting the rich, painterly qualities of charcoal and chalks, as well as crayons. Rubbed, wetted, sponged or scratched, these materials were ideally suited to the textual effects that naturalist and realist artists sought to achieve in drawings of landscapes and other subjects. Developments in technology added to the array of fabricated chalks and crayons that were available for artists' use, while the emergence of a ready market for finished drawings added further impetus to this trend.[21]

16. Jean-François Millet, *Watering Horses, Sunset*, 1866
Pastel and conté crayon on paper, 38.1 x 48.3 cm
Boston, Museum of Fine Arts (CAT. 39)

The 'natural' medium of charcoal enjoyed particular prominence and its merits were discussed and promoted in various pamphlets and manuals. In his 1869 essay on charcoal Maxine Lalanne noted that charcoal could be used to realise a whole range of values 'from the most delicate to the most vigorous tones'.[22] Fantin-Latour was one of many artists to exploit the evocative qualities of the medium in drawings such as his portrait of his sister Natalie (Plate 17).[23] There is no evidence that Seurat could have seen this particular work, but it offers a striking parallel to his handling of charcoal in *The Seamstress* (Plate 7). Both artists manipulate the powdery greys

of the charcoal, rubbing and reworking the shifting material to create various textural effects and using its evanescent quality to convey a tender image of quiet domesticity.

Works by artists specialising in charcoal – the *fusainistes* – appeared in increasing numbers at the Salon exhibitions from the 1860s. This is reflected, for example, in the career of Léon Lhermitte, who was able to establish his reputation largely on the basis of his drawings. From 1864 Lhermitte exhibited his charcoal drawings at the Salon and in 1880 one of these was regarded as sufficiently important to be purchased by the State. At the 1883 Salon (in which Seurat made his debut with

17. Henri Fantin-Latour, *A Woman sewing*
(Mademoiselle Nathalie Fantin-Latour), 1857
Charcoal touched with white chalk on paper, 30.0 x 29.6 cm
Oxford, Ashmolean Museum (CAT. 35)

18. Albert Lebourg, *Reading (Evening)*, c.1879
Black chalk heightened with white on paper, 43.2 x 28.1 cm
London, British Museum (CAT. 36)

19. Léon-Augustin Lhermitte,
Bathers at Mont-Saint-Père, 1884
Charcoal on paper, 30.7 x 47.5 cm
New York, Private Collection (CAT. 37)

his crayon portrait of Aman-Jean, (Plate 20) Lhermitte showed
no less than ten works in charcoal.[24] His accomplished drawing
Bathers at Mont-Saint-Père (Plate 19) – one of his numerous
rustic bathing scenes – was exhibited at a 'black and white'
exhibition at the Louvre in 1885. This was the first of a series
of exhibitions organised as a 'Salon of drawing and engraving'
in imitation of the popular 'black and white' shows held in
London from 1873.[25] The exhibition was successful enough to
warrant the publication of a lavish catalogue and the exercise
was repeated in following years, with Lhermitte serving as a
member of the jury of admissions.

20. *Portrait of Aman-Jean*, 1883
Conté crayon on paper, 62.2 x 47.5 cm
New York, Metropolitan Museum of Art (CAT. 33)

Bathers at Asnières
Georges-Pierre Seurat 1859–1891
Oil (identified) on canvas, 201 x 300 cm
THE NATIONAL GALLERY

intensity to develop his distinctive drawing style. He first showed the result of this labour in public at the Salon in 1883 where he exhibited his portrait of Aman-Jean (Plate 20). This virtuoso piece, which is twice the size of most of his early drawings, was described by a reviewer as, 'an excellent study in light and dark, a meritorious drawing that cannot be the work of a newcomer'.[29] As befits a work conceived for public exhibition, some of the more daring elements of his technique are held in check. The vigorous interwoven lines that animate many of his drawings are condensed into a simple, luminous background which provides a delicate foil for the darker tones in the figure. With layers of crayon Seurat skilfully rendered the tufted hair, wispy beard and pointed features of his friend. The carefully crafted lights and darks are perfectly in tune with the portrayal of artistic concentration. As a portrait it is utterly convincing, yet as an image of quiet determination and introspection it seems to tell us more about Seurat than about his sitter.

1. Kahn 1928, 1971, p. v.
2. Kahn 1891, p. 108.
3. Coquiot 1924, p. 27.
4. Signac 1939, p. 81.
5. Boime 1971, p. 24f., and Boime 1977, p. 13.
6. Herbert 1962; Paris, Grand Palais, 1991; see also Franz and Growe 1983–4.
7. On differing techniques for the manufacture of conté crayons see; Julia de Fontenelle and Poisson 1828, pp. 213–27; Entry for 'crayon' in Larousse, Paris 1869, p. 458; Meder, 1978, p. 105; see also Watrous 1957, pp. 118–22. We are grateful to Harriet K. Stratis for sharing her expertise on this subject (see also n. 20 below).
8. Paper was available in a wide range of standard sizes. Although there was always some variation in the sizes of handmade papers due, for example, to shrinkage during drying, Seurat was probably dividing up sheets of a size known as Royal (480 x 630 mm). We are grateful to Peter Bower for information about Michallet paper.
9. Paris, Grand Palais, 1991, pp. 37, 40ff.
10. Coquiot 1924, p. 136.
11. De Hauke, i, p. xxix; for the other albums see Paris, Grand Palais, 1991, p. 13.
12. Erich Franz in Franz and Growe 1983–4, p. 61.
13. Herbert 1962, pp. 8off.; Paris, Grand Palais, 1991, pp. 33ff.
14. Huysmans 1879, 1880 edn., p. 118.
15. De Goncourt 1864, p. 8; cited also in Zimmermann 1991, pp. 110–11.
16. Kahn 1891 pp. 109–10
17. Coquiot 1924, p. 29.
18. The contents of the Seurat Folio were first noted by Robert Herbert in 1958 and they are listed in Paris, Grand Palais, 1991, pp. 378ff.
19. See Murphy 1984, p. 173.
20. Cartwright 1896, p. 114.
21. See Stratis 1994–5, p. 354f.; Watrous 1975; Jirat-Wasiutyński 1980, pp. 128–35; Jirat-Wasiutyński 1990, pp. 121–4.
22. Lalanne 1869, p. 11.
23. See Paris, Grand Palais, 1983, no. 18, p. 89.
24. See Cleveland 1981, p. 302. The drawing is no. 428 in the catalogue by Le Pelley-Fonteny, *Lhermitte*, Paris 1991, p. 400.
25. See *La Chronique des Arts et de la Curiosité*, 21 March 1885, p. 90, and 13 Feb. 1886, p. 50
26. Coquiot 1924, p. 183.
27. On the drawings of Charles-Albert Lebourg (1849–1928) see Marx, 1903, pp. 455–66 and 1, 1904, pp. 66–82; Bénédite 1923.
28. See Jamot 1911, p. 177. On evening classes at the Academy see Lemaistre 1889.
29. Roger Marx 1883, cited in Paris, Grand Palais, 1991, p. 49.

Paintings and Studies in Oil

Compared to Seurat's rapid maturity as a draughtsman his development as a painter seems more hesitant and less dramatic. Only a handful of paintings, including some copies, may be dated to his years as an art student in the 1870s.[1] He is said to have destroyed some of his earliest efforts in oil but, even so, we may assume that most of his works during these years were directed towards drawing.[2] By tradition the Academy gave precedence to drawing over painting in the training of an artist and when he was a student in Henri Lehmann's atelier Seurat probably received relatively little formal instruction in the skills of oil painting and the secrets of colour.

By contrast, in the years following his return from military service Seurat produced a substantial group of works in oil which testify to a determined effort to learn the material processes of painting. The scale of these works is modest and the subjects are often unassuming, but as a group they amount to a rigorous apprenticeship. Of the eighty or so paintings that may be reasonably assigned to these years (not including the studies for the *Bathers*) more than half are landscapes. These are mainly of suburban or rural sites and there are a small number of urban views. The remainder focus on figures or animals in various settings in the country or in the fringes of

21. *The Stone Breaker*, c.1882–3
Oil on wood, 15.4 x 24.9 cm
Washington, DC, Phillips Collection (CAT. 46)

the city, with, for example, stone breakers (Plate 21), peasants, mowers or gardeners. Sometimes the subjects are not easily classified, since the backgrounds are often only summarily indicated; a painting of a riverside scene (Plate 22) might evoke the Seine on the outskirts of Paris, but the vaguely indicated structures in the background could be either industrial or domestic. Another river view (Plate 23) seems deliberately featureless and only the intrusive detail of a striped pole, probably a flood marker, adds some sense of a specific place and a trace of human activity.

Some of Seurat's early works are on canvas, but the majority of his paintings were executed on small, thin panels (Plate 24). In the same way that he evolved a favourite size for his drawings, he found a format for his oil studies that he used almost without variation. In the literature on Seurat these panels are frequently referred to as cigar-box lids. The idea that the artist might have transformed the ephemeral packaging of a modern trade into works of art is an attractive one and it seems in tune with the spontaneity that we associate with painting in the open air. Yet his panels seem to be mainly mahogany or walnut not the lightweight and insect-repelling cedar that was commonly used for cigar boxes. It is difficult to

22. *Fisherman in a Moored Boat*, c.1882
Oil on wood, 16.5 x 24.8 cm
Private Collection on extended loan to the
Courtauld Institute Galleries, London (CAT. 41)

23. *The Seine at Asnières*, c.1883
Oil on wood, 15.8 x 24.7 cm
London, National Gallery (CAT. 45)

imagine that Seurat would have been prepared to remove the paper labels that covered the boxes or to avoid the trademarks that were often branded on to the lids.[3] Seurat bought good quality paper for his drawings, and there is no reason why he should have stinted on his panels, which he probably bought from an artists' supplier. Contemporary trade catalogues indicate that these small panels were available in a range of sizes and thicknesses.

In a guide to the practice of oil painting, published in 1878, Karl Robert noted that good, thin panels could be purchased to fit easily into a hand-held painting box (*boîte à pouce*) (Plate 25).[4] According to Robert, the outdoor painter could carry a

number of these tiny panels to the motif and make several 'impressions' in a day. Several of Seurat's contemporaries noted that he used one of these small painting boxes. Charles Angrand, for example, referred to the little *boîte à pouce* studies that he saw hanging in quantities on the walls of Seurat's studio.[5] These ingenious small boxes provided a very practical way to transport materials to and from the motif. Seurat would have bought his panels in a size that fitted behind slats in the lid of his painting box and, indeed, many of his panels display marks or grooves at the edges from being held in place in this fashion.

As Karl Robert's comments suggest, many nineteenth-century artists used small panels for outdoor work, including

24. *Houses among Trees*, c.1883
Oil on wood, 16 x 25 cm
Glasgow Art Gallery and Museum (CAT. 47)

25. Detail from a nineteenth-century trade catalogue showing a *boîte à pouce*

for example Daubigny, Diaz and Théodore Rousseau. The consistency of Seurat's choice of materials is, however, unusual, and just as the collaboration between conté crayon and paper is crucial to his drawing style, so Seurat seems to have depended on the particular qualities of his chosen support for painting. Occasionally he added a layer of white ground to his panels but more often he painted directly on to the wood. He could exploit the natural grain of the wood for its textural effects and he seems to have enjoyed the way that wet paint could be manipulated on the hard, slippery surface. Often small areas of the warm brown of the wood are left exposed and it becomes an active part of the colour scheme. The format of the small panel might seem restricting, yet Seurat's approach was surprisingly varied. He could use the panels for rapid open-air work, working wet-into-wet to capture a motif in a single session. Sometimes he used the panels as a kind of notepad, with swiftly observed figures or details assembled in an informal way. Other works are more developed and seem to have been painted in stages with an accumulation of several paint layers. At the Indépendants exhibition in 1884 he described his studies as 'croquetons', an invented word which must derive from 'croquis' (the academic term for a quick sketch).[6]

When Seurat went on his painting excursions to the banks of the Seine and to the villages outside Paris he was following an example set by several generations of artists. His studies of modest suburban scenes or of quiet riverbanks belong to a tradition of open-air painting in France that stretches back to the beginning of the century. In the later eighteenth century painting in oils out of doors was an activity primarily associated with northern artists working in Italy and the sight of a painter at work in the French countryside must have been comparatively rare. This changed rapidly in the first decades of the nineteenth century, and in the summer whole colonies of artists began to develop, notably on the Normandy coast and in the environs of Paris, including the areas around Sèvres, Saint-Cloud and, of course, the 'colony of colonies' at Barbizon in the Forest of Fontainbleau.[7] An oil sketch that Paul Huet made during his student years provides one distinguished example of early nineteenth-century *plein-air* painting in the Paris region (Plate 26). This small study of horses watering in

the Seine was sketched on the Ile Séguin near Saint-Cloud. This rapidly brushed exuberant sketch conveys the excitement and freshness of vision that was often associated with studies made directly from nature.

Throughout the nineteenth century the practice of sketching landscape motifs in oils was promoted by various academic theorists and teachers. The influential treatise on landscape painting published by Pierre-Henri de Valenciennes in 1800 was followed by many similar discourses that stressed the value of outdoor *études* for training the hand and eye of the artist and as part of the preparatory process.[8] By making such studies the student became familiar with the raw material of nature, creating 'trial fragments' that could be useful in the development of finished, studio-based paintings.[9] However, for the academic theorists there was a clear distinction between the direct observation of nature in freely handled studies and the intellectual ordering and artistic vision that could only result from sustained toil back in the studio.

Towards the middle of the century this traditional division between *plein-air étude* and studio composition began to become less distinct. The caricaturist Daumier, for example, produced some small landscape sketches showing bathers or watering horses that were neither painted out-of-doors, nor made as studies, but simply as modest compositions in their own right (Plate 27). Corot was one of many landscape artists who experimented in what might be described as the middle ground between a rapid study and a finished tableau. Some of the sketches that he made on his numerous travels across

26. Paul Huet, *L'Ile Séguin, Watering Place*, 1820
Oil on canvas, 12.5 x 34.5 cm
Château de Sceaux, Musée de L'Ile de France (CAT. 52)

27. Honoré-Victorin Daumier, *The Bathers*, c.1846–8
Oil on wood, 25.4 x 32.1 cm
Glasgow, Burrell Collection (CAT. 51)

France are vivid notations, painted in a fluid and spontaneous style (Plate 28). Other studies that he made from nature were the result of more substantial labour and repeated visits to the motif. Yet Corot rarely exhibited his *plein-air* sketches and in his lifetime he was best known for his pastoral and ideal compositions produced in the tranquillity of the studio. In the 1870s working in the open air became an essential activity for the Impressionists and they began to exhibit works that retained the qualities of a sketch; yet the private, small-scale study could still play a role, and even Monet in the 1870s sometimes mapped out his design for a picture with a hastily executed sketch (Plate 29).

Seurat would have been aware of the traditional role of the oil sketch from his readings in art theory and from his days at the Ecole des Beaux-Arts. His master, Henri Lehmann, was not a landscapist but he did make some *plein-air* oil sketches,[10] apparently for personal pleasure rather than artistic gain, and he might have encouraged his students to adopt this practice. Seurat must also have known the more informal works of the Barbizon generation of landscape painters from his visits to art sales and to dealers' shops. While works by these artists frequently appeared in exhibitions, the posthumous studio sales of such prominent painters as Corot, Daubigny and Diaz unleashed large numbers of studies and sketches on to the market in the second half of the 1870s.

28. Jean-Baptiste-Camille Corot,
River Scene with a Bridge, 1834
Oil on paper mounted on canvas
25 x 33 cm
Washington, DC, National Gallery of Art
(CAT. 53)

29. Oscar-Claude Monet,
The Railway Bridge, Argenteuil, 1874
Oil on canvas, 14 x 23 cm
Paris, Musée Marmottan (CAT. 54)

30. *Sunset, c.*1881
Oil on wood, 15.2 x 24.8 cm
Bristol Museums and Art Gallery (CAT. 40)

The subjects and the technique of many Seurat's early oil studies confirm his interest in the work of the mid-nineteenth-century landscapists. In one *croqueton* (Plate 30) he sets a humble orchard against a sunset sky in a work that recalls some of Théodore Rousseau's moody, autumnal views. In another panel (Plate 22), where a fisherman is silhouetted against a background of misty, silvery tones, both the motif and its treatment are reminiscent of Corot, whom Seurat later singled out as an important formative influence. Around the time of Corot's death in 1875, he had obtained a text which recorded some advice from the great landscapist about painting methods and procedures. This text, which Seurat dictated later to Fénéon, stresses the importance of a harmony of tones: 'What one should see in painting, or rather what I look for, is the form, the whole, the value of the tones; colour for me comes afterwards.'[11] This rather conservative advice echoed ideas on the handling of tone and colour that Seurat would

have read elsewhere. It is certainly in line with Seurat's practice, for many of his early pictures – including the *Bathers* – were first laid in with muted colour to establish the main tonal relationships. Brighter combinations of colour were applied on to this tonal base.

Seurat's debt to Corot extended beyond the details of technique; both artists found inspiration in seemingly banal corners of a landscape. One of Seurat's most accomplished early landscapes depicts nothing more dramatic than the view across a field to some unassuming buildings. By tradition it was painted at Ville-d'Avray, an area that was intimately linked to Corot. Although the geometry of the composition and the sharply edged forms of the houses belong to Seurat's vision, aspects of the earlier artist's influence linger in the soft treatment of the trees and foliage. Seurat extracts a gentle mood of melancholy from this most ordinary scene, comparable to the *triste* mood of many of Corot's later landscapes.

It is often assumed that Seurat's dependence on the Barbizon generation of painters was gradually displaced by a growing interest in Impressionism. Thus, a tendency to sombre naturalism was superseded by a more vigorous touch and a more sophisticated handling of colour as he began to study the chromatic adventures of Monet and his contemporaries. This might be useful as a general description of the pattern of Seurat's development in the early 1880s, but only a few of his panels can be dated with any certainty and their experimental quality tends to foil any attempt to place them in a logical chronological sequence. Seurat could be flexible in his

approach, trying out different methods of brushwork and colour and adopting the style that best suited his subject.[12] The studies that he made along the banks of the Seine in 1882 and 1883, for example, are usually linked to Impressionism, yet as a group they are varied in technique. In one sketch (Plate 31) the figure of a boatman is coarsely brushed in with thin fluid paint over a white ground. The pale tonality of this luminous work is comparable to the oil sketches of Corot (see Plate 28). In another study of a similar subject (Plate 32) the water, riverbank and trees are painted in patterns of small dabs of paint in what seems like an essay in the manner of Monet and

31. *Man in a Boat*, c.1884
Oil on wood, 17.6 x 26.8 cm
Private Collection on extended loan to the
Courtauld Institute Galleries, London (CAT. 43)

Renoir. A third study, which depicts a man painting his boat (Plate 33), recalls Manet's particular version of riverbank Impressionism. The swift touches of paint in the foliage are combined with longer, more graphic strokes which define the figure and the fence. Alongside the more intense colours, such as the greens and yellows, there are mixtures of whites, blacks and blues which provide a tonal anchor for the composition.

These are all confident studies. While they might date from different sketching campaigns along the river, the differences between them seem to result from a wide-ranging experimentation rather than from a sequential development where one approach is rejected in favour of another.

It is difficult to define with precision the extent of Seurat's knowledge or interest in Impressionism during the early 1880s. If he had chosen to, he could have seen a wide range of Impressionist works on exhibition and with dealers such as Durand-Ruel. Small paintings by middle-of-the-road landscape painters such as Stanislas Lépine were also in common currency, representing suburban sites in a freely brushed style (Plate 34). There is, however, only the one report of a visit to an Impressionist show recalled, many years later, by one of his friends.[13] Seurat acknowledged his admiration of the 'intuition'

32. *A Boat near the Riverbank, Asnières*, c.1883
Oil on wood, 15 x 24 cm
Private Collection (CAT. 44)

33. *Man painting a Boat, c.*1883
Oil on wood, 15.9 x 25.0 cm
London, Courtauld Institute Galleries (CAT. 42)

of Monet and Renoir but the tone of this comment in his 1890 letter to Fénéon seems designed to play down their influence.[14] Signac also stressed that Seurat knew nothing of Impressionism in the early 1880s, although he had his own motives for making such a claim.[15] It is important to note also that many aspects of his technique that might tempt a comparison to the Impressionists could also derive from other artists, notably Delacroix, or from readings in colour theory. Nevertheless, the treatment of a study such as *Man painting a Boat* does have affinities with the impulsive brushwork and colour of the Impressionists. There are parallels too between the regular, criss-cross strokes that Seurat used in some of his

panels and canvases and the tightly woven brushstrokes adopted by, for example, Pissarro in the later 1870s. The dry, textured surfaces of *Ville-d'Avray, White Houses* (Plate 35) could also be compared to the gritty technique which Camille Pissarro used in some of his rustic subjects and which he later described disparagingly as 'rough and rasping'.[16]

There is what appears to be a more direct connection to the precedent of Impressionism in Seurat's painting of fishermen on the banks of the Seine (Plate 36). This work seems to derive from pictures of similar subjects by Monet such as *Anglers on the Seine at Poissy* (Plate 37) which was on view at Durand-Ruel's gallery in early 1883.[17] Like Monet, who looks down on

34. Stanislas-Victor-Edmond Lépine,
The Seine at La Garenne Saint-Denis,
*c.*1874–8
Oil on canvas, 34.5 x 54.5 cm
Hamburg, Kunsthalle (CAT. 55)

35. *Ville-d'Avray, White Houses, c.*1883
Oil on canvas, 33.5 x 46.0 cm
Liverpool, Walker Art Gallery (CAT. 48)

36. *Men fishing on the Banks of the Seine*,
1883
Oil on wood, 16 x 25 cm
Troyes, Musée d'Art Moderne

37. Oscar-Claude Monet,
Anglers on the Seine at Poissy, 1882
Oil on canvas, 60 x 82 cm
Vienna, Osterreichische Galerie Belvedere

the anglers from a high viewpoint, Seurat sets the dark, simplified forms of the figures against the light reflecting off the river. Both artists close off the bottom right-hand corner of the composition with a glimpse of the riverbank and they use the reflections of unseen trees or buildings to suggest depth and to articulate the surface of the river. But if Monet seems concerned to evoke a chance arrangement that will change as the boats move and fishing rods whip backwards or forwards, Seurat's composition seems more static and more structured. His sensitive observation of light is combined with a more insistent design, with the blocky shapes of the anglers and the curving lines of their fishing poles dividing the surface of the small panel into a compact two-dimensional pattern.

This degree of artifice is often apparent in the works that Seurat made in the years before the *Bathers*. He may have borrowed elements of his style from Impressionism and he certainly absorbed aspects of other tendencies linked to naturalism, but he remained loyal to an idealising tradition where the artist remains firmly in control, actively imposing his vision upon nature. Some of his panels are better described as small pictures rather than spontaneous studies in oil, and even in his most modest works there are insistent reminders of the intellectual intervention of the artist. The rhythmic, criss-cross strokes that animate studies such as Plate 24 create a convincing atmospheric shimmer but they also bind the forms into a taut, surface pattern. The poplar trees at the centre of the composition seem like an extension of the buildings beneath them, continuing the line of a gable to create a strong vertical accent. Tone and colour are carefully controlled and manipulated. The sky is lightened next to the dark silhouette of the poplars but darkened where it meets the pale wall at the right. Overall one senses the artist imposing unity on the diversity of nature.

As a group, the array of small canvases and panels that Seurat produced in the early 1880s might offer few clues to the scale of ambition that would be revealed in the *Bathers*. Yet each of these little studies betrays the quiet potential of Seurat's methods, and close study reveals the careful decisions and calculations that underpin even those pictures that appear to be direct and spontaneous. Perhaps his greatest achievement in these years was his mastery of colour. Seurat inherited the academic view that colour was subordinate to form, but his paintings indicate that study of this element in his art was one of his main preoccupations.

1. See Paris, Grand Palais, 1991, pp. 103ff.
2. Rewald 1948, 1990 edn., p. 30.
3. We are grateful to Robert Emery and Simon Chase for information about nineteenth-century cigar boxes.
4. Robert 1878, p. 19.
5. Charles Angrand in Coquiot 1924, p. 39.
6. According to Signac, Seurat derived the term from the writings of the Goncourt brothers. See Paris, Grand Palais, 1991 p. 106, and Seyrès 1991, p. 91.
7. Henriet 1876, p. 13
8. For a bibliography of academic theory see Paillot de Montabert 1829, I, p. 233ff. See also Boime, 1971.
9. Paillot de Montabert 1829, I, p. 158
10. See Aubrun 1984, nos. 344–5.
11. Fénéon 1970, I, pp. 290ff; Paris, Grand Palais, 1991, p. 394.
12. See Zimmermann 1991, pp. 61, for a discussion of style and content in Seurat's early work.
13. Rosenthal 1911, p. 66.
14. Paris, Grand Palais, 1991, p. 383.
15. Signac 1939, p. 82.
16. Camille Pissarro to his son Lucien, 4 May 1883, repr. in Bailly-Herzberg 1980, p. 202.
17. Signed and dated 1882, Wildenstein, II, no. 748, p. 74; see also Zimmermann 1991, p. 109.

Seurat and Colour Theory

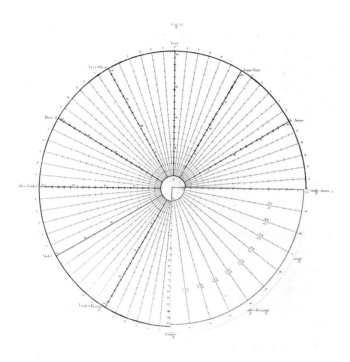

38. Chevreul's chromatic circle, from M.-E. Chevreul,
De la loi du contraste simultané des couleurs (Paris 1839)

39. Blanc's illustration of complementary colours, from C. Blanc,
Grammaire des arts du dessin (Paris 1866, 2nd edn. 1870)

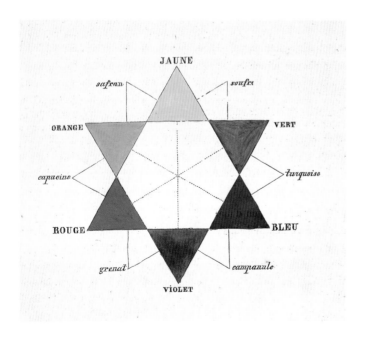

Although the development of Seurat's painting technique clearly owed much to his study of other artists, by his own admission Seurat relied relatively heavily on the written word. In his letter to Fénéon (see above, p 15) he listed the names of several authors whose works had influenced him, among them the aestheticians Charles Blanc and David Sutter, the chemist Michel-Eugène Chevreul, the physicist Ogden Rood and the mathematician and aesthetician Charles Henry, whose work Seurat did not know until 1886, two years after he had exhibited the *Bathers*. In his search for what he described as an 'optical formula' it is not surprising that he turned to the work of scientists, partly as interpreted by other authors, for assistance. His study of how colours interact with one another in practice drew principally upon Chevreul's observations on complementary and contrasting colours, but also, through Rood, on the work of Hermann von Helmholtz and James Clerk Maxwell on the behaviour of the human eye and its response to light of particular wavelengths. However, in many ways Charles Blanc was the most fundamental influence of all: Seurat read Blanc's *Grammaire des arts du dessin* (Paris 1867) and his article on Delacroix in the *Gazette des Beaux-Arts* (1864) during his student days.[1] What Seurat learned from Blanc about the theory of art, the importance of drawing and the handling of colour and of chiaroscuro remained of central importance to him throughout his career.[2]

Chevreul's work on the optical effects achieved by placing one colour next to another was carried out after he became Director of Dyeing at the Gobelins tapestry workshops in 1824. Asked to look at the apparent dullness of certain textile dyestuffs, he found no fault in the technical quality of the dyeing; the lack of brightness lay in the optical mixture of the hues of adjacent threads. It is useful to remember that the primary colours as understood by Chevreul, Blanc and most painters during the nineteenth century were red, yellow and blue; the complementary secondary colours produced by mixing pairs of these primaries are well known to be green (blue + yellow), violet (red + blue) and orange (red + yellow). Chevreul found that where adjacent threads were of complementary colours – yellow and violet, for example – the overall appearance to the eye was greyish. He formulated his observations as the law of simultaneous contrast of colours, which stated that if the eye saw two contiguous colours at the same time, they would appear as dissimilar as possible, both in hue and in tone.[3] Thus, the effect of placing a light and a dark shade of the same colour (including, of course, grey) side by side is to enhance the lightness of one and the darkness of the other, the effect being most marked at the boundary between the two. In the case of two different colours, the hue of each is modified by the effect of the complementary colour of the other: for example if red is placed next to blue its colour will appear a more orange red than it would if used alone or placed next to yellow, say, because orange is the complementary colour to blue. The blue, meanwhile, appears more green than if used alone, because green is the complementary colour to red. The effect is most marked if the adjacent colours are themselves complementary (red and green), as the complementary colours induced then reinforce the colours present. If the patches of colour are small – fine tapestry threads, for instance – the colours appear to merge, resulting in the greyish appearance observed. (The reason is discussed below.) Chevreul first lectured on the contrast of colours in 1829, but his work was only published ten years later in the much reprinted *De la loi du contraste simultané des couleurs, et de l'assortiment des objets colorés* (Paris 1839), in which pages of plates and examples illustrated the effects described; the variables of hue and tone, indicating the primary and complementary secondary colours and six intermediate colours, were shown in a diagrammatic chromatic circle (Plate 38).

Chevreul extended his discussion to successive contrast, which arises as a result of looking at a coloured area for a period of time and then looking away; momentarily the fatigued eye perceives the respective complementary colour. If, under these circumstances, the eye then looks at a new colour, the colour actually perceived is the resultant of the new colour and the induced complementary of the first colour.[4] This explained the already well-known observation of coloured after-images, which had been observed in nature by Goethe and others and recorded by observant painters such as Delacroix. Chevreul also discussed the appearance of individual colours and pairs of colours with white, black and grey. However, much of the book was devoted to examples of the effects of the various types of contrast in painting, weaving, interior decorating of all types (including picture frames), horticulture and even the observation of natural phenomena: the orange light of the sun on the horizon illuminating an object causes it to cast a blue shadow, for example.[5] These practical observations helped to give the book its popularity among a very wide range of readers. Chevreul's principal concern was the achievement of colour harmonies of both contrasting and analogous colours: between tones of the same colour; between a particular hue and its neighbour on his colour wheel; between a dominant colour and others around it. His intention was to avoid glaring contrasts or unwanted optical mixture resulting in the greys he had observed in the dyed textiles.

It is likely that Seurat was first introduced to the essential elements of Chevreul's work, along with the conventionally accepted notion of primary colours and colour mixing, through the pages of Charles Blanc's *Grammaire des arts du dessin*. Here he would have seen complementary colours illustrated in

40. *Bathers at Asnières*. Detail of torso of the central seated bather, showing the contrast in tone between the light-coloured paint of the shoulder and upper arm and the deep blue water. A line of light paint scumbled thinly over the pale blue of the water provides a tonal contrast with the mauve shadow along the figure's back.

Blanc's star-shaped diagram (Plate 39). He would have learned also that the simultaneous contrast between stripes of two complementary colours was particularly marked along the boundary between them, a feature he recreated in many of his paintings; on the other hand, if the stripes were very narrow both the individual colours and the stripes tended to become indistinct and 'optical mixture' – a term coined by Blanc, not Chevreul – resulted in a greyish or neutral tint, different to either of the parent colours.[6] An even more successful result was obtained if the dividing line between the bands was punctuated by small, even serrations.

41. *Seated Boy in a Meadow*, c.1882–3
Oil on canvas, 63.5 x 79.6 cm
Glasgow Art Gallery and Museum (CAT. 49)

Whether or not Seurat read Chevreul's book in its entirety, he made a copy of the chromatic circle and noted down several paragraphs from the section on painting, including those on the raising and lowering of tones of different colours by their juxtaposition to achieve harmony, and the attainment of chiaroscuro by the juxtaposition of different tones of the same colour.[7] Certainly the emphasis of tonal contrast, exemplified in the *Bathers* by the pale, heavily reinforced outline of the shoulder and upper arm of the boy seated on the bank against the strong blue of the water (Plate 40) is a feature found throughout Seurat's work: not only in the finished picture, but also in several of the painted studies, including those now in Kansas and Chicago (Plates 59 and 60). Here, and in many other instances, it is combined with a contrast in colour, but the effect of simultaneous contrast that may be seen in, for example, the touches of blue and orange in the water (Plate 45), appear to be subordinated to the contrast in light and shade. The use of the sort of colour harmonies and contrasts discussed by Chevreul can be found throughout the finished painting, but subtly used, not quite as striking as the yellows and oranges contrasted with the purplish blue seen in the *Seated Boy in a Meadow* (Plate 41). It is worth pointing out

42. Detail of the figure seated at the left of the *Bathers at Asnières*. The softly blended mottled colours of the figure's clothes and streaks of bright yellow, orange and blue paint within the overall green of the grass give a constantly shifting effect. In no area of the painting is simple unmodulated colour used.

that Seurat would have observed many examples of the use of colour contrasts and harmonies that he could have drawn upon in Delacroix's work and, also, in the work of the Impressionist painters, Monet, Pissarro and Renoir, which he must have seen.

The paintings of Eugène Delacroix had the most profound influence on Seurat's work, as they had had on the development of the Impressionists a generation earlier. During 1881 Seurat made notes on Delacroix's palettes and a number of paintings, including *The Fanatics of Tangier* (Plate 43), in which he commented on the red and green harmony of the street and a number of passages where tones of blue and orange play against one another. In other paintings by Delacroix, too, he noted reds and greens, yellow and violets, often in terms of the harmony given by such pairs of complementary colours rather than the contrast.[8] He saw Delacroix's great mural paintings of *The Struggle of Jacob with the Angel* and *The Expulsion of Heliodorus* (Paris, Saint-Sulpice, 1849–61); the chapel containing these paintings, with their rather dry, scumbled surface texture and open brushwork, giving the effect of broken, interwoven colour, had been a place of pilgrimage for the young Impressionist painters some twenty years before. It is easy to imagine that the interlaced

43. Eugène Delacroix, *The Fanatics of Tangier*, 1838
Oil on canvas, 97.8 x 131.3 cm. Minneapolis Institute of Arts

webbing of brushstrokes that Seurat used in works painted in the earlier years of his career, such as the *Bathers* and the *Seated Boy in a Meadow* of about 1882, was influenced by what he saw of Delacroix's work.[9] In the *Seated Boy in a Meadow* (Plate 41), the texture of the corn is evoked by fairly long strokes of yellow, green and white paint, giving a modulated golden yellow colour, slightly darker and greener in the distance behind the figure and with more white in the foreground. The colour is dominated by the contrast between the yellow cornfield and the purplish-green figure of the boy, but within that overall scheme flickering accents of mauve and orange bring out subsidiary contrasts. The gaze of the spectator cannot focus on the diffuse, shifting painted surface, a characteristic shared by the *Bathers* (Plate 42) and a particular feature of Delacroix's painting technique.

What Seurat learned from his observations of Delacroix's paintings was supplemented by his reading. Blanc wrote that Delacroix's vibrant colour effects were carefully planned, and to some extent this is true: for his later paintings Delacroix spent much time planning the precise colour needed in the half-tones, the harmonies and contrasts. Finally he had the palette prepared accordingly, thus saving much time in the execution of the final work.[10] Delacroix's use of contrasting colours – red and green, for example – in half-tones rather than simply adding black, was undoubtedly influential, whether it was based on theory or, more likely, on close observation. Seurat also read Achille Piron's *Eugène Delacroix: sa vie et ses oeuvres* (Paris 1865), in which some observations Delacroix made on colour whilst at Dieppe in 1854 were noted, for example his mention of violet shadows with green reflections.[11]

Blanc offered a detailed examination of the *Women of Algiers in their Apartment* (Paris, Louvre), painted in 1834, which had been in the Louvre since 1874. He gave examples of Delacroix's apparently scientific understanding of colour effects that, he implied, were partly derived from Chevreul, including the use of optical mixtures of contrasting colours to give tints that were effectively grey. This was exemplified by the soft colour modelling the white garment of one of the women, a muted echo of its embroidered decoration of red and green flowers. Although Delacroix is known to have shown some interest in Chevreul's work late in his career, it is not at all clear that he was influenced by it at the time he was painting the picture, which was based on watercolour studies made during a visit to north Africa. It seems that Blanc, interpreting Delacroix's work in the light of Chevreul's findings, considerably exaggerated the influence of scientific theory on the painter; nevertheless his interpretation of the painter's methods, however false, must have impressed Seurat;[12] the young painter would have interpreted what he saw in Delacroix's work in the light of Blanc's writings.

The importance of the use of simultaneous contrast to increase chiaroscuro, the sculptural quality of an object, while also isolating such an object from its background – summarised in a paragraph from Chevreul that Seurat copied out – was perhaps reinforced by a short description of 'irradiation' in one of a series of articles by the Swiss aesthetician David Sutter, which appeared in the journal *L'Art* in 1880. Sutter described irradiation as a luminous phenomenon that separated one object from another while simultaneously giving it a high relief. He gave as example a white wall standing out against the blue sky: the viewer would

44. Additive and subtractive mixing. White light is obtained by the *additive* mixing of the three primary colours of light: orange-red, green and blue-violet. The *subtractive* mixing of the three ideal primary pigments, magenta, yellow and cyan (conventionally red, yellow and blue), produces black, as the mixture of pigments absorbs light of all colours. Pairs of additive primaries combine to give a colour *complementary* to the remaining additive primary, that is itself one of the subtractive primaries (red+green=yellow, complementary to blue-violet). Similarly, pairs of subtractive primaries combine to give the additive primaries as complementary colours. The fundamental complementary pairs are green and magenta; orange-red and cyan; blue-violet and yellow.

see a white line, whiter than the white of the wall, next to a blue or grey one, darker than the mass of the sky; this effect was an example of irradiation.[15] This increase in the definition of the form certainly describes very well the characteristic 'detached' appearance seen in the bathing figures in the *Bathers* (see, for example, Plate 40), many of Seurat's other paintings and his drawings, for example the *Crouching Boy* (Plate 12). The figure is detached from the dark shadow behind him by the diffuse band of lighter grey on the crown of his head and along the line of his back, while the part of his face in deep shadow and the dark outline of his right arm stand out sharply from the background, here rendered in paler grey, less dense strokes of conté crayon. The optical effect to which the name of irradiation is usually given is defined as the apparent enlargement of the edges of a strongly illuminated object when seen against a dark background. It was so described by Helmholtz in an article entitled 'L'optique et la peinture', published in Ernst von Brücke's *Principes scientifiques des beaux-arts* (Paris 1878), a book aimed at the general reader.[14] The effect has its maximum intensity near the object, diminishing strongly at a greater distance, giving the appearance of a halo; it can be still be seen if the object (Helmholtz used a lighted match as an example) was blocked out by holding a finger, say, between the object and the eye of the observer. The appearance described is quite close to that seen in some of Seurat's drawings, such as *The Nanny* (Plate 8), discussed above.

Seurat was also interested in another part of Sutter's text, where he discussed the proposition that, like science, art was governed by laws and that one should look for the scientific rules governing the harmonies of line, light and colour. By the

1880s there were many inexpensive books in which the essentials of recent work on colour – Helmholtz's research into the fundamental primary colours of light (based on the work of Thomas Young some fifty years earlier) and Maxwell's research into the way in which colour could be measured – were explained. Young had suggested that the primary colours of light were red, green and violet, but did not realise that the mixing of beams of coloured light and that of pigments were two fundamentally different processes.

It was in fact generally believed that the primary colours of light were red, yellow and blue, as they were with pigments; Chevreul, for example, assumed this. The mixing of pigments and dyestuffs is subtractive: a yellow pigment, for example, appears yellow because it absorbs light from the blue and violet regions of the spectrum, reflecting the remainder, and a mixture of red, yellow and blue, the colours commonly taken to be the three subtractive primaries, should yield black, or a greyish colour. Mixing a primary (red) with its complementary secondary colour (green) will also give grey or, ideally, black. This is the reason underlying Cheuvreul's explanation for the unsatisfactory appearance of the dyed tapestries. The ideal subtractive primaries are, in fact, magenta (which absorbs the green region of the spectrum of light, reflecting red and blue light), yellow and cyan blue (absorbing red light, reflecting blue and green), the colours used in the printing and photographic industries (Plate 44). The optical properties of conventional artists' pigments and also printing inks are not always so simple or predictable; the subtractive primaries as commonly known to and used by painters are still simply red, yellow and blue, as they were for nineteenth-century painters.

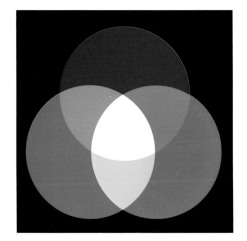

ADDITIVE MIXING

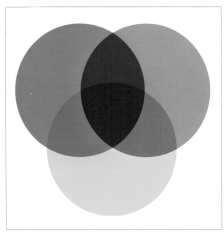

SUBTRACTIVE MIXING

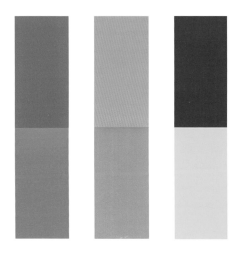

COMPLEMENTARY PAIRS

45. *Bathers at Asnières*. Detail of bather standing in the water, right. An example of complementary contrast as described by Chevreul is that between the bather's orange-red trunks and the blue water; the contrast is reinforced by streaks of orange paint on the edge of the bank. Seurat appears to have been influenced by Chevreul's emphasis on harmonies arising from the use of contrasting colours, rather than simple applications of the use of complementary contrast.

46. Detail of the brushstrokes forming the shadow in the grass behind the seated bather. Strokes of purple, mauve, blue, pink and cold green in the shadow form a complementary contrast (as Rood describes) with the lighter green and lilac paint used in the surrounding grass.

The mixing of coloured light to give white light is, however, additive, as demonstrated by Helmholtz in 1852.[15] The so-called additive primary colours of light are orange-red, green and blue-violet (or, to a near approximation, red, green and blue). If light of these colours is mixed in the correct proportions, white light is obtained; yellow light results from mixing red light and green light. The link between the additive and subtractive primaries can easily be seen, as each complementary pair (magenta and green, for example) consists of an additive and a subtractive primary (Plate 44).[16]

Maxwell's great contribution was to define an objective method of colour measurement, using algebraic colour-matching equations, thus enabling the precise quantity of each of the three additive primary colours needed to match any spectral colour to be specified. For this a source of monochromatic red, blue and green light was necessary, and Maxwell designed a form of colorimeter (which he called a 'colour box') for this purpose. However, he also used a very much simpler method which consisted of discs of red, green and blue papers, slit radially so that they could be interleaved, attached to a spinning top. The size of the coloured sectors exposed could be altered (unlike the painted sectors used by Young) and measured using a protractor. By spinning the top rapidly until the individual colours could no longer be discerned, Maxwell found he could obtain results identical to those obtained by mixing red, blue and green

light projected on a screen. A smaller disc of colour for which a match was desired could be added, leaving the original sectors still visible as a border; by spinning the top and adjusting the sectors as necessary, the colour could be defined algebraically in terms of the amounts of red, blue and green needed to match it.[17]

It seems unlikely that Seurat looked very far into the writings of such scientists as Helmholtz and Maxwell for explanations for the way colour appeared to the eye and should, perhaps, be represented on the canvas; but in fact it was not necessary for him to do so. As far as the painter was concerned, the clearest and most relevant explanations were given in Ogden Rood's *Modern Chromatics, with Applications to Art and Industry* (New York 1879). Rood carried out many colour-matching experiments under different lighting conditions, many based on spinning discs of papers painted in different colours, others using coloured glass filters,. Like Maxwell, he used red, green and blue papers (painted using vermilion, emerald green and artificial ultramarine), together with smaller black and white papers to make a neutral grey, but he also allowed for the fact that the three colours were not equal in luminosity. He was also able to construct an accurate diagram of contrasting colours (Plate 47), from which it can be seen that, for example, vermilion is complementary to a greenish blue; green is complementary to purple.[18] For much of what he had to say about colour saturation and harmony

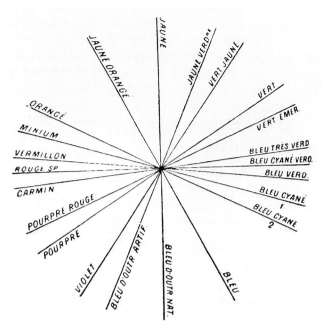

Fig. 120. — Diagramme des contrastes d'après O. Rood.

47. Rood's chromatic circle, from O.N. Rood,
Théorie scientifique des couleurs (Paris 1881)

Rood followed Chevreul's work quite closely, harmony being related to the angle between one colour and another on the colour wheel. Angles of less than 80° or 90° between colours gave rise to effects of contrast that were unsatisfactory or even discordant; sets of three colours separated by angles of about 120° were often particularly successful. The association of colours separated only by a small interval (for example red and orange-red) was, however, very effective under certain circumstances, such as where it was necessary to represent small gradations in colour. The placing of small dots or lines of colour side by side so that, when viewed from certain distances 'the blending is more or less accomplished by the eye of the beholder' was another method of achieving such gradation, and the tints observed were identical to those obtained by the method of spinning discs of coloured paper, rather than by mixing pigments on the palette. Rood described this method as giving 'true mixtures of coloured light', the nearest the artist could get to the additive mixture of colour explained by Helmholtz and Maxwell.[19] As we have seen, 'blending to the eye of the beholder' had been described by Cheuvreul and Blanc: their discussions had not been restricted to greys resulting from complementary contrast.

Seurat apparently purchased the French edition of *Modern Chromatics* shortly after it was published in 1881, and at some time he copied out the colour wheel and made notes from one of the experimental sections of the book.[20] He could well have made use of the colour wheel in constructing some of the contrasts and harmonies visible in the *Bathers*, as it was exhibited in 1884 – there are, for example, many based on cold viridian green and purple, which are complementary colours according to Rood's system (for example Plate 46) – but at this stage he had yet to investigate the possibilities of 'optical mixture' opened up for him by Rood or to develop the dotted brushwork so characteristic of his later paintings. It is, however, important to emphasise that, whether Seurat constructed his colour harmonies and contrasts in the *Bathers* on the basis of the work of Chevreul, Rood, Blanc or Delacroix, he was not necessarily aiming to reproduce a more scientific or naturalistic reworking of outdoor light. The earliest sketches for the *Bathers* may have been painted from what he observed on the riverbank; the colour in the later studies and in the final painting has been ordered and contrived as part of the intellectual process of the construction of the picture.

1. Blanc 1864, pp. 5–27, 97–129.
2. For discussions of how far Seurat's approach to painting was indeed scientific see Homer 1964; Lee 1987, pp. 203–26; Gage, 1987, pp. 448–54; Smith 1990, pp. 381–5.
3. Chevreul 1839, pp. 1–16.
4. Chevreul 1839, pp. 49–67. See also Padgham and Saunders, 1975, pp. 146–7, 152.
5. Chevreul 1839, para.961 p. 680–1.
6. Blanc 1867, 2nd edn. 1870, pp. 610–12.
7. Paris, Grand Palais, 1991, pp. 388–91; Chevreul 1839, paragraphs 335–40, pp. 197–201.
8. Paris, Grand Palais, 1991, pp. 394–6. For *The Fanatics of Tangier* see Johnson 1986, cat. 360, pp. 171–3, pl. 176.
9. Johnson 1989, pp. 159–92, pls. 62–9. For Seurat's reaction see pp. 171–2.
10. Blanc 1864, pp. 115–6; Piot, 1931.
11. Piron 1865, 1923, I, pp. 71–4.
12. Blanc 1864, p. 115; Johnson 1986, cat. 354, pp. 165–70, esp. p. 169.
13. Sutter 1880, pp. 74–6, 124–5, 147–9, 195–7, 216–20, 268–9. For irradiation and chiaroscuro see paragraphs xlv–xlvii, p. 216.
14. Helmholtz 1878, esp. pp. 207–9.
15. For Helmholtz's work in general see Helmholtz 1924. In 1852 Helmholtz thought that it was only possible to match all spectral colours if the number of colour receptors in the retina was five; ten years later he realised that if the sensitivities of three receptors, responsive to red, green and blue light (or, more accurately, long, medium and short wave illumination) overlapped, all spectral colours could be matched successfully.
16. McLaren 1983, pp. 63–73; Padgham and Saunders 1975, pp. 67–74. A useful introductory book on colour is Rossotti 1983. For nineteenth-century colour theory in general see Sherman 1981; other titles are listed in London, National Gallery, 1990, pp. 221–2. For colour theory with reference to painting see Kemp 1990, pp. 306–22, and Gage 1993, pp. 171–6.
17. Maxwell's work is discussed in the general references cited in n. 16 above; see also Maxwell 1890, I, pp. 119–54.
18. Rood 1881, p. 215, see also pp. 138–53.
19. Rood 1881, pp. 117–8, 235–45, esp. pp. 241–4.
20. Paris, Grand Palais, 1991, pp. 390–1.

2 The Bathers: Making a Masterpiece

Seurat probably began his preparatory work for the *Bathers* (Plate 178) during the spring or summer of 1883. The painting must have been finished by early in the following year, in time for submission to the jury of the Salon exhibition. The artist left no documents that shed light on the genesis of the picture but the studies illustrated on the following pages offer some record of his extensive preparations for his first major oil painting.

Seurat's painstaking research for the *Bathers* can be related to his early training at the Ecole des Beaux-Arts. The process of making studies of various kinds in preparation for large-scale compositions was central to the academic programme. An artist was expected to clarify his ideas for a picture by making a series of preliminary sketches and studies, gradually imposing intellectual order upon raw inspiration, for as Charles Blanc declared, 'composition is in no way improvised'.[1]

The notion of the artist leaving nothing to chance, carefully planning every detail of his canvas, also fits in well with Seurat's reputation as a disciplined and ponderous craftsman. Emile Verhaeren, who knew the painter in the later 1880s described him as an 'organiser', who never began his pictures 'without knowing where he was going . . .'.[2] When Seurat's output is viewed as a whole, there is much to endorse this observation. However, a close examination of the *Bathers* and its related studies suggests that the systematic or the conventional nature of its production should not be over-stressed. As we might expect for a young artist tackling a work on this scale, there are signs of hesitation and doubt alongside the obvious confidence. There are indications too that if his methods were in many respects traditional they could also be fluid and improvised. In some respects it is the informality rather than the precision of Seurat's preparations that is surprising.

The following survey of studies and drawings for the *Bathers*, shows the gradual development of Seurat's ideas for his first major canvas. We can follow how the young artist wrestled with different approaches to technique and subject matter and, while it is impossible to reconstruct exactly how he worked, we can get a sense of how the painting grew out of a process of selection and refinement. A technical examination of the canvas itself offers new information about how the picture evolved and, in particular, about the role of the preparatory drawings. The artist himself would later refer to his first large works as his 'canvases of combat'.[3] Modern methods of scientific analysis do indeed reveal signs of a struggle as Seurat worked to adapt his technique to a grand scale.

1. Blanc 1867, 2nd edn. 1870 p. 552.
2. Verhaeren 1891, cited in Seyrès 1991 pp. 280–1.
3. In a draft letter of 1890 to the journalist Maurice Beaubourg, cited in Paris, Grand Palais, 1991, p. 381.

The Oil Studies

The catalogue raisonné of Seurat's work compiled by César de Hauke groups together fourteen works as oil studies for the *Bathers*,[1] all of which are reproduced here except one that appears to represent a site further upstream and should be set apart.[2] The studies are all painted on Seurat's customary wooden panels, but in spite of their shared format they vary considerably in their technique and in their approach to the subject. Several of them have the appearance of rapid, open-air sketches which record figures or animals along the riverbank. Other panels have more considered compositions and are painted with a careful, measured touch. Three of the panels concentrate solely on the landscape, either as a general view or as a close-up fragment, while other studies concentrate on figures. The scale and the treatment of many of the panels suggest that Seurat painted them in front of the motif at Asnières, using his hand-held painting box. However, he may have reworked some of them back in his studio. And, as we will see, there are certain studies which have a distinctly schematic character, which suggests that they may have been painted entirely in the studio using information from other studies.

48. *The Riverbanks: Study for 'Bathers at Asnières'*, 1882–3
Oil on wood, 15.9 x 25.1 cm
Glasgow Art Gallery and Museum (CAT. 2)

It is tempting to try to arrange the studies into an exact sequence to recreate the step-by-step development of the artist's ideas.[3] It is certainly possible to suggest some general order of working, yet, even taking into account the variety and differing status of the studies, Seurat's ideas seem to have shifted back and forth in a way that undermines any effort to establish a precise or logical evolution from one panel to another. Ultimately, Seurat could have had them all to hand as he worked on the final picture. Visitors to his studio would later describe how he kept his *croquetons* hanging on the walls

and, according to Charles Angrand, they were his 'chief delight'.[4] As a group the studies must have had a cumulative impact, providing general information about effects of light and atmosphere as well as specific reminders about the site near Asnières. Even a study which must count among the first relating to the *Bathers* (Plate 48) was consulted for the small but important detail of the cloud of steam from a train passing over the bridge in the background in the final picture.

The earliest studies that can be related to the *Bathers* may have been made as part of Seurat's wider campaign of

49. Map of Asnières and the Grande Jatte

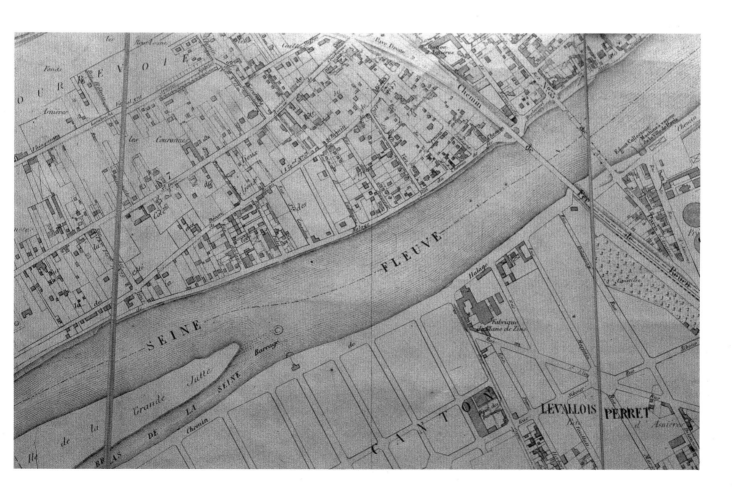

50. *Bathers: Study for 'Bathers at Asnières'*, 1883–4
Oil on wood, 15.5 x 25.0 cm
Private Collection (CAT. 4)

sketching along the banks of the Seine and perhaps even
before he had evolved the idea of creating a large picture of
this subject. One of these (Plate 48) seems to date from 1882
rather than 1883. The handling of paint is more tentative than
in the other studies of this site while the limited colour range
and the autumnal foliage also distinguish it from the rest of
the group. Nevertheless, this work establishes the general vista,
which became the basic setting for the *Bathers*. The view
along the riverbank at the left is interrupted by a sandy gully.
We know from other studies that this inlet was used for
watering horses, and it may be the indentation in the
riverbank that is clearly shown on a near contemporary map
(Plate 49). As the map indicates, this stretch of the riverbank

51. *Horse and Boats: Study for 'Bathers at Asnières'*, 1883–4
Oil on wood, 15.2 x 24.5 cm
Private Collection (CAT. 5)

52. *Horses in the Water: Study for 'Bathers at Asnières'*, 1883–4
Oil on wood, 15.2 x 24.8 cm
Private Collection on extended loan to the Courtauld Institute
Galleries, London (CAT. 3)

53. *The Rainbow: Study for 'Bathers at Asnières'*, 1883–4
Oil on wood, 15.5 x 24.5 cm
London, National Gallery (CAT. 6)

between Seurat's viewpoint and the Asnières railway bridge in the background was dotted with suburban dwellings. Many of these would have been obscured from Seurat's view as the bank curved away from the artist, and in this study, as in the final picture, we have only a glimpse of some villas nestling among the trees at the left. Behind them, the railway bridge leads across to the chimneys of the gas plant and factories at Clichy on the opposite bank. The horizon is closed at the far right by the clump of trees on the tip of the Ile de la Grande Jatte. A small dab of white paint just to the left of the island stands for the little round tower that appears in several other studies and the finished painting. On the map this appears as a free-standing structure forming part of a weir next to the island.[5]

There are two lively, open-air studies (Plates 50 and 51) which also must belong to an early stage in the development of

Seurat's ideas for the *Bathers*. Both were painted on panels with white grounds which enhance the brightness of the colours. Seurat rarely abandons himself to the physical pleasure of manipulating oil paint but here there is a real sense of an artist enjoying the inherent textures of his medium. A flick of a loaded brush produces the reflection of a sail; a smear of paint renders the hull of a moving boat; a few deft strokes produce a convincing notation of a figure. Even as he works at speed, Seurat carefully constructs the tonal relationships throughout the picture. The pale backs of the boys in the water are set off by patches of dark blue while the white horse also has a blue silhouette. These contrasts are at their most contrived in the seated figure at the centre of the composition. His white coat is set against dark touches of blue but the dark tones of his hat and trousers are surrounded by patches of pale yellow and white in the water.

54. *The Black Horse: Study for 'Bathers at Asnières'*, 1883–4
Oil on wood, 15.9 x 25.0 cm
Edinburgh, National Gallery of Scotland (CAT. 7)

The horses in these sketches are a reminder of the nearby presence of industry and commerce and that we are close to what must have been a busy towpath. Yet these are not weary nags being watered by exhausted workers. The mood is one of recreation and pleasure rather than toil. The combination of boating and watering horses appears again in another panel (Plate 52) which also has the spontaneous qualities of an outdoor study. This time painting over bare wood, Seurat began with his usual thin washes of underpainting with grey in the water and green in the riverbank and trees. This was overlaid with small dabs of broken colour. This vivid study has often been compared to the river scenes of Monet and Renoir. However, next to the forceful contrasts of orange and blue in, for example, Renoir's *Boating on the Seine* (Plate 129), Seurat's handling of colour seems conventional, based around patterns of light and dark rather than scintillating effects of colour

contrast. With his mixtures lightened or darkened by the addition of white and black, the colouring seems closer to Manet's adopted Impressionist palette (Plate 128).

The panel known as *The Rainbow* (Plate 53) retains some of the spontaneity of these early studies, although on close examination it is apparent that it is elaborately painted and artfully composed. The picture still conveys a convincing sense of a particular effect of light and atmosphere, yet even the rainbow arching down from the exact centre of the panel seems highly contrived and was added over dry paint in the sky. The three seated figures all face the same direction and are ranged across the foreground. Their presence was planned from an early stage and they are carefully integrated into the rhythms of the landscape. So for example, the head, upper torso and legs of the figure at the left are each locked into different bands of the landscape behind. The final effect is

55. *Bathers in the Water: Study for 'Bathers at Asnières'*, 1883–4
Oil on wood, 15.5 x 25.0 cm
Paris, Musée d'Orsay (CAT. 8)

quite unlike the apparently haphazard groupings of people and
horses in motion that feature in some of the studies for the
Bathers. The measured design and the controlled handling of
paint add to a feeling of calm, verging on lassitude, that would
be carried over into the final painting.

The Rainbow may be one of the earlier studies for the
Bathers, but its studied arrangement suggests that Seurat was
already working out ideas for a definitive composition. There
are other panels, however, in which Seurat not only experiments
with different combinations of figures but also with contrasting
approaches to the subject. In the picture now in Edinburgh
(Plate 54), he focuses on the industrial aspect of the site. The
pose of the man at the left of *The Rainbow* is adapted to
become a brooding presence in the foreground. His dark,
practical clothes and his powerful arms seem to link him with
the environment depicted in the background, where the sky is

56. *Study for 'Bathers at Asnières'*, 1883–4
Oil on wood, 16 x 25 cm
London, National Gallery (CAT. 11)

57. *Study for 'Bathers at Asnières'*, 1883–4
Oil on wood, 15.7 x 25.0 cm
Cleveland Museum of Art (CAT. 10)

58. *Clothes on the Grass: Study for 'Bathers at Asnières'*, 1883–4
Oil on wood, 16.2 x 24.8 cm
London, Tate Gallery, on loan to the National Gallery (CAT. 13)

darkened by the clouds of smoke from the factory chimneys.

By contrast, another panel (Plate 55) presents a similar view as an image of leisure rather than industry. The chimneys are edited out and the industrial buildings seem to dissolve into a distant, sun-soaked haze. Nude boys bathe in an attractive river and a sail appears in the distance. As usual, Seurat painted directly on to his wooden panel, which shows through as a base colour in several areas, including the river, where it sets up a warm orange-brown contrast to the vivid blues. Unlike the dark accents that predominate in the Edinburgh study, the colour scheme revolves around light tones. The figures are delicately modelled with pale blue shadows worked into the highlights in a technique that is similar to that employed in the final picture. Touches of red, green and yellow enliven the background and a streak of pink in the roofs is answered by a complementary tinge of green in the sky. The study now in

Cleveland (Plate 57) is equally luminous and was painted in a similar, shorthand style. The landscape setting is very close to that of the final picture, and here Seurat experiments with a single figure dominating the foreground. The same figure would later reappear in the background of the *Bathers*, but this time wearing a white jacket.

Seurat eventually chose to combine key elements from the Edinburgh, Paris and Cleveland panels in a compositional study now in Chicago (Plate 60). The setting is closest to the Cleveland picture but the seated figure becomes a bather whose pose is based on yet another rapid sketch (Plate 56). Several details from the Paris picture are retained, including an indication of the dog in the foreground, the bundle of clothes and boots and one of the bathing figures. The dark-clothed figure from the Edinburgh picture also reappears, but he has been placed further back and given a straw hat instead

59. *Two Seated Figures: Study for 'Bathers at Asnières'*, 1883–4
Oil on wood, 17.5 x 26.3 cm
Kansas City, Nelson-Atkins Museum of Art (CAT. 12)

of a cap. The factories and gasworks reassert their presence, but the river belongs to boaters and bathers and, as in the final picture, industry and leisure, or in today's terms, pollution and pleasure, exist side by side.

The Chicago picture is an elaborate and carefully considered study but it was not necessarily Seurat's final essay in colour before he began work on the final painting. A study now in Kansas (Plate 59) is closely related to the Chicago panel and may have been developed alongside it. It has been noted that Seurat had scored several lines across the surface of the Chicago study.[6] Before he began this picture, he used a straight edge to score horizontal and vertical centre lines on to the panel. When the painting was under way he then added some more lines which are scored freehand into the wet paint, probably with the end of his brush. These extra lines correspond to the limits of the Kansas study and it has been

suggested that they were drawn to assist with the incorporation of information from that study.[7] It is also possible that having embarked on the Chicago panel, Seurat then decided to experiment further, marking out a section of his composition which he developed as the Kansas study. A rather schematic view of the empty landscape setting (Plate 58) also relates closely to the composition of the Kansas panel and may have been painted as part of this experiment.

The Kansas study is one of the most fully developed for the *Bathers*, and an illustration of a detail of this work reveals Seurat's painstaking brushwork. The shadowed area of the bather's eye is worked through with tiny strokes of pink, while the shadows of the roofs and chimneys are depicted with minuscule dots of blue and pink paint that anticipate the precision of the artist's later technique.

If the Kansas panel represents an alternative idea for the

60. *Final Study for 'Bathers at Asnières'*, 1883–4
Oil on wood, 15.8 x 25.1 cm
The Art Institute of Chicago (CAT. 9)

arrangement of the final picture it was not pursued. The lines gouged into the surface of the Chicago panel (Plate 60) are partly obscured by further layers of paint, which suggests that Seurat returned to this composition. The reclining man in the foreground seems to have been added at this later stage. Although Seurat established the basic layout of his composition in the Chicago panel he may have gone on to produce further notes for his picture. A study of the left-hand side of the picture (Plate 61) is painted with the same deliberation as the Kansas picture. It is both a study for the still life of the clothes piled up on the bank and an exercise in colour where he experiments with the pale, luminous surfaces that characterise the finished painting.

As a group the oil studies for the *Bathers* display a remarkable variety. This stems in part from their different functions. Using the pedantic terminology of the nineteenth-century Academy, some might be described as *études* (studies that provided information to be incorporated into a finished picture) while others might best be described as *esquisses* (studies that are in effect trials for the basic arrangement of whole composition). For example the study of five figures (Plate 56) is an *étude* in which Seurat uses his panel like a reporter's notepad, accumulating ideas for his composition. There is only a cursory indication of the landscape background and the figures on the right are drawn to a different scale to those on the left. As we have seen, however, there are other studies which may have been drafts for the arrangement of the entire composition. In these works we become aware of how the artist seems to sift his material, imposing structure and order on the raw data of nature.

This process of editing and selection would be familiar to any artist working within the broad confines of an academic

61. *The Seine with Clothing on the Bank: Study for 'Bathers at Asnières'*, 1883–4
Oil on wood, 17.1 x 26.4 cm
Private Collection (CAT. 14)

tradition. As noted above, Seurat, through his academic training and his study of authors such as Charles Blanc, was familiar with accepted ideas about how the vocabulary of the real world was transformed by the grammar of art through prolonged study and deliberation. Yet there is something novel and idiosyncratic about Seurat's dogged pursuit of his subject in these small panels. Poised between observation and invention, between the record of particular nuances of light and mood and the imposition of intellectual order, these vivid notes seem to assert his determined independence rather than his passive allegiance to traditional methods.

1. De Hauke, i, pp. 198–9.
2. H. 83: see Zimmerman 1991, pp. 154–5.
3. See, for example, Nicolson 1941, p. 140–5; Cooper 1946, pp. 12–14, Thomson 1985, p. 79f.; Zimmermann 1991, p. 154f. and Paris, Grand Palais, 1991, p. 152f. for suggested sequences for the oil studies fot the *Bathers.*
4. Cited in Coquiot 1924, p. 39.
5. An old postcard of the tip of the island and the tower is illustrated in Zimmermann 1991, p. 152.
6. Thomson 1985, p. 84; Paris, Grand Palais, 1991, p. 161. We are grateful to Douglas Druick and his colleagues at the Art Institute of Chicago for technical information and for an X-radiograph of the Chicago study.
7. Paris, Grand Palais, 1991, p. 162.

The Drawings for the *Bathers*

62. *Hat, Shoes and Undergarments:*
Study for 'Bathers at Asnières', 1883–4
Conté crayon on paper, 23.6 x 30.9 cm
Cambridge, Mass., Fogg Art Museum (CAT. 15)

There are drawings that relate to all of the five main figures in the *Bathers* and one which depicts the discarded clothes in the foreground (Plate 62).[1] All of these are in conté crayon on Seurat's usual Michallet paper cut to sheets of approximately the same size. During the final stages of the preparation of this catalogue a previously uncatalogued and unpublished drawing came to light (Plate 66).[2] This drawing appears to be Seurat's first draft for the standing bather at the right (the so called echo-boy). A detail of this pose was developed in the famous sheet now at Yale (Plate 67).

There can be little doubt that the drawings for the *Bathers* were made from life in the confines of a studio. An easel appears in the background of one (Plate 63), a skirting board is indicated in another (Plate 65) and in a further drawing (Plate 64) a languid nude seems to be seated on a box rather than a riverbank. In comparison to many other drawings by Seurat, those relating to the *Bathers* are notable for a less synthetic, more naturalistic treatment of the figure. The contours are often clearly defined and the individual figures have a considerable sculptural presence. Where Seurat's broad, tonal style usually encourages generalisation, here he evokes an uncharacteristic level of detail; he takes care to carve out the intricate anatomy of an ear or to suggest the way soft muscle gives way to bone in the forearm (Plate 67). Yet as Benedict Nicolson observed in one of the first detailed discussions of these works, the drawings still manage to combine intricacy with simplification.[3] Although they are drawn from the life we become aware of a process of abstraction, of complex forms reduced to elemental shapes and simple planes. The way that the forms are pressed close to the surface of the paper and are cropped into unexpected details helps to reinforce this underlying geometry.

In the artificial environment of the studio Seurat could control and manipulate the effects of light and shade that would be carried over into the painting. In most of the drawings the modelling of the figure is enhanced by contrasting tones in the background. In the seated nude, for example, the light tones of his arm are answered by a darker tone in the background, while the shadow of his back is set against a halo of light. These contrasts were carried over into the painting although they were clearly harder to contrive in colour than in black and white. The complex patterns of tone that are rendered with apparent ease in *The Echo* (Plate 67), for example, became a confused and much reworked area on the painted surface.

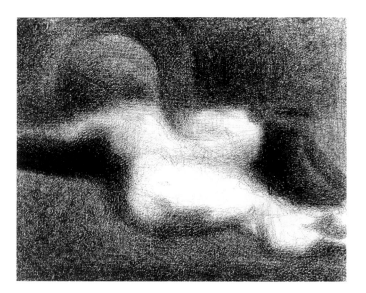

It would be logical to assume that, having established the landscape setting and the arrangement of his figures in his small painted studies, Seurat then decided to make the drawings in order to finalise the details of each pose before he embarked on the painting itself. However, the evidence of an X-radiograph suggests that the painting was already under way before at least some of the drawings were brought into play. This has important implications for the development of the composition and the role of the drawings is discussed below in more detail.

The way that Seurat used these drawings must have had a profound impact on the appearance of the finished picture. As studies from the life they may have reasserted the physical presence of the figures, but the manner in which they were literally grafted on to the composition must surely have emphasised the separation of one figure from another. It is often observed that each individual in the painting seems oblivious to the presence of his companions and, whether intentional or not, Seurat's manner of working must have enhanced this effect. The Chicago oil study (Plate 60) with its lively impressionist brushwork and more alert poses does not convey the same heavy mood of separation and self-containment. Through the medium of the drawings, something of the weariness and boredom of posing in an artist's studio is carried over into the finished picture. The colour and light of the riverbank seems to be an incongruous setting for these passive males who are absorbed in the quiet reverie that often protects life models from interminable boredom.

63. *Boy viewed from behind:*
Study for 'Bathers at Asnières', 1883–4
Conté crayon on paper, 32.0 x 24.5 cm
Private Collection (CAT. 16)

64. *Seated Nude Boy: Study for 'Bathers at Asnières'*, 1883–4
Conté crayon on paper, 31.7 x 24.7 cm
Edinburgh, National Gallery of Scotland (CAT. 17)

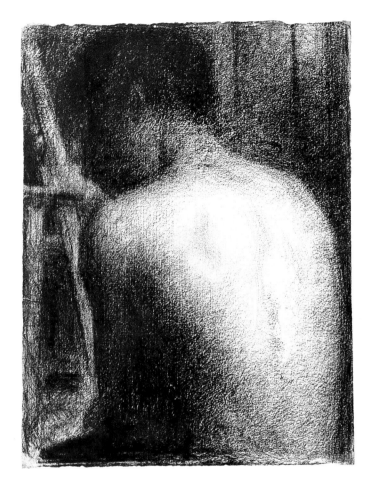

1. On these drawings see esp. Franz and Growe 1983, p. 77 f.; Herbert 1962, p. 104; Paris, Grand Palais, 1991, p. 161f.
2. This drawing is mentioned by Robert Herbert (Paris, Grand Palais, 1991 p. 151 n.6), where the provenance is given as 'formerly collection Henri de Régnier'. Initial examination of the sheet suggests that it is not on Michallet paper. However, on the reverse there is the following inscription, apparently in the hand of Maximilien Luce (one of the compilers of Seurat's studio inventory): 'G. Seurat L. Baignade'. There is also (in another hand) the number '366'. This number can be linked to the numbered inventory in the Signac archives where, under the category 'Croquis et Dessins', Signac noted: '366–372 Baignade'. We are grateful to Robert Herbert for this information.
3. Nicolson 1941, p. 145.

65. *Study of Legs: Study for 'Bathers at Asnières'*, 1883–4
Conté crayon on paper, 24.2 x 31.8 cm
Private Collection

66. *Study for 'Bathers at Asnières'*, 1883–4
Conté crayon on paper, 32.4 x 24.1 cm
Private Collection (CAT. 18)

67. *The Echo: Study for 'Bathers at Asnières'*, 1883–4
Conté crayon on paper, 31.2 x 24.0 cm
New Haven, Yale University Art Gallery (CAT. 19)

Making the Final Picture

The *Bathers* is painted on a single piece of canvas, commercially supplied and pre-primed by the artist's colourman. It was normal practice for huge lengths of canvas to be stretched and primed before they were cut up into the various standard sizes for sale. This one, considerably larger than any of the available standard formats, would presumably have been mounted on its heavy stretcher (which it no longer has) as a special order. It is very close in size to the canvas of *Sunday on La Grande Jatte* (Plate 153) and they may well have been identical before the *Grande Jatte* was expanded to include its painted borders.

The priming is greyish white, composed of lead white tinted with a small amount of carbon black pigment, but it is densely covered by the paint layers and its light, cool tonality plays little part in the final appearance of the *Bathers*. There are no signs of any of the traditional devices, such as squaring-up, which might have eased the transition from studies to final painting, nor is there direct evidence of how Seurat placed and sketched out his composition on the priming.[1] Examination of the edges of the canvas reveals no position lines or squaring-up, but there may be axes fixing positions that are now

68. Composite X-ray photograph of the whole of Seurat's *Bathers at Asnières*, showing the variation in X-ray density of the paint layers in the composition. The dark bands around many of the large-scale elements of the design represent Seurat's initial application of thin layers of paint to mark these out. The paint is very thickly applied in the sky, the figures and the foreground riverbank.

covered by the paint layers. There are traces of carbon black at the base of the paint samples taken from the outline of the seated boy, suggesting that the figures and other principal features of the composition were drawn in individually, perhaps with charcoal or conté crayon. It seems that with the aid of his studies Seurat was able to establish the basic arrangement of the landscape setting, which remained more or less unaltered as the painting developed. The positions of the main figures were also fixed at an early stage although, as we shall see, their exact poses were subject to some revision.

The composite X-ray photograph of the *Bathers* is a striking image – a simplified monochrome version of the painting set out in clearly defined areas of paint separated by dark outlines (Plate 68). This type of X-ray image arises from the artist filling in the composition of a carefully systematised drawing with blocks of dense colour that do not quite meet. The narrow spaces between the blocks, where the paint is thin and only the initial lay-in is present, form the dark outlines. X-rays of the oil sketches are, by contrast, relatively unstructured, with the various areas undifferentiated and the brushstrokes evenly weighted.

Once his drawing was in position on the pale grey priming, Seurat covered the whole canvas with thin layers of colour, setting down the basic tonality of the various areas in many applications of thinly brushed out paint. This was his normal practice in the oil sketches and it is also apparent in the later *Grande Jatte*. This underpainting is visible through the upper layers in many areas and in the outlines of the figures; it seems to consist of a mesh of thin washy strokes rather than the more continuous layer observed in the sketches, and its colour does not always correspond closely to the intended final colour (see below). In the *Bathers* a considerable range of colour and tone, some quite muted, is used in the early stages.

Working within these carefully defined outlines Seurat systematically built up the painted forms with layer upon layer of brushed, dabbed and dragged oil paint. So thick are the accumulations in some areas that a porous honeycomb of paint has resulted where one layer has been pulled across gaps in the layer below (Plate 69). In many places, trapped air bubbles burst through the paint surface while it was still fluid, making small holes and craters (Plate 70). Most of the paler passages of paint are thickly layered and smoothed by repeated brushing: especially heavily worked areas are the dense light halo in the water behind the seated boy's back and certain of the flesh paints.

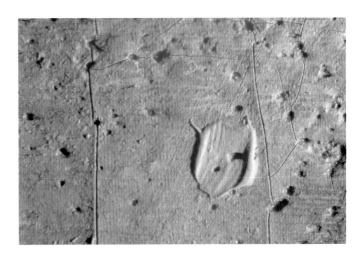

69. Macro detail of the water, centre right, showing air bubbles breaking through the impasto.

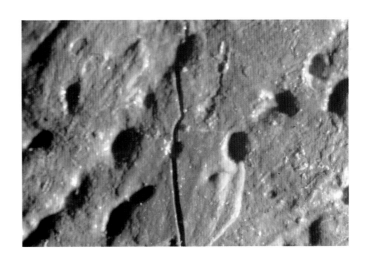

70. Macro detail of the boy's hat, showing air bubbles breaking through the upper paint layers.

1. The idea that Seurat arranged the compositions of the *Bathers* and other works according to the Golden Section has been repeated often in the Seurat literature but is now generally dismissed; see Herz-Fischler 1983, pp. 109–12.

The Evolution of the Composition

An examination of the X-ray photograph (Plate 68) and a comparison with the Chicago sketch (Plate 60) reveal several significant changes that give clues to the ways in which Seurat's ideas developed. The main compositional change is seen in the reclining figure in the left foreground. In the Chicago sketch the legs of this figure were angled steeply out of the bottom edge of the picture. In the final state of the *Bathers* they are more horizontal and wholly visible. In the X-ray image of the *Bathers* both positions of the legs can be seen: Seurat began by painting the legs at the steeper angle of the Chicago sketch and changed their position to that of the final design (Plates 71 and 72). The position and scale of the dog were altered at the same time: the larger dog of the sketch is visible in the X-ray of the final picture, but was then made smaller so that its whole body is visible. A strip of grass in the foreground now conceals brown paint of the earlier working of the dog's body.

The drawing showing the whole reclining figure with legs outstretched (Plate 75) has traditionally been assumed to be a preliminary study for the *Bathers*; the evidence of the X-radiograph, however, suggests that this study was made at an intermediate stage in order to clarify and improve the design for this figure. Seurat made two further drawings to fix the detail of the reclining man's head and hat. The first of these includes careful folds on the model's coat (Plate 73). This was simplified in a subsequent drawing that closes in on the head (Plate 74), which has been turned more to the right as it appears in the final picture.

The red hat of the bather at the extreme right was also changed in style and profile between the broad-brimmed shape in the Chicago oil-sketch (Plate 60) through an intermediate stage with a lower crown, seen clearly in the X-ray, to the more conical small-brimmed hat of the final painting (Plates 76 and 77). This figure seems to have caused some problems. Seurat's first drawing of the nude boy (Plate 66) presumably did not offer enough detail to allow him to paint the complex interaction of the arms, hands and face. A further drawing was needed to clarify this pose (Plate 67). In the final painting this area is much reworked, suggesting that in this case the move from tone to colour was a difficult one.

71. X-ray detail of the reclining figure in the foreground.

72. Detail of the reclining figure in the foreground.

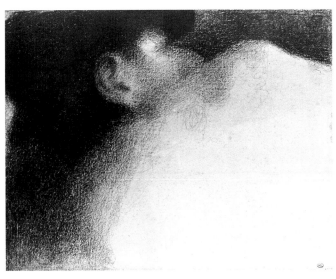

73. *Man in a Bowler Hat: Study for 'Bathers at Asnières'*, 1883–4
Conté crayon on paper, 24 x 30 cm
Berggruen Collection (CAT. 20)

74. *Reclining Man: Study for 'Bathers at Asnières'*, 1883–4
Conté crayon on paper, 24 x 31 cm
Paris, Musée du Louvre (CAT. 21)

75. *Reclining Man:*
Study for 'Bathers at Asnières', 1883–4
Conté crayon on paper, 24.5 x 31.5 cm
Riehen/Basel, Fondation Beyeler (CAT. 22)

76. X-ray detail of the boy on the right.

77. Detail of the boy on the right.

The head of the central bather shows another progression from sketch through intermediate painted stage to final state. In the Chicago study this figure's haircut is short, revealing an ear and brow. The X-ray of the *Bathers* (Plate 78) reveals that a similar head to that seen in the sketch underlies the finished head with its longer hair (Plate 79). This is also a particularly heavily reworked area, with many applications of paint brushed and rebrushed to give a rough, caked texture which has been smoothed over while the paint was still soft. The drawing (Plate 64) again appears to have been made as the painting was developed, in order to envisage the final form of this important element. The flick of hair at the nape of the boy's neck is carried over from the drawing and, since it passes over the already completed paint of the water, it does not register in the X-ray photograph. There are indications in the

X-ray image that Seurat adjusted the outline of this figure and again, the drawing seems to have acted as his final guide. It is in the drawing that we first find the surprisingly long arm, the drooping head and the slight slump of the shoulders that appear in the finished picture.

The principal alteration to the straw-hatted seated figure at the left is that the long trouser legs of the Chicago study are pulled up to the knees in the finished picture (Plate 81). There is no trace of these longer trouser legs in the X-ray (Plate 80), but the image of the flesh paint of his lower legs is so dense that it is impossible to be sure whether this change occurred before or during the painting of the *Bathers*. In any case, the positions of the legs themselves were modified as the painting developed and this is suggested by two intermediate drawings (Plates 65 and 82). Examination of the corresponding area on

78. X-ray detail of the central figure.

79. Detail of the central figure. Note the very thickly applied paint in the head and hair and the flick of hair at the nape of the neck, present in the drawing (see Plate 64).

80. X-ray detail of the seated figure at the left.

81. Detail of the seated figure at the left. Note the alterations in the legs in comparisons between the X-ray image, the drawing and the finished painting (see Plates 65 and 82).

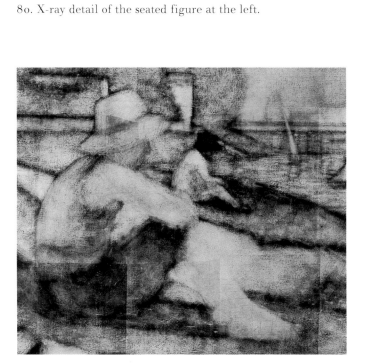

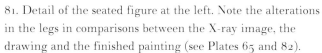

the painting shows that these details posed some problems for the painter and the drawings presumably helped him to determine their final position.

The fingers of the left hand that appear under the right elbow are a late addition, not present in the sketch and not detectable in the X-ray but included in the drawing (Plate 82). In the finished picture the man is seated on what appears to be his folded clothes. The X-ray and close examination of the paint surface show that Seurat did not plan this from the outset, but painted it over the grass in dark shadow: the inclusion of this feature in the drawing confirms its probable status as an intermediate rather than a preliminary study.

Finally, there are some details in the finished picture that are not visible in the X-ray. The straw-hatted figure lying on the riverbank in the middle distance was apparently a late

addition, added perhaps to echo the new position of the reclining man in the foreground. Similarly the skiff at the far right edge and the ferry boat with its prominent tricolour do not appear to have been part of Seurat's original scheme (Plate 83). The X-ray and the technical examination show that the *Bathers* evolved in several distinct phases. It is possible that these details were added after the main body of work on the canvas had been completed, perhaps even after a gap of several years. This is speculation, but it is intriguing to imagine the appearance of the painting without the key details of the ferry and the skiff. These elements add considerable life and movement to the composition. Without them, the solemn, static quality of the painting would surely have been even more apparent. It is also interesting that the ferry, which is sometimes used as a clue to interpreting the social message of

83. Detail of the small ferry in the upper right added by
Seurat at a late stage in the evolution of the composition.

82. *Seated Boy with Straw Hat:*
Study for 'Bathers at Asnières', 1883–4
Conté crayon on paper, 24.1 x 31.2 cm
New Haven, Yale University Art Gallery (CAT. 23)

the painting, did not form part of the artist's first ideas.[1] It
seems possible that Seurat may have returned to the *Bathers*
after he had begun work on the *Grande Jatte*; the issue of how
these two works relate is a contentious one in Seurat studies.[2]
Yet, although there is no direct evidence that he planned the
Grande Jatte as a pendant to the *Bathers*, he may have
contemplated a link between them in both technique and
subject matter. It is well known that Seurat started to repaint
parts of the *Bathers* with the pointillist technique that he used
in the final stages of the *Grande Jatte* (see below). Perhaps the
ferry with its conspicuously middle-class passengers heading
across the river to the pleasures of La Grande Jatte, was added
as part of an attempt to impose a closer link between the two
large compositions. In the end, however, the two works were
never exhibited together in Seurat's lifetime. By the time that

the *Grande Jatte* was shown in 1886, at the last Impressionist
exhibition, the *Bathers* with its strong whiff of the Académie
des Beaux-Arts must have seemed outmoded. Seurat may have
begun to repaint the *Bathers* in an effort to make it match his
new avant-garde credentials, but the attempt was not pursued.

1. See, for example, House 1980, p. 346f.; House 1989, p. 127;
   Zimmermann 1991, p. 139.
2. See House 1980, p. 346f.; Thomson 1985, pp. 125–6; House 1989;
   Zimmermann 1991, pp. 135ff.

Colour and Colour Effect
in the *Bathers*

In spite of the complexity in the design of the *Bathers*, and the many stages in its evolution and execution, Seurat's palette remained restricted in range with certain pigments dominating the colour effects he achieved. Among the more intense colours are cobalt blue and French ultramarine, vermilion and a strongly coloured pinkish-red lake, viridian green and two yellows, chrome and cadmium (Plate 85).[1] Many of the paint layers are lightened in tone by the addition of lead white, and this pigment is used widely in all the light-coloured passages. In addition there is some restrained use of perhaps three types of earth pigment — a red, a brownish red and a yellow-brown — but on the whole these occur in the lower paint layers, particularly in the structure of the preliminary design laid out in the thinnest underlayers, as described above, although in a few places earths appear at the surface (Plate 84). (In the final modifications Seurat made when he returned to the painting, probably in 1887, different materials occur.)

Except in one particular section of the composition — the dark shadowed parts of the trousers of the seated figure at the far left — no black pigment was used in the *Bathers*,

the darkest tones being formed from paints containing a high proportion of French ultramarine, which has a very dark intense inky colour when used pure and also when the blue is mixed with red lake pigment to form very dark purples and brownish-purple colours. The boots on the riverbank are an example of this mixture of pigments, while the dark purplish-brown surface paints of the reclining figure's trousers are composed of red lake mixed with a high proportion of French ultramarine, over a solid underlayer of red-brown earth pigment (Plate 86). In the same figure's bowler hat, the ratio of the deep blue to other pigments is even greater, lending a very saturated dark tone to the paint (Plate 87).

The considerable range of colour and colour effect Seurat creates is achieved in the painting with quite few pigments, but with great elaboration in their use. This is particularly evident in his mixture of colour, superimposition of multicoloured paint layers, his use of broken and directional brushstrokes and a complex juxtapositioning of contrasting colour as well as lightness and darkness of tone. These contrasts are created at the level of scale of individual

84. Dark yellow-brown touch of paint of the central figure's hair in cross-section. The surface paint contains a yellow-brown earth and some lake pigment. The understructure consists of separate layers containing vermilion, cobalt blue and a yellow earth. The lowermost two layers of pale blue and pale green represent the thin initial lay-in paints for the head. Magnification, 205x.

85. Detail of the yellow flowers near the signature, lower left, painted in cadmium yellow. A similar group of flowers can be seen to the lower right, near the water's edge.

86. Purple-brown of the reclining figure's trousers. Paint cross-section showing the surface glaze of French ultramarine and red lake over a dark blue-green of cobalt blue and viridian. Beneath this there is a solid red-brown layer containing earth pigments and vermilion. The mid-yellow green of the early stages of the riverbank passes under the paint of the trousers. Magnification, 205x.

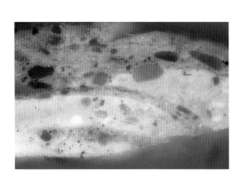
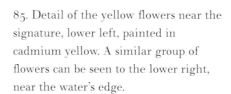

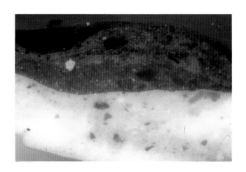

87. Detail of the reclining figure's bowler hat, finished at the surface in a paint rich in dark, inky blue French ultramarine.

88. Detail of the foreground riverbank, showing the mesh of surface brushstrokes.

89. Detail of the foreground riverbank, showing the final strokes of strong colour.

brushstrokes as well as between adjacent broader areas of the painting. The complexity of execution is taken to its greatest degree of development in the colour and structure of the sunlit grass on the foreground riverbank seen in relation to those areas of the bank cast in shadow (see Plate 46). The scintillating effects of light on the water are achieved in a similar way, although for the river's surface the brushstrokes are largely horizontal and parallel, rather than constructive of form and running in all directions, as they do in the foreground.

Where several coloured pigments are incorporated into mixed paints in the *Bathers*, these were kept simple in constitution to retain the purity of tone that is generally lost when many different pigments are combined. For example the cobalt blue used for the sky and the water occurs either only in pure form or mixed just with white; the applications of greyer-blue tints containing French ultramarine were kept quite separate. The most intense green colours are made of viridian green or simple mixtures of this pigment with white or with a strongly coloured yellow, such as cadmium or chrome. Viridian with cobalt blue provides another colour variation in the greens. These different paint mixtures juxtaposed with purer colour are interwoven in criss-cross brushwork over the surface of the foreground, layer over layer, to create the vibrant and powerful colour effects Seurat achieved (Plates 88 and 89). Among the green brushstrokes of the grass are touches of intense blue (cobalt blue) and grey-blue (French ultramarine and white) as well as mauves and purples (cobalt blue, French ultramarine and red lake), yellow (cadmium and chrome yellows), pink and red (vermilion, red lake and white) and

90. Detail of the river in the middle distance and the railway bridge beyond.

91. Detail of the thin band of multicoloured paint beneath the central figure's thighs. These blurred brushstrokes represent Seurat's initial delineation of the main element of the composition in the first paint layers to be applied over the ground.

orange. The pigment mixtures remain simple, as in, for example, the brightest orange streaks in the grass, which consist of roughly equal proportions of vermilion and chrome yellow, carefully blended to a homogenous colour, so much so as to suggest a manufacturers' mixture of pigments.[2] The yellow flowers growing on the bank are pure cadmium yellow (Plate 85).[3]

Where a colour is modified it is most usually by superimposition of paint layers, such as a glaze of French ultramarine to darken the intensity of vermilion of the discarded garment on which the figure to the far left sits, or the use of a translucent combination of French ultramarine with red lake to create the purple and blue shadows on the grass behind the principal figures. Elsewhere, a yellow-brown earth was applied to subdue the stronger colours of the hair – vermilion and cobalt blue – of the central figure seated on the riverbank, an unusual case of an earth colour used at the surface of the picture (Plate 84).

The general lightness of tone in the painting results from the incorporation of a large proportion of lead white in many of the paint layers, not only in the last applications of paint at the surface. To some extent in the grassy bank of the foreground, the strongly coloured, light-toned, yellow pigments also raise the general key of the painting and this helps to

provide the luminous effect and, in conjunction with Seurat's open brushwork, something of the quality and look of painting in *buon fresco*, to which the *Bathers* has been likened. This overall rather bland lightness conceals an extraordinarily complex paint structure beneath, part of which is exposed in the very thinly painted areas, particularly those outlining the figures, the discarded clothing on the riverbank and the distant railway bridge (Plate 90). These are part of Seurat's initial planning of the composition; even at this early stage the application is surprisingly complex. For example the horizontal band of thin greyish-green paint indicating where the thigh of the central seated bather meets the grass of the bank consists of blurred brushstrokes incorporating green, cream, pale blue, pink and reddish-brown paint barely covering the texture of the canvas (Plate 91). Equivalent effects can be seen in other areas blocking out the principal elements of the composition, although the overall appearance varies from place to place: it is for example greyish blue along the outline of the bridge and reddish purple around the bowler hat. These register as the broad dark lines described above, which are such a striking element in the X-ray image (Plate 68).[4]

The evidence of cross-sections suggests that during the early stages of the evolution of the composition Seurat paid little

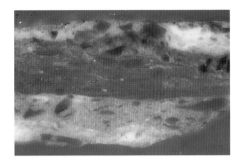

92. Cross-section of deep blue-green shadow of the riverbank behind the seated figure, far left. The paint is applied in a great many layers. The main pigments are viridian green, cobalt blue, chrome yellow and lead white, with lesser amounts of French ultramarine. There is even an intermediate layer containing vermilion and some red lake pigment. Magnification, 240x.

93. Detail of the river to the right edge, showing light-coloured underlayers visible through the stronger surface colour.

attention to his intended final local colour, which he had to a large extent already planned in the preparatory small oil sketches on panel. The paint of the riverbank is built up using freely applied strokes of green, yellow and blue paint, in a series of superimposed opaque layers based on viridian, chrome yellow and cobalt blue mixed with lead white (Plate 92). In this area, therefore, the overall effect achieved would have been green even at an early stage; in the build up of the figures, however, the paint structure includes applications of pale greens, light yellows, mauves and pale blues before the overall pinkish colour of the flesh was worked over the surface. Light green even occurs at an early stage in the paint structure of the white shirt of the reclining figure in the foreground and under the brown paint of the hair of the central seated figure (see Plate 86) as well as in an initial layer for his swimming trunks. The blue of the sky is underpainted in pink and that of the water with pinks, pale greens and creamy yellows (Plate 93).

The painting was then modified in a number of different ways as Seurat laboured to obtain the colour and tonal effects that enliven the surface. Many of these changes aimed to emphasise the tonal contrasts between areas of lightness and darkness, to the extent of a contrived and artificial use of colour rather than close observation of the conditions of light

and shade that obtained in the real setting. There is an element of this artificiality even in the earliest studies such as *The Rainbow* (Plate 53) and *Bathers in the Water* (Plate 55). He also at this stage deliberately brought out contrasts of colour, either reinforcing those that were already present or introducing touches of new colour. Over the picture surface as a whole the effects obtained are not inordinately strident even though the individual touches of colour may be extremely bright. Thus in the middle tones of the grass there are strokes of intense blue (cobalt), cold green (viridian), orange (vermilion and chrome yellow) and bright yellow (cadmium) laid over the meshwork of green paint below, intensifying its colour and introducing a note of contrast by the use of orange (Plates 94 and 95). It is clear from paint cross-sections from this area that Seurat returned to the picture after a short delay to add these final accents of colour (Plate 96). There is, however, no evidence that this hiatus was extended; the paint below had had time to dry sufficiently for it not to be disrupted by the strokes applied on top, but this process could have taken place in a matter of days or weeks.[5] In the areas of strongest shadow in the foreground, typified by that extending from the pile of clothes behind the seated bather, the darker undercolour is reinforced by the cold green of pure viridian

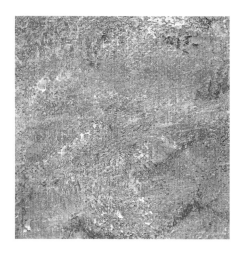

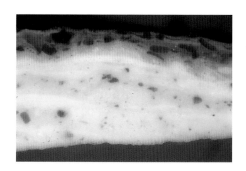

94. Detail of the foreground riverbank, showing Seurat's construction of colour contrasts of orange, green and mauve in the surface brushwork.

95. Detail of the foreground riverbank, showing Seurat's construction of colour contrasts of yellow, pink and green in the surface brushwork.

96. Cross-section of deep blue-green surface brushstroke over bright orange from the foreground riverbank. A cold stroke of cobalt blue and viridian passed over an orange paint made from a combination of vermilion and chrome yellow. The layer structure shows that the orange paint had dried partially before the surface colour was added. Yellow-green layers of the understructure lie beneath. Magnification, 190x.

97. Detail of the colour contrasts used in the body of the dog, lower left.

and by the powerful colours of cobalt blue and intense purples mixed from red lake and French ultramarine. In this treatment of colour Seurat constructs contrasts, such as the purple colours of the shadow with the yellow touches of the surrounding sunlit grass, according to Charles Blanc's interpretation of Chevreul, as discussed in the section on colour theory above. Within the shadowed area itself, however, it is tempting to see the effect of the use of the Helmholtzian contrast of juxtaposed green and violet. This colour effect may be one which Seurat would have been able to derive from even a cursory reading of Ogden Rood's *Modern Chromatics* (discussed above); his attention was drawn to the book when it

was published in 1881 and at some time he made a copy of the colour wheel (Plate 47). In the extreme foreground the paint of the dog, laid in using a strongly coloured red-brown earth pigment, is completed with touches of much brighter spectral colour, for example vermilion, chrome yellow, and pinks that contain vermilion and red lake, with blue and mauve in the shadows (Plate 97). This serves to bring the dog forward in the composition. In a slightly more subdued way, touches of colour on the trousers of the reclining man serve a similar purpose.

Interwoven with these brightly coloured touches are more muted mauves, greyish blues, pinks and soft yellows designed to push back the stridency of the middle ground without reducing the frieze-like quality of the placing of the figures. These effects are carried over into the water where greyer blues, pinks and creamy colours are used to an ever-increasing extent as the water meets the buildings and bridge on the horizon. The overall visual effect is to unite the figures on the bank with the pale pinks and creams used for the buildings in the background and the indeterminate pale blue sky.

Similar colour effects are used in the bodies of the figures although here the paint has been applied in a smoother and more blended manner (Plate 98). In the figure of the central seated boy the shadows on the pale flesh contain light blues, mauves, pinks and creamy yellows blurring one into another (Plate 99), a technique seen in the other figures and also to some degree in the white clothing of the reclining man and in the pile of discarded linen. Although warmer in overall tone,

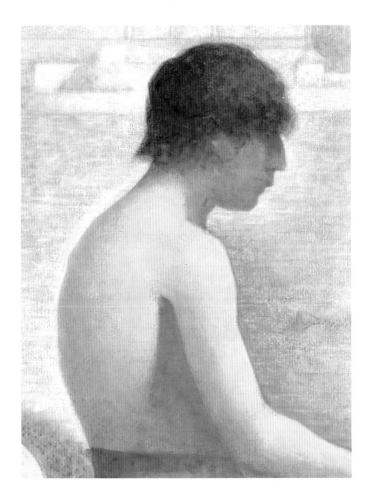

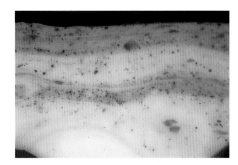

99. Cross-section of the flesh paint of the central seated figure, showing the multilayered application of paint containing lead white with cobalt blue, French ultramarine, red lake and chrome yellow. Magnification, 135x.

98. Detail of the central seated figure, showing the thick smooth brushwork of the flesh paint, the dark blue band of water outlining the front of the figure and light-coloured paint outlining his back. Note the paler, desaturated colour contrasts of pink and pale mauve with cream and pale yellow and the late application of orange and blue dots in the shadow of the lower back.

the trunks of the bathers make use of a similar pattern of the application of mottled colour. It is interesting to see that Seurat's enthusiasm for Delacroix and his reading of Charles Blanc's eulogies to this artist did not extend to the use of pinks contrasted with greens to construct his flesh tones in the *Bathers*.[6] However, he does make use of a soft colour contrast between the smooth cream-coloured flesh in strongest sunlight and the mauves of the shadows cast on the bodies.

In addition to Seurat's exploitation of contrasts of colour in the painting, contrasts of lightness and darkness are brought out using another aspect of contemporary optical theory, based on Chevreul and on David Sutter's description of the phenomenon of 'irradiation', as earlier discussed. This is seen most clearly in the treatment of the central figure. Seurat paints the water in front of the figure a strong dark blue, contrasting with the intensified cream of the flesh of his arm, deliberately outlined by a final passage of smoothly applied paint. The lilac-mauve shadow of his back adjoins lighter, cream-coloured paint scumbled over the surface of the water, following the curve of the boy's spine. Another contrast is developed between the boy's face in shadow and the paint of the water (Plate 98). These effects of non-naturalistic,

differential lighting are seen in monochrome in the drawing for this and other figures (see, for example, Plate 64). Seurat has employed the same device throughout the painting, as in the junction between the trousers of the reclining figure and the grass immediately above, and in the light haloes surrounding the straw hat and discarded clothing.[7]

There was a last stage in the evolution of the *Bathers* which took place, probably around 1886 or 1887, over two years after the picture was first exhibited.[8] This drew on optical effects that Seurat had explored in his final working of the *Grande Jatte* (Plate 153) and involved his application of dots of colour principally to the bathers in the foreground and their immediate surroundings. The effects obtained are not particularly striking since the areas treated in this way are not extensive and the dots of paint are small and sparsely distributed; as described above, the motivation for this last reworking may have been to provide a visual link between the two paintings, although there is no evidence that the *Bathers* and the *Grande Jatte* were destined to be exhibited together. John Gage has commented that the addition of dots to various parts of the painting perhaps served more to enliven the surface than as an application of the additive mixture of colour.[9]

100. Detail of the boy on the right, showing Seurat's late application of orange and pale yellow dots (now faded) on the hat.

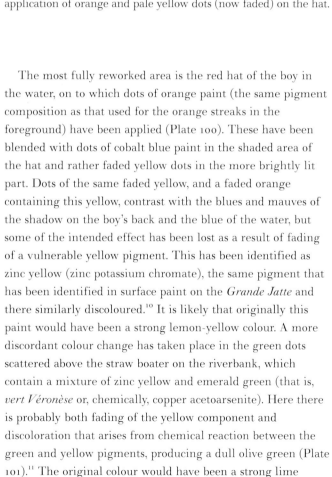

The most fully reworked area is the red hat of the boy in the water, on to which dots of orange paint (the same pigment composition as that used for the orange streaks in the foreground) have been applied (Plate 100). These have been blended with dots of cobalt blue paint in the shaded area of the hat and rather faded yellow dots in the more brightly lit part. Dots of the same faded yellow, and a faded orange containing this yellow, contrast with the blues and mauves of the shadow on the boy's back and the blue of the water, but some of the intended effect has been lost as a result of fading of a vulnerable yellow pigment. This has been identified as zinc yellow (zinc potassium chromate), the same pigment that has been identified in surface paint on the *Grande Jatte* and there similarly discoloured.[10] It is likely that originally this paint would have been a strong lemon-yellow colour. A more discordant colour change has taken place in the green dots scattered above the straw boater on the riverbank, which contain a mixture of zinc yellow and emerald green (that is, *vert Véronèse* or, chemically, copper acetoarsenite). Here there is probably both fading of the yellow component and discoloration that arises from chemical reaction between the green and yellow pigments, producing a dull olive green (Plate 101).[11] The original colour would have been a strong lime green. Precisely this colour change has been recorded also for the *Grande Jatte*. As part of this last campaign the shadow on the lower back of the seated boy has been reinforced with contrasting spots of blue and orange, using the same cobalt

101. Detail of the application of dots of paint around the straw hat on the riverbank, probably applied by Seurat in 1887, which have undergone colour change. The olive green is a discoloured mixture of emerald green (copper acetoarsenite) and zinc yellow (zinc potassium chromate), while the brownish-orange colour is based on zinc yellow. The zinc yellow paint was clearly a poor quality product and contains wheat starch as an extender.

blue and chrome–vermilion mixture as on the hat. At the same time Seurat added a scattering of pale yellow and pink dots enlivening the surface of the water around the figure.

In terms of technique, the *Bathers* might be described as a combination of the traditional and the modern. Seurat's extensive preparations with oil studies and drawings, his carefully wrought composition and his devotion to clearly articulated, sculptural figures are all aspects of the painting that serve to link it to a Beaux-Arts tradition. By contrast, his varied application of paint and his exploration of colour and colour theory seem to relate the painting to more contemporary concerns and, in particular, to Impressionism.

Technical analysis of the painting and its studies reveals that the marriage between old and new was not easily achieved. There are signs of improvisation as the painting developed. The paint surface that we now see covers layers of colour in different combinations, which suggests a degree of freedom and experimentation in the early stages of the execution. Several, if not all of the drawings of individual figures seem to have brought into play when the painting was already well underway, while the reworking of certain key passages may also indicate a measure of uncertainty on Seurat's part.

From the first vivid studies after nature to the simple resolute forms of the final picture, Seurat's method might seem to entail a relentless idealisation where the 'individual accents of nature' as Charles Blanc described them are gradually distilled in a search for the essential and the permanent. Modern authors have stressed the intellectual clarity and the formal harmony of the work, suggesting that as he evolved his ideas Seurat gradually discarded the 'trivial' and the 'superfluous'.[12] Yet, the scientific examination shows that, as the painting progressed, the tendency towards the general was held in check by the re-introduction of closely observed detail. The central bather was repainted to become an individual rather than a type. The nose of the echo boy in the water was repainted so that it wrinkles upwards against the weight of his cupped hands. The little tabs on the heels of the boots on the bank also seem to have added at a late stage. Even the static quality of the composition was disturbed by the addition of the ferry and the fast-moving skiff. These adjustments were small yet significant, shifting the picture back towards the particular, adding a sense of the momentary and reminding us of its origins in a specific location on the banks of the Seine. As Roger Fry commented, 'in spite of the exactitude and rigour of its harmony, this picture retains also something of its quality of immediacy, of a thing that was actually seen and seized on by the imagination in a single ecstatic moment'.[13]

As he painted the *Bathers* Seurat had to reconcile several, often conflicting elements. He had to balance his interest in draughtsmanship and tone with the seductive qualities of colour. The evocative generalisation of his conté drawings was not readily translated into the unforgiving medium of oil paint, while the compelling and often disparate pieces of advice that attracted his attention in writings on colour theory were not easy to put into practice. Similarly, his search for the simple and the monumental co-existed with an attachment to reality and an eye for naturalistic detail.

To the modern observer Seurat's *Bathers* seems to radiate with calm and assurance. Refined by the passage of time, and accorded the status of a major work in the National Gallery, the picture hangs confidently in a collection dominated by Old Masters, a short distance away from, for example, the works of Piero della Francesca – an artist with whom Seurat has often been compared by Roger Fry and others.[14] In the last century, however, those critics who noticed the picture found it more difficult to assess. It was likened to an Italian fresco yet also described as a modern, Impressionist painting.[15] While a technical analysis of the painting will not explain the meaning of the picture nor clarify the artist's motives, it can help us to perceive some of its original awkwardness, reminding us that this masterpiece was the work of a young and relatively inexperienced artist.

1. Based on analysis of paint samples.
2. This homogeneous mixture of pigments has been found in a number of works by Seurat of this period, including oil sketches for the *Bathers* and also for the *Grande Jatte*, reinforcing the conclusion that this is a ready-mixed paint; manufacturers' catalogues of the period are not informative on this point. The colour of the mixture is similar to certain varieties of orange earth pigment (natural or artificial). The evidence of one of the versions of the letter from Seurat to Fénéon of June 1890 suggests that Seurat sought to eschew the use of earth colours; see Paris, Grand Palais, 1991, p. 383.
3. Cadmium yellow is fairly unusual in later nineteenth-century French painting, perhaps because it was an expensive imported colour: in the 1883 catalogue produced by Lefranc et Cie, for example, a size 1 (40 ml) tube of cadmium yellow is listed as costing 1 franc, four times the price of a size 2 (55 ml) tube of chrome yellow. Seurat's intention here may have been to use an intense bright yellow known for its stability.
4. In the *Bathers* the contrast in the X-ray image between the bands defining the major elements of the composition and those elements themselves is largely the result of differences in the thickness of the applied paint.
5. Examined under the microscope, cross-sections from these areas show a slight but distinctive division between the series of paint layers applied initially, which merge one into another, and those applied rather later, as the next sequence.
6. Blanc 1864, p. 116; Blanc 1867, 2nd edn. 1870, pp. 610–11.
7. See the discussion in the section on colour theory and also Zimmermann 1991, p. 44.
8. The *Bathers* and the *Grande Jatte* were presumably together in Seurat's studio and it seems likely that his reworking of each composition was effected at this time, using materials that proved to be unstable. According to Signac the reworking took place in 1887: see Rewald 1949, p. 114. See also Fiedler, 1989, pp. 173–9, esp. p 178.
9. Gage 1987, pp. 450–2.
10. Zinc yellow identified in the *Bathers* by EDX analysis. The same pigment identified by Inge Fiedler in the *Grande Jatte*, see Fiedler 1989, pp. 176–8. In an earlier article she notes the presence of wheat starch as an adulterant or extender in zinc yellow-containing passages in the *Grande Jatte*: see Fiedler 1984. This unusual additive occurs also in the limited applications of zinc yellow in the *Bathers*, suggesting the same material was used on both pictures, purchased from the same source and at roughly the same time. Zinc yellow is not particularly stable and has a tendency to lose its colour: see Kühn and Curran 1986, pp. 187–204.
11. Emerald green had a reputation for poor stability, particularly when mixed with yellows, although there is no reference to problems with zinc yellow specifically. Pissarro found the mixture with cadmium yellow (a sulphide pigment), to be unstable, even more so than with chrome yellow. In a letter to his son Lucien, dated 31 May 1887, he suggested that Seurat be informed: see Bailly-Herzberg 1986, no. 431, pp. 177–8. His pigments had been supplied by the colour merchant Contet.
12. Cooper, p. 12.
13. Fry London 1926, p. 191.
14. Ibid., p. 191; for discussions of Seurat and Piero see Boime 1965; Venturi 1953.
15. For example the anonymous review of Durand-Ruel's Impressionist Exhibition in New York in *The Art Amateur*, 14 May 1886; Roger Marx, *Voltaire*, 10 Dec. 1884.

3 Seurat's Choices: The Bathers and its Contexts

Adapting the Ideal

Bathers at Asnières is the result of a long process of choices and decisions on Seurat's part. This began with the kind of art education he opted to follow, the teachers he had and books he read, continued with the methods of painting and drawing he decided to develop and the types of subject he selected, and culminated in specific decisions he made about his first exhibition painting: should it be executed in a conventional or modern style? should it represent a traditional or contemporary subject? how large should it be? where should it be exhibited? which set of aesthetic criteria should it seek to satisfy? to which publics should it appeal? This process of forging oneself as an artist in the years around 1880 was complicated by the confusing pressures and tensions of the French art world, themselves symptomatic of broader national issues. By exploring Seurat's choices, the decisions he made and the contexts in which he made them, we can perhaps further our understanding of Seurat's serene, mute masterpiece.

Seurat's schooling, choice of artistic career and training at the Ecole des Beaux-Arts took place during a period of considerable social and political instability in France. Pressures within the body politic to restore order and rebuild confidence in the national identity had a distinct impact on the art world. In September 1870 the Second Empire, its armies defeated by the invading German forces led by Prussia, collapsed and gave way to the Third Republic. The new regime was powerless to prevent the gruelling siege of Paris and the inevitable capitulation to Bismark's Germany early the following year. The insurgent Paris Commune that emerged from the defeat was aroused in part by opposition to the conservatism of the newly elected government, but was fiercely suppressed by Republican troops in May 1871, leaving over 20,000 Parisians dead. In the wake of this national humiliation and fratricidal civil war the Third Republic, led by an alliance of conservative interests under the ironic sobriquet of the 'République des ducs' because reactionary rather than progressive policies were to the fore, pushed forward schemes of national regeneration. Among these were cultural projects. On his installation as Director of Fine Arts in 1874, the marquis de Chennevières initiated the decoration of the Panthéon by the leading mural painters of the day, among them Alexandre Cabanel, Elie Delaunay, Jean-Paul Laurens and Pierre Puvis de Chavannes. Chennevières's aim was frankly nationalistic in its fusion of imagery and culture.[1] Grand decorative cycles in one of Paris's noblest monuments would restate France's cultural primacy, he claimed, and the representation of heroic figures from the nation's past – Sainte Geneviève, Clovis or Joan of Arc – would apply history painting to its proper role: the articulation of uplifting moral values.

Since the seventeenth century the system of art education in France had been predicated on the notion of the primacy of history painting. Students were taught that *la grande peinture* was the most elevated form of expression because the orchestration of a number of scrupulously executed figures into a narrative composition derived from the great stories of Greek and Roman mythology or history, or from the Bible, demanded the highest technical and organisational skills from the artist in order to achieve a grand image broadcasting an universal truth. Such paintings should be based on the great paradigms of past art: the sculpture of classical Greece and Rome and the masters of the High Renaissance. Students' training was designed to instil these examples, from elementary copying of plaster casts, through the life and painting classes to the Prix de Rome competition, which allowed the winner several years' study in Italy to polish his elevated style. Seurat was educated in this idealising tradition between 1876, when he enrolled at the Ecole Municipal de Sculpture et de Dessin in his local *arrondissement*, and the summer of 1879, when he left France's senior art college, the Ecole des Beaux-Arts, apparently having failed a competition.[2] The causes of this failure are not known, but they may have involved mutual disenchantment with his teacher Henri Lehmann and the desire to explore other pictorial paths. Nevertheless, Seurat's creative thinking was imbued with the ethos of the Ecole, and thus of history painting – even at the height of Seurat's avant-garde reputation Pissarro complained that 'Seurat is from the Ecole des Beaux-Arts, he's impregnated with it'.[3]

Throughout Seurat's career history painting stood on shifting sands. At one level it was subject to political change. The reactionary governments of the 1870s supported *la grande peinture*, returning control of the Prix de Rome to the conservative Académie des Beaux-Arts in 1871, manipulating the annual Salon exhibitions to favour history painting over the lesser genres of landscape and everyday subjects, and commissioning murals for the Panthéon and other public buildings. Elite aided élite. However, in 1879 the Republican president Jules Grévy was elected and a new political climate emerged with a rhetoric of modernisation and *liberté, égalité et fraternité*. Nowhere is the impact of this on history painting more clear than in the interior decorations of the Parisian town halls, which in the 1870s often involved noble but rather arcane allegories of *Lex* (law) or *Justitia* (justice), but in the 1880s began to promote more legible and populist social values such as *Famille* (the family) or *Travail* (work).[4] At another level, wider social changes were at play. In 1888 Georges Lafenestre, a civil servant at the Ministère des Beaux-Arts, listed some of the pressures subverting *la grande peinture*: 'the weakening of religious traditions and the decline in philosophical studies, the decadence of classical education . . . the spread of a titillating press and saucy novels, the pressing demands of the struggle for life, the almost absolute lack of leisure and meditation in most lives...'[5] By such an account, the cultivated standards necessary to sustain history painting were jeopardised by the progress of modernity and democracy. What choices was a young artist, schooled in *la grande peinture*, to make?

Seurat's training had not just involved the development of technical skills. He also read about art, itemising his studies in a letter of 20 June 1890 to the critic Félix Fénéon (see p. 15).[6] The general tenor of his reading as a student echoed the idealising ethos of the Ecole. The aesthetician David Sutter, for instance, argued in his *Esthétique général* (1865) that the artist had to choose from nature elements that could be harmonised into a work of art, and should follow specific aesthetic rules rather than be improvised. French art, Sutter held, was at its best with such artists as Poussin and David, whose compositional discipline and elevated subject matter emulated the ideal forms Sutter traced in classical sculpture by detailed descriptions and diagrams.[7] As we have already seen, most important to the young Seurat was Charles Blanc's *Grammaire des arts du dessin* (1867). Blanc had been Chennevières's predecessor as Director of Fine Arts, a committed Republican at odds with the marquis's reactionary politics but sharing his dedication to *la grande peinture*. Blanc's support for history painting was austere and selective. An admirer of both Ingres and Delacroix, he disdained as superficial the work of such academicians as Cabanel and Jean-Léon Gérôme:[8] a salutary reminder to us today that it is misguided to see history painting of this period as a homogenous 'academic' entity. As Director, Blanc attempted to establish in Paris a Museum of Copies, a project at once democratic – great Renaissance art would be available to any student, obviating the privileged Italian tour – and autocratic, as Blanc would select the examples. The *Grammaire* was a pedagogical exercise, running through the fine arts with ordered descriptions of styles and techniques, and setting up totemic examples for emulation: Phidias the master of line, Rembrandt of light, Veronese and Delacroix of colour. Blanc equated art with the ideal – 'the artist is charged with recalling the ideal to us, that is to say revealing to us the fundamental beauty of things' – and, like Sutter, expected the artist to transform nature into a work of art. Such idealism was not élitist, the Republican Blanc giving his promotion of *la grande peinture* a politico-moral twist by insisting that 'painting preaches to peoples with its mute eloquence'.[9]

This idealism undoubtedly formed Seurat's intellectual background. How consciously he was aware of such abstract notions as he planned and executed the *Bathers* is impossible to tell, but perhaps some pictorial indication of Blanc's significance can be traced in the line drawing by Ingres of two nudes illustrated under the final sentence of the *Grammaire* (Plate 102). Both poses – the seated figure resting arms on bent knees and the reclining figure, head turned away and cradled on the hand – reappear in the *Bathers*. However, it was through Poussin that Blanc's theoretical importance for Seurat and the *Bathers* took visual form. As a student Seurat made a number of pencil copies after Poussin and, in an act of homage to two masters, copied Poussin's hand from his portrait in Ingres's *Apotheosis of Homer* in the Louvre.[10] Reverence for Poussin, whose seventeenth-century example lay at the foundation of David's Neo-classicism on which Ecole teaching was still based, was hardly exceptional among Seurat's contemporaries. For Sutter, Poussin was the greatest French painter, able to synthesise classical Greek and later Italian art, while Georges Berger, in a lecture given at the Ecole des Beaux-Arts in 1877, praised the way in which his knowledge of the antique harmonised with his observation of nature. Both echoed Félibien's seventeenth-century account of how Poussin walked along the banks of the Tiber gathering material that might be useful in paintings.[11] Two centuries later this story had acquired mythic status among Ecole-trained French painters concerned to integrate figure and landscape, and Poussin's promenades served as a subject for pictures, at least from Paul Flandrin's lost Salon painting of 1843 to Alfred de Curzon's canvas of 1886.[12] At the Salon of 1857 Léon Benouville, a winner of the Prix de Rome, mythologised this further with a canvas showing Poussin watching Roman washerwomen by the riverside, one of them bathing a baby (Plate 104).[13] Benouville's landscape, with its bridge arching across the rear space and the horizon broken by two standing women, would have been recognised by the cultivated Salon visitor as an allusion to Poussin's *Finding of Moses* of 1638, well known from the Louvre's collection (Plate 103). In the *Grammaire* Blanc made much of this mythic moment of observation and creativity in Poussin's work, citing it at the beginning of his volume as a salient example of how art should transform and idealise nature: 'This is how a scene from everyday life suddenly becomes raised to the dignity of a history painting'.[14]

The *Bathers* is far from the historicising anecdotalism of Benouville, of course, but it bears striking resemblances to the 1638 *Finding of Moses*; both the format and the relation of figures to landscape are similar. In the foreground, both Seurat

'il est de leur essence d'être immortels; et, bien que dar ériodes de décadence on les croie menacés de périr, ils r que sommeiller, semblables à cet évangéliste que la poé ige nous représente comme endormi dans son tombeau bercé par les songes, celui qui doit venir l'éveiller.

102. Jean-August-Dominique Ingres, *Study for 'The Golden Age'*, c.1840–5. Pencil on paper. Paris, Musée du Louvre. Reproduced from Charles Blanc, *Grammaire des arts du dessin* (Paris 1867), p. 713.

and Poussin's canvases have a reclining male figure seen from behind and another male to the right up to his waist in water; both puncture the horizon off-centre with a head; both have a flat-bottomed boat traversing the current to centre right; and both span the river with a distant bridge, a block-like building on one bank and trees on the other.[15] Perhaps these are no more than coincidences, the subliminal traces of a picture known from the Louvre. It would certainly seem that the kind of stately spacing of figures in a serene landscape exemplified in this work by Poussin lingered in the imagination of Ecole-trained artists at this time; witness Luc-Olivier Merson's *Saint Antony of Padua preaching to the Fishes* (Plate 105) from the Salon of 1881.[16] Merson, whose contemporary religious paintings might employ flowing movement or great detail,

here opted for calm and austerity, qualities he too had found in the *Finding of Moses*. Perhaps, though, Seurat, on the banks of the Seine, found himself reminded of Poussin by the Tiber and chose to recast his composition in the vernacular of the 1880s. If the *Bathers* is in this sense a homage to Poussin it surely is also to Blanc, whose *Grammaire* had celebrated this particular instance of the history painter achieving the ideal through the transformation of nature. The *Bathers* is no history painting; there is no heroic incident or uplifting moral, but it was imagined in the intellectual climate of history painting and executed on the scale of *la grande peinture*. One way of understanding the *Bathers* is to respect its allegiance, willed or not, to the idealism and the mythologising of the Ecole.

During the time Seurat was a student at the Ecole, it was an institution under pressure. The conservative regime of the

103. Nicolas Poussin, *The Finding of Moses*, 1638
Oil on canvas, 93.5 x 121.0 cm
Paris, Musée du Louvre (CAT. 56)

104. Léon Benouville, *Poussin on the Banks of the Tiber, inventing the Composition of his 'Finding of Moses'*, 1855
Watercolour, gouache and pencil, 227 x 395 cm
Amsterdam, Historisch Museum

105. Luc-Olivier Merson, *Saint Antony of Padua preaching to the Fishes*, 1880
Oil on canvas, 88.5 x 152.0 cm
Nantes, Musée des Beaux-Arts (CAT. 65)

106. Hippolyte Flandrin, *Young Male Nude seated by the Sea*, 1836
Oil on canvas, 98 x 124 cm
Paris, Musée du Louvre

107. Adolphe-William Bouguereau, *Seated Nude*, 1884
Oil on canvas, 116.5 x 89.8 cm
Williamstown, Mass., Sterling and Francine Clark
Art Institute (CAT. 58)

1870s had sponsored grand public history-painting projects, but Grévy's Republic, equally ideologically driven and responding to those forces of a modern capitalist democracy that Lafenestre outlined, was less supportive. Indeed, in 1882, Antonin Proust, who had been Minister of Fine Arts in Léon Gambetta's short-lived radical government of 1881–2, went so far as publicly to question the validity of the Prix de Rome, the linchpin of the Ecole's curriculum.[17] The Ecole's primacy as a teaching institution was then under threat from students trained at the unaffiliated Académie Julian by such teachers as William Bouguereau, arousing jealousies that led to rumours that Cabanel, a professor at the Ecole, had used his influence to reject work by Julian pupils from the 1881 Salon.[18] The general standard of history painting, which it was the duty of the Ecole to sustain, was seen to be weakening, even by sympathetic conservative critics. In a stocktaking of French art written in 1877, Eugène Veron upbraided the Ecole for promoting history painting without encouraging in young painters the imaginative reflection necessary to achieve it successfully; the result was academically 'correct' figures juxtaposed as individual units, rather than coherently composed as an ensemble, and large canvases inadequately filled.[19] Eight years later Gustave Ollendorff, the director of museum administration, regretted that social pressures had weakened the Ecole's Neo-classical principles, luring young artists into 'anecdotal and bourgeois painting'.[20] By this he no doubt meant the representation of contemporary subjects, but that passage from Ecole-trained history painter to a painter of modern life was well-worn by 1880, having been taken by the likes of Degas and Tissot in the 1860s and Béraud and Bastien-Lepage in the 1870s. The professors at the Ecole fought back, even from beyond the grave. In 1885 Gustave Boulanger published a lecture, 'To our Pupils', attacking the neglect of beauty for naturalist 'vulgarity', while the year before Seurat's teacher Lehmann had established by his will a triennial prize at the Ecole for the painting that demonstrated the most emphatically *anti*-modern characteristics.[21]

The specific impact of Lehmann's teaching on Seurat is far from clear. Born in 1814, Lehmann had a distinguished career as a history painter, with a number of substantial decorative projects to his credit. The last major commission he completed was *Law prevails over Force* for the Ecole de Droit in 1872. Poor health led him to decline a rôle in the Panthéon project in 1874, and despite a devotion to his senior institutional duties it is probable that at the time he taught Seurat Lehmann felt deeply the threats to *la grande peinture*, for which he had striven so long.[22] A devoted pupil of Ingres, he constantly invoked his master in his teaching, as Seurat's fellow pupil Ernest Laurent remembered, using the *Apotheosis of Homer* as an example of the 'equilibrium of masses'.[23] A rare instance of Seurat's response to Lehmann again suggests the retrospective nature of his teaching. About 1878 Seurat copied a figure from one of Lehmann's compositions decorating the Galerie des Fêtes of the Hôtel de Ville. Executed in 1852, these had been destroyed during the Commune and Seurat must have been given one of his professor's preparatory cartoons, made twenty-five years earlier, from which to work.[24] Lehmann's work, with its confident foreshortening and energetic gestures, may not have appealed to the young Seurat, but his devotion to Ingres was shared by his student.

Seurat made a number of copies after Ingres, including a scrupulously worked oil after the female figure in the Louvre's *Roger and Angelica*.[25] The sheet with the copy of Poussin's hand from Ingres's *Apotheosis* also includes an outline of the figure of the Iliad from the same composition. There two female figures flank the central Homer, the Iliad clasping her knees in her outstretched arms and the Odyssey in stricter profile. These two figures are not only crucial to Ingres's 'equilibrium of the masses'; they seem to have acted as models for subsequent artists working in the Neo-classical tradition. The seated figure posed in profile, the curve of the spine counterpointed by the triangle of knees bent and raised to the chest, creating an ideal of the human figure at once harmonious, disciplined and calm, achieved its acme in the *Young Male Nude seated by the Sea* (Plate 106) painted in 1836 by Ingres's favourite pupil Hippolyte Flandrin, a canvas on display in the Louvre while Seurat was a student. This 'triangular' seated pose remained a stock figure in the traditionalists' figurative canon throughout the century, taking its conventional nude turn in a canvas by Bouguereau (Plate 107) executed at the same time as the *Bathers*. While this image is typical of academic idealisation, by the 1870s a number of artists who worked variations on it were opting for more naturalistic treatment of the model and associating the pose with melancholy subjects; Alphonse Cornet's *Repentant Magdalene* (1870) or Bastien-Lepage's *Diogenes* (1877) come to mind.[26] The figure who sits beneath his straw hat to the left of the *Bathers* corresponds to this pose. Lightly clad rather than nude, set in no heroic location, he nevertheless exudes a tranquil dignity and self-control conveyed by the steady

108. Hippolyte Flandrin, *Priam's Son, Polytes, observing the Greeks approaching Troy*, 1834
Oil on canvas, 205 x 148 cm
Saint-Etienne, Musée d'Art Moderne (CAT. 57)

'triangular' pose. Head up and sunlit, Seurat's youth is hardly melancholy; rather, like Ingres's own description of his *Odyssey* figure, he 'observes and meditates'.[27] Just as the *Bathers* is no history painting, this figure is no hero, unlike Flandrin's muscular nude of his similarly poised Polytes (Plate 108). But the pose of Seurat's straw-hatted boy, steeped in the ordered idealisation promoted at the Ecole, is a reminder once again that Seurat's academic training played an active rôle in the *Bathers*.

Lehmann's reactionary instruction did not appeal to all his students. In late 1875, before Seurat joined his atelier, malcontents burned one and painted the other of the pair of slippers the professor wore in the studio, caricatured him on the wall and demanded his resignation. On his refusal, half his class deserted to other teachers, some Lehmann students apparently approaching Edouard Manet, then still very much a

109. Pierre-Cécile Puvis de Chavannes, *Solitude*, c.1879–82
Pastel on paper mounted on canvas, 32.0 x 41.3 cm
Manchester, Whitworth Art Gallery (CAT. 50)

controversial artist, for instruction.[28] Another symptom of certain young painters' dissatisfaction with the teaching at the Ecole was their gravitation towards Pierre Puvis de Chavannes. Born in 1824, Puvis's career had a slow start. Gradually during the 1860s and 1870s he made a name painting mural decorations for public buildings in such provincial centres as Amiens, Marseilles and Poitiers, though as late as 1872 the Salon rejected one of his submissions. With the exhibition in 1876 and 1877 of *Sainte Geneviève in Prayer* and *The Pastoral Life of Sainte Geneviève*, both destined for the Panthéon, followed in 1879 by two easel paintings, *The Prodigal Son* (Zurich, Bührle Collection) and *Young Women by the Sea*

(Paris, Musée d'Orsay), Puvis increasingly won admirers at the Salon and among young painters.[29] For the latter Puvis represented an alternative master to follow. Almost self-taught, he was no academic; indeed, the Ecole professor Boulanger chided him for not being able to draw.[30] But Puvis's work, often large canvases of classical or historical subjects suggestive of noble values and destined for public spaces, did maintain the ideals of *la grande peinture*. These great projects were executed in a modern manner, with blanched clear tones broadly and mattly applied, simplified modelling and strongly outlined, somewhat naïve drawing. These last characteristics are evident if we compare his pastel known as *Solitude* (Plate

109) to Bouguereau's *Seated Nude* (Plate 107); for all the difference of medium and size, Puvis's more personal, less schooled and precise manner is markedly indistinct.

By 1881 the young poet-critic Jules Laforgue, himself briefly an Ecole pupil of Lehmann, could list 'a whole pleiad of artists' in Puvis's orbit, among them Paul Baudoüin, Alexandre Séon and Henri Daras.[31] There is uncertainty about whether the connection with Puvis at this time extended to Seurat and his fellow former Lehmann students Ernest Laurent, Edmond Aman-Jean and Alphonse Osbert, who then formed a close circle. Aman-Jean's son claimed that Seurat and his father helped Puvis square-up drawings for *Le Bois Sacré* (The Sacred Grove), the great mural painting destined for the Musée des Beaux-Arts at Lyon, which was shown at the Salon of 1884, though Robert Herbert has questioned whether Seurat and Puvis ever met.[32] Puvis planned a portrait of his young *confrères* about 1880, which would have included none of Seurat's immediate friends, and although he gave small works as presents to his 'pleiad', Puvis does not seem to have done so to Seurat or his friends in the early 1880s.[33] As Seurat moved from the Lehmann studio towards the development of the *Bathers* it would appear that although he turned his attention to Puvis's work he had no personal connection with the older painter.

What was Seurat's response to Puvis's work? In 1881 he painted from memory a small copy of Puvis's Salon painting that year, the *Poor Fisherman* (Paris, Musée d'Orsay). While this has often been taken as a homage, Herbert has recently argued that Seurat's misspelling of 'Puvisse' on the copy was a deliberate irreverence.[34] Certainly Puvis, celebrated and patrician, was a sure target for student jokes. He was regularly pilloried in the *Expositions des arts incohérents*, which, beginning in 1882 and profiting from the more relaxed press regulations and scope for anti-hierarchical attitudes allowed in the changed political climate of the eighties, mocked him as 'Pubis de Cheval' or 'Pue Vice de Chats (Vannes)'.[35] In similar spirit Toulouse-Lautrec led a group of students at Fernand Cormon's atelier in painting a full-scale replica of *Le Bois Sacré*, the muses's reverie being disturbed by bohemian revellers.[36] This parody, it would seem, was directed at the idealism of Puvis's serene classical composition and motivated by the commitment to naturalism that many of Lautrec's generation upheld. Was this so in Seurat's case? On the other side of the panel used for the copy after Puvis, itself painted over a landscape study, Seurat had painted a sketchy river vista, which Aman-Jean remembered was made at Saint-Ouen, in the north-western suburbs of Paris.[37] This juxtaposition might be taken as inferring that by 1881 Seurat was coming to value close observation of nature over the idealism represented by the *Poor Fisherman*. On the other hand, Sutter's *Esthétique générale* used a Saint-Ouen motif to demonstrate how the rules

of art insist that one half or other of a picture should be dominant, a trait Seurat's sketch rehearses.[38]

On the first public appearance of the *Bathers* in 1884 a critic loosely linked it with Puvis's work, as we shall see. The year before Seurat started work on the *Bathers* Puvis had exhibited at the Salon of 1882 *Doux Pays* (Pleasant Land), a large canvas intended to hang as a decoration in the house of his friend the painter Léon Bonnat (Plate 110). Seurat would undoubtedly have seen *Doux Pays*, and the correspondences between the two canvases are evident enough. Both are large works, some two metres by three. In relation to the spectator, the figures are more or less life-size, so the two canvases have the physical authority of *la grande peinture*. Within the picture space the disposition of landscape elements – bank sloping from upper left to lower right, water shown to centre and right – and staffage – a combination of figures arranged as horizontal and vertical accents – are similar. They have certain spatial caesurae and markers in common, notably the figure breaking the horizon just right of centre and the distant curving sail. Puvis opted for the seated 'triangular' pose, as Seurat did, in both cases an appropriate decision for works whose overall mood, defined by structure, pose and matt, chalky colour, is essentially one of poise and reflection, slightly inflected by boys grappling or hallooing. Of course, there are distinct differences too. The figures in Puvis's canvas are more modelled than in Seurat's, indicative of the older artist's traditional instinct to render the body sculpturally. Puvis's colour was frankly decorative, its unnaturalistic ochre sky determined by function rather than observation, whereas Seurat paid greater respect to local colour, to the play of sunlight and the evocation of summer warmth, indicative of the younger artist's desire to respond to physical nature. In sum, such differences were primarily those of generation. Nevertheless, it is hard to escape the likelihood that at one level the *Bathers* was a response to *Doux Pays*. But was such a response one of respect for a senior figure, as Auburtin's copy after *Doux Pays* (Plate 111) evidently was, or was it some kind of parody of a style in common currency, or an aggressive attempt to carve out an individual identity, what Griselda Pollock has called an 'avant-garde gambit'?[39] The differences between the two paintings would seem to deny slavish pupillage, and at the same time the similarities might appear too evident to support the idea of insolent subversion. Seurat's public profile in 1883–4 was so negligible that he would have been happy just to win some notice; it was only with the *Grande Jatte* (Plate 153), made in the wake of the *Bathers*, that he made a calculated 'play' for priority as an avant-garde artist. The *Bathers* sought neither to copy nor to combat Puvis's work. Rather it is at once a respectful recognition of Puvis's place in the idealist tradition of *la grande peinture* and a purposeful

110. Pierre-Cécile Puvis de Chavannes, *Doux Pays*, 1881–2
Oil on canvas, 230 x 430 cm
Bayonne, Musée Bonnat

exercise in adapting his example to a contemporary subject and a more modern response to light and colour.

In this context it is perhaps best to understand the *Bathers* as Seurat's masterpiece, in the traditional sense of the term. It was painted to prove mastery of his craft by demonstrating equality with, and a degree of difference from, the master. However, Puvis was not the only master, *Doux Pays* not the only point of pictorial reference. To a considerable extent Seurat's choices, as he prepared and executed the *Bathers*, had been informed by his experiences at the Ecole des Beaux-Arts. There he had been taught to copy and revere painters such as Poussin, whose seventeenth-century classicism, embodied in canvases like the *Finding of Moses* (Plate 103), was itself an ideal formulation derived from the study of the Antique and the Renaissance. This formula had been relayed by Blanc and other theorists, and sustained by the neo-classical aesthetic of Ecole teachers such as Lehmann. Some of Seurat's choices

were negative: not to pursue Lehmann's retardataire but energetic manner, for instance. Others showed initiative. Opting for Puvis as an exemplar – a non-Ecole figure, still controversial in some quarters, but a painter with a definable visual identity – gave the inexperienced Seurat a foundation on which to build. Puvis's example at once justified Seurat's existing principles and challenged him to confront new ones. On the one hand, *Doux Pays* is an idealising image rooted in sculptural representation derived from classical antiquity. On the other, its credentials as a history painting are slightly shaky, for it conveys no noble narrative, rendering its figures discrete in their decorative balance. This isolation of the figure, a symptom of decay in *la grande peinture* according to Véron's diagnosis, together with harmonised touch and unnaturalistic chromatics, rendered *Doux Pays* modern, although its subject of Mediterranean antiquity emphatically did not. It is to the modern and subject-matter that we should now turn.

111. Jean-Francis Auburtin after Puvis de Chavannes,
Doux Pays, c.1885–90
Oil on paper pasted on canvas, 50.5 x 99.0 cm
Private Collection (CAT. 59)

1. Chennevières 1979, pp. 24–6; Mainardi 1993, pp. 58–9.
2. Paris, Grand Palais, 1991 pp. 399–400.
3. Bailly-Herzberg 1986, p. 248 (letter 503, late August 1888).
4. Levin 1986; Mainardi 1993; Paris, Petit Palais, 1986.
5. Lafenestre 1888, p. 643.
6. De Hauke, I, pp. xxi–xxiii; Paris, Grand Palais, 1991, p. 383.
7. Sutter 1865, pp. 3–4, 177–94; Paris, Grand Palais, 1991, pp. 387–8.
8. Flax 1989. p. 99.
9. Blanc 1867, pp. 14, 513; Zimmermann 1989; Zimmermann 1991, pp. 28–41; Paris, Grand Palais, 1991, pp. 384–6; Mainardi 1993, pp. 40–6.
10. H. 224, 225, 285.
11. Sutter 1865, pp. 185–6, 191; Berger 1877, pp. 73, 76, 108, 131.
12. Chavanne and Gaudichon 1988, no. 221.
13. Verdi 1969, pp. 742, 745; Plate 35, p. 744.
14. Blanc 1867, p. 10.
15. Thomson 1985, p. 87; Clark 1985, p. 202.
16. Thomson 1994, p. 92.
17. Proust 1882, p. 537.
18. Silvestre 1881, p. 325.
19. Veron 1877, pp. 177, 227–9.
20. Ollendorff 1885, pp. 910–12.
21. Boulanger 1885; 'Cours et Expositions' 4 Oct. 1884, p. 429.
22. Aubrun 1984, I, pp. 34, 37; Thomson 1985, p. 18.
23. Rosenthal 1911, p. 65; Paris, Musée des Arts Decoratifs, 1970, p. 14.
24. Paris, Grand Palais, 1991, no. 5.
25. H. 1, 309, 314; Paris, Grand Palais, 1991, no. 8.
26. Riom 1981, no. 45; Aubrun 1985, no. 119.
27. Montrosier 1882, p. 35.
28. Weir Young 1960, p. 89; Rivière 1921, pp. 55–6.
29. Amsterdam 1994.
30. Germain 1891, p.207.
31. Laforgue 1881, p. 278.
32. Paris, Musée des Arts Decoratifs, 1970, p. 18; Herbert 1959, p. 29.
33. Boucher 1979, pp. 70–2; Baudoüin 1935, figs. 2, 5, 6; Angoulême 1986–7, pp. 43–4.
34. H. 6; Paris, Grand Palais, 1991, no.77.
35. Paris, Musée d'Orsay, 1992, p. 65.
36. London 1991–2, no. 23.
37. H. 7; Paris, Grand Palais, 1991, no. 76.
38. Sutter 1865, p. 122–3.
39. Pollock 1992, pp. 29–31; Paris, Grand Palais, 1991, pp. 148–9; Mathews 1994, p. 271.

Representing the Modern

If certain crucial elements of the *Bathers* – compositional order or conventional poses – reveal Seurat's Ecole-ordained idealism, the painting's subject is unashamedly modern. We are shown men and boys relaxing on a riverbank which the title tells us is at Asnières, in the suburbs of Paris. They wear contemporary clothes, and behind them we see some of the trappings of the modern city: smoking factory chimneys, a train crossing an iron bridge. When Seurat chose a modern subject for his first major exhibition picture he was not breaking new ground, for such subjects had been on the increase at the annual Salon exhibition, at least since the 1860s. However, to do so on such a large scale could still be a matter of controversy and experiment, for the modern subject remained a controversial topic at the Salon and in the wider art world.

Many of the modern subjects exhibited at the Salon were paintings of modest, portable size. The same was true at the Impressionist exhibitions, where paintings on the scale of

Gustave Caillebotte's *Pont de l'Europe* (1876; Geneva, Modern Art Foundation) or Auguste Renoir's *Luncheon of the Boating Party* (1881; Washington, Phillips Collection) were the exception rather than the rule. This was for a number of reasons. Canvases of modest dimensions were generally priced to reach a prosperous bourgeois market, and scaled to fit the domestic space conveniently. They tallied with one particular account of the 'modern': that it was something glimpsed *en passant* in the flux of contemporary experience, the momentary observation matched by the compact format of representation. Also the long-standing aesthetic dictum – that as 'lesser' art, genre painting should be on a smaller scale than *la grande peinture* – was upheld. Nevertheless some paintings of modern life were executed on a big scale, even with life-size figures. Such canvases were intended first for the essential showcase of the Salon, from which the artist hoped they would be purchased for a museum or some other public building. A painting such as Alfred Roll's *Floods in the Suburbs of Toulouse*

112. Alfred Roll, *Floods in the Suburbs of Toulouse (June 1875)*, 1877. Oil on canvas, 140 x 180 cm
Le Havre, Musée des Beaux-Arts

113. Jean-Charles Cazin, *Judith in prayer at the Camp*, c.1882–3
Black chalk and oil on canvas, 250 x 300 cm
Tours, Musée des Beaux-Arts

(June 1875) (Plate 112), measuring almost one-and-a-half by two metres, was unlikely to find a private buyer; it was purchased by the museum at Le Havre. Conservative voices spoke out forcefully against large paintings of modern life, which transgressed the regulations of the academic canon. Boulanger, acting as mouthpiece for the Ecole, condemned in his 1885 lecture 'scenes of banal current facts on canvases of colossal proportions', while Henry Houssaye, in his review of the Salon of 1882 for the establishment *Revue des Deux Mondes*, levelled the same charge, resenting 'the intrusion of banal or vulgar scenes of contemporary life into *la grande peinture*'.[1]

In his article Houssaye succinctly defined what were commonly seen to be some of the cultural causes of these developments: the rise of naturalism in both the visual arts and literature, supported by Republican institutions and public taste, the decline of which Lafenestre had analysed.[2] These were symptomatic of broader social shifts and fissures which can be swiftly outlined. The extent to which the early 1880s was a time of fractious transition and intense debate in France should not be underestimated. A conservative Republic geared to the restoration of monarchy had given way to more progressive Republican forces apparently dedicated to reform. Church control over education was under dispute; trade unions were legalised; the divorce law was liberalised, giving women a little leeway; censorship laws were relaxed. Nevertheless, more radical forces on the Left pressed their calls for further reform. Agriculture went into a slump as the economic prosperity of the 1870s slipped away. Industry increasingly drew the population from the countryside towards the cities, now perceived as places of enervating pace, rampant consumerism and, in the wake of the Commune, potential social disorder dangerous to the dominant bourgeoisie. Never, it must have seemed, had traditional values clashed with modern pressures in such a complex and febrile combination. The painter was inescapably caught up in this. Making a picture involved decisions and compromises that negotiated a path through, and finally arrived at a position on, these current concerns. Roll, for example, could be accepted by a critic such as Houssaye because his modern subjects respected conventional chiaroscuro. *Floods in the Suburbs of Toulouse* may have used a scene of heroic struggle for survival to justify its up-to-the-minute subject, but this would not necessarily have excused his scale in conservative eyes. With the *Bathers* Seurat too must

have thought through the relationship between scale and modern subject. While his painting was to convey no significant narrative, preach no overt *exemplum virtutis*, and thus be – in the word shared by Boulanger and Houssaye – 'banal', he considered his motif worthy of the scale of *la grande peinture* perhaps because he was creating a modern idyll structured in accordance with Ecole-ordained classicism. With a different subject, methods and results, Seurat was nevertheless effecting some kind of compromise between the demands of the modern and the traditional, just as Roll and many others sought to do in their various ways.

While there was no single solution to the problem of painting a modern subject on a substantial scale, a number of examples and options were being explored during the first half of the 1880s. One of these was pioneered by Jean-Charles Cazin. At the Salon of 1880 he had presented two large canvases, *Tobias and the Angel* (Lille, Musée des Beaux-Arts) and *Hagar and Ishmael* (Tours, Musée des Beaux-Arts), which put traditional religious subjects in a broadly brushed landscape setting typical of his native Pas-de-Calais rather than a contrived evocation of the Holy Land. They had an impact on younger painters, among them Seurat's friend Aman-Jean, whose *Saint Julian the Hospitaller* (Carcassonne, Musée des Beaux-Arts), shown at the Salon in 1883, derived its high horizon and high-key palette from Cazin's example.[3] At the same Salon Cazin exhibited *Judith leaving the Ramparts of Bethulia* (location inknown), which had been commissioned by the state-run Gobelins factory as a tapestry design together with a second, *Judith in prayer at the Camp* (Plate 113). The subject was biblical once more, although the use of figures in quasi-modern garb and Pas-de-Calais settings confused and irritated the reviewer of the *Gazette des Beaux-Arts*: 'What! Are we in Judaea with these costumes taken from our age and our country?'[4] It would be intriguing to know if Seurat had seen or heard of the less finished design, *Judith at the Camp*. Much the same size as the *Bathers*, it shares a roughly similar composition, with figures on the bank to the left and an expanse of water to the right, although the narrative relationship Cazin set up between the protagonists is quite different to Seurat's isolated individuals. Here then we can identify some options Seurat rejected. He did not mollify his modernity by using it merely as a veil for a history painting; he did not play his figures' gazes and gestures off each other, however subtly.

114. Ernest Laurent, *Study for 'Scene at the Brook'*, 1883
Conté crayon on paper, 24 x 27 cm
Paris, Musée d'Orsay

Another option of which Seurat would certainly have known is exemplified by his friend Laurent's *Scene at the Brook (Beethoven, op. 68)*, exhibited at the Salon of 1884. Belying its somewhat oblique title the painting, now lost, represented a crowd listening to the Pastoral Symphony at one of the Sunday afternoon concerts given by the conductor Edouard Colonne at the Théâtre du Châtelet. Laurent prepared it carefully with many drawings (Plate 114) – the Louvre alone holds some fifteen – made during the autumn of 1883, when Seurat would have been working on the *Bathers* and its preliminary drawings for the same Salon. Such reliance on preparatory drawings Lehmann would have taught them, though their recently deceased professor would have disliked the lineless, tonal tenebrism of the draughtsmanship that Seurat and Laurent had developed together during the first years of the decade, when they had practised working by lamplight, Laurent later recalled.[5] An image of attentive faces peering out of the gloom of the concert hall, *Scene at the Brook* continued that interest, whereas Seurat's recent *plein-air* colour studies of landscape motifs had put him on the path that led to the *Bathers* and beyond. That the two painters were aware of each other's working up of Salon submissions is clear from the fact that Seurat posed for one of Laurent's studies (Plate 4); their fellow Lehmann student Alphonse Osbert sat for another. It seems reasonable to assume that they discussed their subjects as well as methods.

Laurent's attitude to the subject matter of his exhibition pictures was an equivocal one, typifying the uncertainty young painters felt; in 1883 he exhibited at the Salon a costume piece taken from Samuel Richardson's eighteenth-century English novel *Clarissa*, in 1884 his contemporary concert audience and in 1885 *The Annunciation* (Musée de Nérac), which was purchased by the State.[6] Although ostensibly so different, the *Bathers* and *Scene at the Brook* do have significant points in common. The Colonne concerts were cheaply priced and intended to foster an interest in classical music in the young.[7] Colonne had worked against the odds to support Wagner's music in a hostile Paris and, as one who had Wagnerian interests, it seems likely that Seurat would have accompanied Laurent to the concert hall.[8] Both the canvases on which the two colleagues worked over the winter of 1883–4 represented on substantial scale young men at leisure, on the riverbank or at the concert. In each picture the figures face the same way, in silence and apparent harmony. Their leisure is represented as being both individual and communal; in a word, both paintings can be construed as democratic.

Finally one might consider *At the Organ* by Henri Lerolle (Plate 115). This is a slightly later painting than the *Bathers*, and was shown at the Salon of 1885. However, the exhibition history of the two paintings soon coincided, because both canvases were on display the following year at the *Works in Oil and Pastel by the Impressionists of Paris*, staged by the art dealer Paul Durand-Ruel at the American Art Association and National Academy of Design in New York.[9] A pupil of Louis Lamothe, himself taught by Hippolyte Flandrin, Lerolle had received a training in the same academic tradition as Seurat. Lerolle had private means, collected as well as painted, and moved in sophisticated *haut-bourgeois* circles outside Seurat's social range. But in attempting a large-scale canvas of a modern subject Lerolle arrived at several of the conclusions Seurat adopted for the *Bathers* and the *Grande Jatte*, both of which had been resolved before *At the Organ* went on show in May 1885. All three canvases range emphatic figures in profile against a distinct diagonal, achieving images in which the modern subject is forced into a somewhat over-determined stylistic discipline. It is as if both Seurat and Lerolle independently agreed that the modern had to be subjected to a style, to a legible order which would be the proof of the artist's transformation of nature, his obedience to the idealism of his training and his ability to give pictorial cohesion to the confusion of contemporary experience. The subjects of the *Bathers* and *At the Organ* are quite different, but Lerolle's interior is executed in high-key tones of grey and buttery yellow, which caused the critic André Michel to complain of its 'blanched starkness', a comment he might equally have applied to the *Bathers*.[10]

However partial, a survey such as this indicates that the *Bathers* was a far from isolated attempt to represent modern subjects on a grand scale, and that while artists such as Cazin, Laurent and Lerolle by no means shared a single style, there were significant, if various, points in common with Seurat's ambitions. The common motivation behind such pictures was, to use the term in its broadest sense, political. The Republican administrations under Grévy's presidency in the early 1880s inevitably turned their anti-élitist and reforming zeal on the art world. Just as they were determined to win control over the education system by wresting influence from the clergy – 1880 was the year the Jesuits were expelled from France – so Republican governments sought to reduce the authority of the Académie des Beaux-Arts and reform the structure of the Salon. These initiatives brought artistic issues squarely into the cockpit of political debate. Patricia Mainardi has recently drawn attention to a striking example of this: an 1880 debate in the Chambre des Deputés on the future of the Salon, at which a right-wing deputy attacked the Under-Secretary of State for the Fine Arts, Edmond Turquet: 'I understand that the Under-Secretary might want to democratise the arts, that he might want to apply the principles of 1789 to the organisation of the Salon', the deputy charged,

> but may I be permitted to tell him that he has taken the wrong path; art is an aristocracy, an aristocracy so much the more legitimate as it owes nothing to birth ... The Revolution has happened, and the new social strata have invaded the exhibition, and the pressure from the bottom upward is such ... that little by little the great names of painting have been pushed out of the catalogue and are staying away from the Salon.[11]

This was a shameless transposition on to the art world of a conservative reading of society, craftily introducing the radical Republican Léon Gambetta's slogan for the lower classes, the 'new strata' (*nouvelles couches sociales*), into cultural debate. The effects of this ideological impetus were clear to the artistic community. Houssaye, defender of *la grande peinture*, saw behind the rise of naturalist subjects at the Salon 'the State and the City of Paris', while Louis de Fourcaud, somewhat more sympathetic to modern themes, was convinced of the political manipulation of pictorial culture. 'The reason for the overspill of scenes from the life of the lower classes [is] ... due to democracy and democratic mania', he told the readers of the *Gazette des Beaux-Arts* in his review of the 1884 Salon: 'Universal suffrage has ... introduced plebeian influence into general morality and the arts'.[12]

Some artists moved swiftly to establish their Republican credentials. At the Salon of 1881 Cazin exhibited an allegory

115. Henry Lerolle, *At the Organ*, 1885
Oil on canvas, 225.4 x 363.2 cm
New York, Metropolitan Museum of Art

entitled *Souvenir of a Fête in Paris: Courage, Science and Work combine to establish the Reign of Concord* (Paris, Petit Palais). Consistently with his recent work, it combined tradition – classically draped allegorical figures – with naturalism – a nocturnal panorama over Paris. The title only elliptically masks the ideology. The fête was the celebration of 14 July; the figures are draped in red, white and blue; and Concorde was synonymous with the Republic. The following year Roll showed a vast canvas almost ten metres across representing the first official Bastille Day celebrations in 1880 (Plate 116). He depicted almost countless masses in the place de la République pressing forward to watch troops march past the new monument of the Republic by Léopold and Charles Morice. Roll's canvas was a paean to the regime. Broadly brushed in high-key *peinture claire* it matched its modern execution with its contemporary subject. The crowd is depicted as euphoric in mood and harmonious despite its class make-up, for here street urchins and *haut bourgeois*, domestics and *rentiers*, and in the foreground the painter himself and his wife, mingle in unanimous praise of the national fête. Technique, subject and ideology seamlessly elided the Third Republic with the modern, the energetic and the egalitarian.

The most important artistic initiative taken by the Third Republic to instil in its citizens the regime's ideological values was the campaign to decorate France's town halls (*mairies*). Starting in the mid-1870s, the *mairies* of the Paris *arrondissements* and suburbs were decorated with mural and ceiling paintings in a campaign that lasted into the early years of this century. This is not the place to discuss this policy in detail, but it is of significance here because it was in its stride as Seurat worked on the *Bathers*. By filling its public spaces with images promoting Republican values – communal labour and family life, civic defence and respect for the law – the regime hoped to replace the influence of the Church with its own; to paint a *mairie* decoration was in a sense to paint a secular altarpiece. These were prestigious commissions for an artist to win, guaranteeing critical attention and work on permanent display, and in the 1880s the competitions for them were enthusiastically disputed. The influences on and options open to decorators were much the same as with large Salon canvases. Both conservative and more progressive critics,

for example Lafenestre or Roger Marx, worried about the excessive reliance on Puvis's example.[13] Among even politically advanced commentators there was division about how modern these decorations should be. Edmond Jacques in the radical *L'Intransigeant* argued that they must be 'truly modern', representing 'our period, its movement, character and fever', while in the Gambettist *Le Voltaire* Marx cautioned against the 'exclusively' modern, the merely descriptive.[14] Another anxiety was that decorations would represent a sterile stylistic mélange, what Lafenestre described as 'classical memories and realist evidence, Pompeii and Millet, Italy and Montmartre, the cap of Arcadian shepherds and the hood of suburban market-gardeners'.[15] Although Seurat was not planning a decoration, these were issues which must have run through his mind.

116. Alfred Roll, *14 July 1880*, 1880–2
Oil on canvas, 645 x 980 cm
Paris, Musée du Petit Palais

Seurat would have been well aware of the various *mairie* projects in train at this time. He made a drawing of a painter, who has recently been identified as Aman-Jean, up a ladder at work on a large canvas;[16] it is an image that recognises the ambitions current in his circle of friends. In 1883 Laurent entered the competition to decorate the *salle des mariages* in the town hall of Saint-Maur-des-Fossés, in the eastern suburbs of Paris, eventually won by Baudoüin.[17] A drawing that probably relates to this submission represents a rural scene with a mother and baby and a little girl welcoming the father on his return from work in the fields, a celebration of family and gender-ordained labour apt for such a setting (Plate 117).[18] The following year Laurent also competed unsuccessfully for the *salle des mariages* at the *mairie* at Courbevoie, the commune adjacent to Asnières, Roger Marx reckoning

117. Ernest Laurent, *The Family*, c.1882–3
Black chalk heightened with white on grey board,
39.5 x 73.5 cm. Private Collection, sold Atelier Ernest Laurent,
14 November 1993, lot 20

118. Alexandre Séon, *Summer*, 1884–5
Oil on canvas
Courbevoie, Hôtel de Ville, Salle des Mariages

119. Alexandre Séon, *Study for 'Summer'*, c.1884
Red chalk on paper, 15.6 x 18.3 cm
Formerly Gallery Arnoldi-Livie, Munich

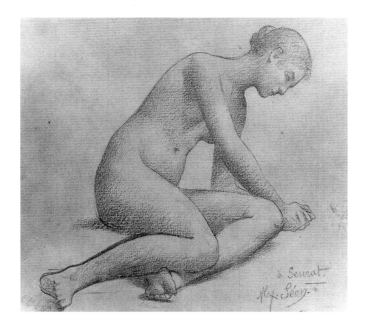

his work 'as rich in promise as in inexperience'.[19] That competition was won by Séon, whose ensemble included a four-panelled ceiling representing the seasons (Plate 118) and a series of eight mural canvases promoting woman's rôle as mother, nurse and educator of children.[20] This decoration is very marked by Puvis's style, notably in the slightly naïve drawing of the figures and the spare landscape settings. However, Séon's use of colour was considerably more adventurous than his master's, with an active use of secondary harmonies and some sharp accents. He dedicated a red chalk drawing of a figure for *Summer* (Plate 119) to his friend Seurat, an interesting choice because not only is this figure a variant on an academically impeccable source, the classical sculpture *Nymph with a Shell* in the Louvre, but also because of all Séon's Courbevoie paintings the bathing scene of *Summer* is closest to the *Bathers*.[21]

Surprisingly, Seurat himself seems never to have competed for a *mairie* decoration despite the fact that these commissions helped make a name, and almost all of the artists mentioned here tried their hand, often with ultimate success. Perhaps Seurat's modest but adequate private means obviated the necessity, though it did not deter the wealthier Lerolle. It may be that Seurat did not want to appear bounden to Republican ideology. The reactionary Catholic Aman-Jean, a monarchist who in 1880 hurled tomatoes at the gendarmes evicting the Jesuits from their college in the rue des Postes, seems never to have competed for a *mairie* commission, though a few years

120A and 120B. Adrien Karbowsky, *Repose* and *Navigation*,
1889–91
Oil on canvas
Nogent-sur-Marne, Hôtel de Ville, Salons d'Honneur

later he was happy to accept one for a stained-glass window in
Orléans cathedral.[22] Possibly Seurat considered himself too
inexperienced, as Laurent was judged to be. It is conceivable
that the *Bathers* was an attempt on Seurat's part to show his
credentials at the Salon, to demonstrate how he could
orchestrate the forms and harmonise the colour of a large-scale
painting, fuse grandeur and modernity on a single canvas, with
a view to entering future competitions. In the event, his failure
at the Salon of 1884 disillusioned him from pursuing such a
course and led him in another direction. When we look at
Repose and *Navigation* (Plates 120A and 120B) with which
Adrien Karbowsky decorated the *salle des mariages* at the
mairie of Nogent-sur-Marne it is not difficult to imagine how
the painter of the *Bathers* could have adapted his superior
talents to such a task.[23]

These large-scale public decorations are symptomatic of one
way in which ambitious painting in France continued its shift
in the 1870s and 1880s away from *la grande peinture* towards
more 'banal' subjects. Karbowsky's decoration is certainly
grande and it conveys a certain civic 'ideal', but it has neither
the historical subject nor the moral authority of the scenes
from the childhood of Sainte Geneviève with which Puvis had
decorated the Panthéon fifteen years earlier. Another symptom
of this shifting pattern can be traced over a longer perspective
in the subject of bathing figures, itself the very nub of the
Bathers. The theme of the male bather has a long tradition in
European painting, dating from the Renaissance's rediscovery
of the human body as an ideal form. This was the elevated

aesthetic in which Seurat had been trained, centring on the
harmonised and 'perfect' nude, its forms derived from the
examples of classical sculpture and the Italian masters, which
the artist was expected to adapt for his history painting. At the
beginning of the nineteenth century the male bather of heroic
Antiquity featured in countless Neo-classical canvases, in the
guise of drowning Leander, cowering Marius or bewitched
Hylas. By the 1870s the male nude with heroic associations
had become a rarity, supplanted by the female nude, itself
increasingly treated in an anodyne, perhaps titillating, manner
devoid of the classical values. This shift, motivated by political
ideology and public perception which implicitly agreed that
the pressures of modern industrial, urban existence were no
longer effectively articulated by a visual language from a
pastoral pre-capitalist past, is typified by Raphaël Collin's
Summer (Plate 121), exhibited at the Salon of 1884 and in
many ways a counterpoint to the *Bathers*. In this canvas life-
size figures also pose on a peaceful verdant riverbank. There
comparison ends. These are female figures, and their poses are
designed to display women's bodies from different viewpoints,
their torsion – quite absent in Seurat's models – emphasising
their feminine charms. Collin's painting jars, naturalistic
replication of flesh and foliage clashing with the wishful
implausibility of this fantasy. No doubt he felt the circle was
squared because this is an image of grace and calm, its claim
to ideal status somewhat spuriously upheld by the posing of
the standing figure to the left in the pose of the Callipygian
Venus, as some critics noticed.[24]

121. Raphaël Collin, *Summer*, 1884
Oil on canvas, 312 x 413 cm
Göteborg, Konstmuseum

122. Charles Meissonier, *Summer:
Bathers at Carrière-sous-Poissy*, 1888
Oil on canvas, 200 x 300 cm
Poissy, Musée d'Art et d'Histoire

123. Jean Seignemartin, *The Bathers*, c.1875
Oil on canvas, 20 x 28 cm
Montpellier, Musée Fabre

124. Jean-Charles Cazin, *Riverbank with Bathers*, 1881
Oil on canvas, 131.2 x 147.0 cm
Boston, Museum of Fine Arts (CAT. 66)

Such developments caused alarm in conservative cultural circles with the representation of the nude a topic of dispute in Salon criticism. Reactionaries such as Boulanger and Houssaye feared the debasement of beauty's 'sovereign expression', arguing that history painting alone justified the nude.[25] Others pointed out the growing tendency to replace the nude – nature corrected in accordance with aesthetic principles, ideal and pure – with the *déshabillé* – the unclothed, either naked or half-dressed, revealing the frank imperfections of the body and its actions.[26] In his *L'Art moderne*, published in 1883, the naturalist novelist-critic Joris-Karl Huysmans argued that the *déshabillé* represented an honest modern ideal, that depicting the body candidly should give the viewer evidence of the figure's age, health and status, and that the naked figure occurred infrequently in daily life; he allowed in bed, bathing, posing in the studio and in the dissection room.[27] Middle-of-the-road critics, André Michel among them, were torn between residual respect for a tradition they recognised as in decline and a naturalism that risked pushing honesty into impropriety.[28] It was in this atmosphere of critical debate that Seurat composed the *Bathers*.

Alongside the grand tradition ran another thread of 'nude' subjects, works claiming to be no more than genre pictures representing everyday bathing scenes. In mid-century Daumier had applied his remarkable visual memory and masterful rendition of movement to small panels of 'banal' riverbank subjects, at least one of which Seurat might have seen at the retrospective exhibition staged by the dealer Durand-Ruel in 1878 (see Plate 27).[29] Such casual compositions of men and boys swimming were commonplace, cropping up in the work of artists whose work Seurat is unlikely to have known, among them Cézanne and the Lyonnais Jean Seignemartin, one of whose little canvases coincidentally prefigures the *Bathers'* juxtaposition of bathers and distant train crossing a bridge (Plate 123). As a quotidian subject river bathing was tackled also in naturalist literature, of which Seurat was an avid reader.[30] He would probably have read Edmond and Jules de Goncourt's *Renée Mauperin*, first published in 1864, in which the heroine demonstrates her emancipated attitudes by swimming with a man in the suburban Seine near the Ile Saint Denis, not far downstream from Asnières. This equivocal idyll, with its industrial setting, was illustrated by James Tissot in a de luxe edition of the novel which, published in 1882, could have been noticed by Seurat.[31]

Such motifs were by no means limited to the urban environs. Lhermitte, one of Seurat's mentors as a draughtsman, drew a scene of peasants bathing in the Marne near his native Mont-Saint-Père in 1884 (see Plate 19), which – again coincidentally – bears a resemblance to the *Bathers*, this time in its distribution of figures within the diagonal composition. Lhermitte's drawing has an obvious anecdote, bathing the baby, which renders it more immediately legible than either the *Bathers* or another contemporary bathing subject, *Riverbank with Bathers* (Plate 124), which may have been among the paintings Cazin showed in 1882 at the Salon des Arts Décoratifs, which were compared by Antonin Proust to Puvis.[32] Cazin's painting combines very disparate elements – ideal (graceful female figures, tranquil landscape), naturalistic (autumnal dusklight, building work under way) and incongruous (the maid bearing a glass, the blithely interfering boatman) – into a confection that balances serenity and ambiguity, thus alerting us to the difficulties we may find in reading such paintings. By contrast, Charles Meissonier's *Summer* (Plate 122), which shares with the *Bathers* both dimensions and title (its subtitle is *Baignade à Carrière-sous-Poissy*), is engagingly direct in its scene of men swimming in the Seine. This too was a confection, put together from photographs and the result of three years' work.[33] Like all these ostensibly naturalistic images, which try to persuade us that they are the record of something seen, Meissonier's canvas also conveys an ideal, no longer one based on notions of classical proportion and heroic purity, but one that peddles more modern values concerning the healthy body, family and friendship, and the balm of bountiful nature.

Such a survey allows us to see the *Bathers* in some sort of perspective. In a cultural climate that could regret the passing of the nude, the academic ideal, or that could sanction the everyday if it conveyed modern, even Republican, values and avoided vulgarity, the bather figure ran the risk of criticism from one quarter or another, as did the group of pastels of women washing and dressing that Degas exhibited at the 1886 Impressionist exhibition.[34] There was no such debate about the *Bathers;* it aroused little press attention on exhibition in 1884, and no significant mention of its subject. This should not be taken as evidence that the *Bathers* is uncomplicated. For Seurat's bathers are extraordinarily equivocal. We are shown half-naked young men, stripped off for a swim. Yet they do not act in 'manly' ways: running, diving, swimming. They are not strapping figures; there is nothing tactile, sensuous, or detailed about the rendition of their bodies. None of them attracts the viewer's gaze by eye contact, for this is a bashful, bachelor, fundamentally decorous painting, pioneering a highly individual path between ideal and natural beauty.

1. Boulanger 1885, pp. 6–7; Houssaye 1882 p. 561.
2. Houssaye 1882, p. 561.
3. Thomson 1985, p. 75; Marlais 1989, p. 154.
4. Bigot 1883, pp. 471–2.
5. Jamot 1911, p. 177.
6. Repr. Jamot 1911, p. 175; Dorra and Rewald 1959, pp. xxxix, xl.
7. Baedeker 1881, p. 36.
8. Brody 1987, pp. 141, 179; Smith 1991.
9. Nos. 29, 170; Dinnerstein 1980.
10. Michel 1885, p. 495.
11. Mainardi 1993, p. 79; Aquilino 1993.
12. Houssaye 1882, p. 561; Fourcaud 1884, p. 466.
13. Lafenestre 1886, p. 586; Marx 8 Dec. 1884.
14. Jacques 16 April 1884; Marx 8 Dec. 1884.
15. Lafenestre 1886, p. 588.
16. H. 602; Persin 1993, p. 19.
17. 'Concours et Expositions' 17 Feb. 1883, p. 49; 21 April 1883, p. 126.
18. Granville 1993, no. 20.
19. Marx 8 Dec. 1884.
20. Paris, Petit Palais, 1986–7, no. pp. 181–3.
21. New York, Shepherd Gallery, 1977–8, no. 96; Haskell and Penny 1981, no. 67.
22. Paris, Musée des Arts Decoratifs, 1970, p. 13.
23. Paris, Petit Palais, 1986–7, pp. 221–4.
24. Haskell and Penny 1981, no. 83; Fouquier 1884.
25. Boulanger 1885, p. 22; Houssaye 1882, p. 562.
26. Olmer and Saint-Juirs 1889, p. 27; Thomson 1988, pp. 58–72.
27. Huysmans 1929, pp. 263–4.
28. Michel 1885, pp. 399, 478.
29. Maison 1968, no. 17.
30. Coquiot 1924, p. 29.
31. Minneapolis 1978, no. 62.
32. Proust 1882, pp. 543–4.
33. Posssy 1988, pp. 35–43.
34. Ward 1986; Thomson 1988, pp. 128–32.

The 'Modern' Landscape

Throughout the nineteenth century the riverside scene formed a stock category in French landscape painting. Tracing its lineage back to Dutch prototypes of the seventeenth century, this flexible motif challenged the painter to balance land, sky and water, and it was often handled simply, relying on minimal idealisation and the reduction of picturesque elements. The views Corot made in the 1850s of Château-Thierry might stand as paradigms of this sub-genre. A canvas such as that in the 'Am Römerholz' Collection, Winterthur, fills the foreground with a diagonal expanse of earthy bank, with houses in trees to the left and to the right of the gently flowing river. On the far bank, in the central distance lies the unobtrusive town. There is little movement is this contented landscape, which represents in vignette the 'natural' ideal of human habitation in the benevolent clasp of nature, handled with 'natural' candour. Such a paradigm corresponds in broad terms to the landscape of the *Bathers*, and as a convention it could be learned – Stanislas Lépine made a precise copy of Corot's view of Château-Thierry [1] – and variations could be worked upon it. Such manipulation was not simply a matter of artistic practice, but was subject to differing and shifting understandings of landscape. After all, 'landscape' means a number of things. It is a three-dimensional space that we inhabit, and is usually associated with notions of unspoilt natural elements such as forests or pastures. It is also a form of representation, and thus an artifice dependent on conventions which the artist can choose to adapt and order; it this sense it is un-natural. A sense of both social progress and the manipulation of the stock motif is apparent when comparing Corot's *River Scene with a Bridge* of 1834 and Pissarro's *Railway Bridge, Pontoise*, painted some forty years later (Plates 28 and 125) At first sight they appear similar, but closer inspection shows how Corot made much of the rhythmic architectural presence of the stone bridge, setting its regularity against the more haphazard cluster of houses. Pissarro's canvas, like the *Bathers*, represents both a road and rail bridge. The recently built railway bridge, erected in 1863, almost effaces its predecessor, but Pissarro conceals its abrupt horizontal within the close tones of his middle-ground, softening its modern intrusion into the tranquillity of the landscape motif. Structure and mood, modernity and naturalness, were all key elements in the choices Seurat had to make in settling the landscape for the *Bathers*.

Painting landscape provided the artist with many options.[2] During the early 1880s Seurat's oil sketches and small canvases reveal him attempting images of rural labour, the *sous-bois* (a forest motif concentrating on vegetation to the exclusion of sky), a few street scenes; he did not take up seascapes until 1885, the year after the *Bathers* was completed. A consistent element in both his *croquetons* and his drawings from about 1881 was a fascination with the suburbs of Paris and their different characters, for he scouted for motifs in both the commercial and industrial quarters such as La Villette and Saint-Ouen, spread like a yoke across the northern shoulders of the city, and more distantly in the leafy dormitory area of the Forêt de Bondy, to the north-east of the city, where his father had a house. The outlying vicinities would inevitably attract painters. Tied to Paris by the need to be involved with the nexus of the art world – patrons, dealers, exhibition outlets, colleagues, studios and training facilities – artists were furnished by the countryside immediately outside the city with the most convenient opportunities to study nature and the effects of changing weather on various terrains. For the ordinary city-dweller too the suburbs, with their towpaths, forests and châteaux parks, provided the scope for promenades

125. Camille Pissarro, *The Railway Bridge, Pontoise*, c.1873
Oil on canvas, 50 x 65 cm
Private Collection, sold Christie's New York, 16 May 1984

and boating, and were rendered accessible first by steamboats and later the railway.

By Seurat's time the suburbs (see Plate 126) were no longer merely the easily reached bucolic resort that, for instance, Ville-d'Avray had been for Corot in mid-century. In the 1840s three-quarters of France's population lived on the land, but whereas in 1843 town and city dwellers comprised 24 per cent of her people, by 1888 this had risen to 35 per cent. The population of Paris itself had doubled, from about one million in 1850 to two million by 1877.[3] This rapid growth was the result of a number of factors. The increasing importance of industry in the French economy drew people to urban areas, a process hastened by problems in the agricultural sector, which went into serious decline in the 1880s. The spread of railways – France's first main line, from Paris to Orléans, opened in 1843 – facilitated the exodus to the cities, and the capital itself served as magnet, with opportunities provided in both business and manual labour by the Second Empire's rebuilding of the city under baron Haussmann during the 1850s and 1860s. Seurat can hardly have been unaware of the changes wrought by the rebuilding. He was brought up in a recently constructed apartment block on the boulevard Magenta, one of Haussmann's direct modern thoroughfares, and it was successful property transactions that permitted his father, a legal official, to sell his business at considerable profit and retire young in 1854.[4] The rebuilding precipitated changes to the suburbs as well as the city. A combination of rising rents in Paris proper, cheaper goods outside the tax-barrier formed by the ring of the city's fortifications and Haussmann's policy of encouraging big industrial concerns – and thus their workforces – to settle outside the city led the lower classes to mass in the suburbs.[5] The increase in the city's population slackened, growing by over 280,000 between 1876 and 1881, but only 75,000 over the next five years.[6] Correspondingly, suburbs like Asnières developed rapidly. Bald statistics should not mask the volatile social results of such demographic shifts and commercial pressures. Relocating the proletariat to certain suburbs may have been welcome to the Parisian bourgeoisie in the wake of the Commune but it was, to use the wry Victorian prose of *The Boulevard*, a newspaper for English-speaking visitors, 'by no means favourable either for [its] moral or physical condition'.[7] Certainly a Catholic aristocrat with a social conscience, such as comte Otherin d'Haussonville, could see in the early 1880s that low-paid, ill-lodged populations on

the rim of the city were a recipe for disaffection or worse.[8] By the time Seurat came to paint the *Bathers* the suburbs of Paris had long been understood to encapsulate the shifting frictions of society perhaps more tellingly than any other microcosm of France.

Interwoven with the changing relationships between country, city and suburb were representations of these locales. This is an immensely complex body of imagery, but from it can be extracted a broad pattern of transition – from representations of essentially typical 'landscape', via leisured outer suburb, to those of industrial inner suburbs – which took place between about 1860 and 1885. The *Bathers* belongs within, and itself extends, this pattern. The working suburbs of Paris had been occasionally represented at least since early in the century, Constant Troyon painting workshops in the environs of Sèvres and Saint-Cloud during the 1830s, for instance. Broadly speaking, from the 1860s onwards there was a momentum in landscape painting that drew painters step by step inwards, from the outlying countryside to the suburbs immediately abutting the city itself. Daubigny's view of the Seine at Mantes, some forty kilometres downstream from

126. Map of the western suburbs of Paris, from Karl Baedeker, *Paris and Environs* (Leipzig and London 1881)

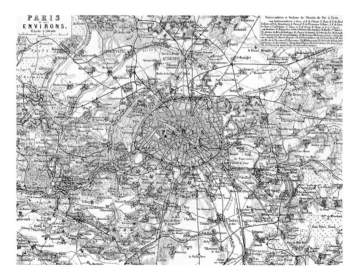

127. Charles-François Daubigny, *The Seine at Mantes*, 1856
Oil on canvas, 48.8 x 75.6 cm
Brooklyn Museum (CAT. 69)

Paris, typifies riverscapes of mid-century (Plate 127). Using a balance of diagonal bank and horizontal river similar to Corot's Château-Thierry pictures and, indeed, to Poussin's *Finding of Moses*, Daubigny gave close attention to nature, binding the disparate elements into a unity under the even summer light. Humanity intrudes into this natural ideal not just in the form of the old bridge and cathedral but also with the smoking factory chimney and the strolling woman, clad in chic rather than rural clothes. This is a scene in which industry and the bourgeoisie, creators and creatures of the modern, discreetly take their turn.

Daubigny's career as a landscapist was peripatetic, but focused chiefly on the Ile de France, the capital's hinterland. Two decades later, several of the Impressionist landscape painters lived and worked closer to Paris, in the outer dormitory suburbs – towns or villages that were increasingly losing their identity as centres as they became subject to the

commercial pull of the capital.[9] Astute critics reviewing the Impressionist exhibitions in the 1870s recognised that the canvases Monet made at Argenteuil or Sisley at Marly were novel and equivocal: 'Ultimately, it is not true nature that they have been looking at', the critic Charles Bigot pointed out in 1877, 'rather the kind of nature that one glimpses from the city or in its outskirts.'[10] By 'true nature' he surely meant what Daubigny represented, where tree and cloud and river dominate, in contrast to landscape interspersed with buildings, penetrated by roads and railways, busied with passing trains, boats and barges. As modern scholars have explained, the Impressionists did not represent a single kind of suburb, for there was no such phenomenon, 'suburb' being almost by definition a locality in constant flux. They painted the suburban experience in its variety, favouring scenes of leisure – the bourgeois populations boating, strolling, relaxing – rather than those of labour. Nevertheless, images of factories, stations

128. Edouard Manet, *The Seine at Argenteuil*, 1874
Oil on canvas, 62.3 x 103.0 cm
Private collection on extended loan to the Courtauld Institute
Galleries, London (CAT. 70)

and new construction did feature in their repertoires as part of their perception of these polymorphous areas, and were frequently made to co-exist more overtly than in Daubigny's case, factory chimneys and newly engineered bridges sharing the pictorial space with 'true nature' and the modestly scaled figures.

It is perhaps significant that the artists of the Impressionist circle whose canvases most closely followed the perception of the suburbs as an arena for comfortable middle-class leisure were those who lived in Paris itself. Manet's *The Seine at Argenteuil* (Plate 128), painted during a visit to Monet in the summer of 1874, shows the latter's wife and son looking at moored sailing boats from the riverbank, while Renoir's *Boating on the Seine* represents two young women in a skiff (Plate 129). In both canvases the spectator is placed on the bank, and is thus a participant in images that equated the suburban Seine – with its smartly dressed women, not workers,

and its pleasure craft, not barges – with leisure rather than labour. However, the paintings do register the made-up towpaths, floating washhouses, prosperous villas and train-carrying bridges that also characterised this kind of landscape. The artists recorded the scenes with a loose gestural touch, which approximated to their perception of the transitoriness of sunlight and moment. Shore up middle-class perceptions as they may, these two paintings still quiver with the equivocation inherent in modernity.

Laurent remembered visiting the 1879 Impressionist exhibition with Seurat, where the two pupils of Lehmann received 'an unexpected and profound shock'.[11] It may have been the suburban subjects that caught Seurat's eye, such as Caillebotte's images of canoeing on and bathing in the River Yerres, or Monet's canvases. Four of Monet's twenty-nine submissions were of suburban motifs, three of which represented the reach of the Seine between Courbevoie and

129. Pierre-Auguste Renoir, *Boating on the Seine*, c.1876
Oil on canvas, 71 x 92 cm
London, National Gallery (CAT. 73)

Asnières.[12] Tiring of Argenteuil, where he had worked for six years, in 1878 Monet had edged closer to the city, experimenting with the new terrain of the inner suburbs before opting to retreat to rural Vétheuil, near Mantes. He had confronted various motifs, some of which, along the island of the Grande Jatte (see Plates 130 and 131), were, with their ramshackle riverbanks and smoking factories, less salubrious than his Argenteuil pictures. His response to this area was clearly equivocal. For the 1879 exhibition he chose to show two works in which the motif is softened by a screen of foliage,[13] and another of strikingly different character. *Men unloading Coal* (Plate 132) represents the view from the railway bridge at Asnières looking north-west to the road bridge, the arch of which spans Monet's canvas. These are the two bridges that cross the horizon of the *Bathers*. Travelling from the Gare Saint-Lazare to Argenteuil Monet would frequently have passed this very spot, but this scene of workers shifting coal from barge to shore is exceptional in his work. Exceptional because it is a direct and uncomfortable confrontation with industrialised labour, the men reduced to silhouetted ciphers as they perform their back-breaking, repetitious task, but also because, as a view from a railway track, it can hardly have been executed *sur le motif* in accordance with Monet's practice, and may have been made from sketches or memory. Whatever the case, here Monet tackled head-on the abrupt realities of labour in the Clichy industrial zone which Seurat set back

130. Oscar-Claude Monet, *Ile de la Grande Jatte*, 1878
Oil on canvas, 50 x 61 cm
Oslo, Nasjonalgalleriet (CAT. 72)

131. Map of Asnières and vicinity, from Karl Baedeker,
Paris and Environs (Leipzig and London 1881)

into the hazy distance of the *Bathers*.

It would be wrong to assume that the 'modern' suburban subject was the exclusive preserve of the 'radical' Impressionist painter. Such motifs appeared at the Salon, in even more uncompromising form than the typical Impressionist canvas. At the Salon of 1874 Antoine Guillemet, friend of Manet and Cézanne, exhibited *Bercy in December* (Paris, Assemblée Nationale), a large, grim-toned painting of the barges and wine warehouses to the south-east of central Paris; the picture was purchased by the State.[14] Four years later Luigi Loir showed *The Quai national at Puteaux* (Plate 133), representing the same left bank of the Seine as the *Bathers*, about two kilometres upstream. Not only did this represent an

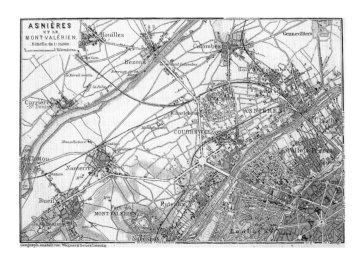

unprepossessing motif, its cloudbank lowering over grimy mudbanks, but also a landscape neither urban nor bucolic. The impermanent embankment and haphazard scattering of buildings give it a transitional character, enhanced by its deliberately scumbled and scratched paint surface. For all Loir's insistent notation of modern labour – telegraph wires and public transport, factories and unloading carts – the painting was shown at the Salon. If these two were large-scale exhibition works, Jean Béraud's *Banks of the Seine* (Plate 134) is an example of how middle-of-the-road naturalist painting around 1880 happily took on a suburban subject for a modestly scaled picture intended for the gallery market, enlivening the drab riverside with a bourgeois couple exercising their dogs.

Guillemet and Béraud's paintings both represent inner suburbs, not the bourgeois dormitory towns typical of contemporary Impressionism but industrialised, lower-class areas of metropolitan Paris. Their two images represented Bercy, just within the ring of fortifications to the south-east, an area where Armand Guillaumin, a loyal exhibitor with the Impressionists since the first exhibition of 1874, regularly worked. By the early 1880s Guillaumin, then a part-time painter who worked for the Département des Ponts et Chaussées, was representing unashamedly industrial subjects with his characteristic, somewhat crude, application of complementary reds and greens, yellows and violets (Plate 135). Both their subjects and something of Guillaumin's

133. Luigi Loir, *Quai national at Puteaux*, 1878
Oil on canvas, 85 x 164 cm
Nice, Musée des Beaux-Arts (CAT. 67)

132. Oscar-Claude Monet, *Men unloading Coal*, 1875
Oil on canvas, 54 x 66 cm
Paris, Musée d'Orsay (CAT. 71)

touch and colour were taken up by the young Paul Signac,
who had met the older artist painting on the *quais*.[15] A native
of Asnières, in 1883–4 the alert and ambitious Signac was
busily apprenticing himself in independent art. This to him
necessitated Impressionist handling and modern subjects,
frequently the kind of industrial motif he found in his
neighbourhood, such as the enormous train-bearing gantry
that dominated the Clichy riverbank just to the north of the
Asnières bridges (Plate 136). If that kind of subject had been
exceptional for Monet, it was commonplace for Signac.

The pattern we have traced has followed artists moving in
towards the city; we have shifted from rural landscapes
scarcely touched by modern intrusions, through motifs from

134. Jean Béraud, *The Banks of the Seine*, c.1880
Oil on canvas, 46 x 56 cm
Paris, Musée Carnavalet (CAT. 68)

135. Jean-Baptiste-Armand Guillaumin,
Quai de Bercy, Paris, c.1885
Oil on canvas, 60 x 92 cm
Copenhagen, Ordrupgaard (CAT. 75)

the outer suburbs in which the leisurely and the sunlit was more inflected by the new, to those embracing the industrial and transitional identities of the inner suburbs. It is a pattern which seems to interweave with a developing socio-political awareness of the changing relationships between country, suburb and city. Within this pattern there were contradictions and ironies. The more controversial and ostensibly 'modern' artists were not necessarily the most daring in their imagery. Perversely, as the suburbs of Paris spread outwards, so many painters of the suburbs were drawn inwards. This was a pattern not just based on changing social conditions or the landscape painters' search for new sites but also on the artist's own awareness of the modern and how it might be represented. This can be seen from the ways in which some of these canvases make a distinct effort to find striking forms of representation for new sites and responses towards them. When Gustave Caillebotte painted the Seine at Argenteuil in

the early 1880s he gripped his chosen features – steam-tug, barge, factory – under the stark iron span of the bridge, almost literally insisting on how this landscape was framed by the modern (Plate 137). Again, Loir's *Quai national* (Plate 133) uses the compositional device of the sharp diagonal, shared – no doubt coincidentally – with certain contemporary images by Monet (see Plate 29), to speed the eye through the pictorial space, thus giving the spectator a sense of passage through the depicted landscape.[16] Such a device gave the motif a rushed, unstable quality, as if it had been 'glimpsed' on the move, to return to Bigot's account of suburban pictures. Perhaps this was a solution at which both Loir and Monet arrived independently because it summarised for them a particular perception of the suburb, as an area to be traversed, a momentary and partial experience just as the suburb itself was transitional. It is notable also how artists of different style and allegiance might concur in their decisions about how to

136. Paul Signac, *Coal Crane, Clichy*, 1884
Oil on canvas, 59.0 x 91.4 cm
Glasgow Art Gallery and Museum (CAT. 76)

represent the flux of suburban societies in the fixed form of the painting. Loir, Signac and Caillebotte might settle on subjects exclusively commercial or industrial, for example, while Béraud or Manet might juxtapose proletarian wage-earning with middle-class recreation.

The topographical precision which Seurat gave to the title of his first exhibition painting – *Une baignade (Asnières)* is how it was listed in the catalogue of the 1884 Salon des Indépendants – is in fact somewhat confusing. His motif does indeed represent the bridges that cross from the direction of central Paris on the right to Asnières behind the trees to upper left (see Plates 126 and 131). It shows a view from about a kilometre south-west of the bridges. On the left bank, where his figures sit, was open ground with a towpath, though nearby properties came down to the waterside. This slope was known locally as the Côte des Ajoux, and the *Bathers'* site was near the end of the rue des Ajoux, which ran down towards the

river. The spot was some two hundred metres from the tip of the island of the Grande Jatte, which can be seen to the upper right of the painting and was perhaps artificially extended by the artist to achieve the balance Sutter's theories advanced (see p. 86). Close inspection of contemporary maps suggests that Seurat finally chose a viewpoint on a shoulder of riverbank which butted into the Seine, a significant choice because this vantage masked most of the riverside properties of Asnières on the left bank. Across the water he opened up a central panorama, with the factories of Clichy beyond the bridges and those of Levallois-Perret to their nearside. His position, it has been argued, was all but in Courbevoie, the upstream commune adjacent to Asnières.[17] The ostensible precision of the title thus dissolves, leaving an image that arrived at its pictorial order by manipulating topography, and in fact depicts several suburbs. By subtitling the painting 'Asnières' Seurat may merely have been concerned to give his public in 1884 a

137. Gustave Caillebotte, *Bridge at Argenteuil and the Seine*,
*c.*1880–5
Oil on canvas, 65 x 82 cm
Private Collection (CAT. 74)

shorthand clue to the character of his motif. He and they
would have been aware that the surrounding suburbs had
different identities, and that these were in constant flux.
But in 1884 how would Asnières and its environs have been
understood by Parisians?

Asnières was an area that had changed a great deal in the
past half century. Around 1835 Joseph Rémond had
represented it as tranquil riparian pastureland, with cows
watering and a single cottage.[18] The construction of a railway
bridge in 1837, built to link Paris to the river port of Le Pecq,
made Asnières the nearest and most convenient stretch of
rural riverside to the capital. Thus it became a centre for
leisuretime pursuits, especially boating, as it could provide a

138. Antony Morlon, *Regatta at Asnières during the Second Empire*, c.1860
Watercolour and gouache on paper, 32 x 47 cm
Château de Sceaux, Musée de l'Ile de France

139. E. Robert, *Railway bridge at Asnières destroyed during the suppression of the Paris Commune*, 1871, photograph. Paris, Bibliothèque Nationale

stretch of river avoiding 'the barges, steamers, coal-boats, public baths and floating washhouses' that cluttered up the Seine nearer the city. Between Rémond's canvas of 1835 and that plaudit from Labédollière's 1861 guidebook to the environs of Paris, the population of Asnières grew from 450 to 3,200. By 1876, when Seurat entered art school, it stood at 8,278, and ten years later, when he exhibited the *Grande Jatte*, 14,778.[19] This expansion can be attributed initially to the boating trade, a leisure industry that brought with it the craftsmen, shopkeepers and restaurateurs who catered for the seasonal trade, the popularity of which was promoted in a multitude of mid-century illustrations (Plate 138). As late as 1886 another guidebook, Barron's luxuriously illustrated *Les Environs de Paris*, characterised Asnières as a lively and picturesque place for boating and strolling, especially at weekends; four years later Périer's matter-of-fact account of the community wrote this off as *passé*.[20] Expanding population, spreading construction and burgeoning industry had long since changed Asnières, forcing the regattas and riverside cafés further from the city, to suburbs in the next ring out such as Argenteuil.

The suburbs around Asnières had been the scene of heavy fighting during the suppression of the Commune in 1871. Communard troops had crossed the road bridge on 2 April as they briefly advanced to attack government forces based on Versailles. They used the railway for an armoured train, which with the counter attack of Ladmirault's Ier Corps was engaged

by government artillery from the garden of a Monsieur Jourdan in Courbevoie. Eventually the Versaillais army crossed the Seine on a pontoon bridge, the road and railway bridges having been destroyed, on its way to crush the Commune in the city itself (Plate 139).[21] The bridges were soon reconstructed and the area rapidly recovered. Local histories and the archives of the *mairie* reveal a prosperous suburban centre in the 1880s. Employment was varied, but there were clear patterns to the local economy; unlike many suburban areas, few were involved in agriculture or market gardening, and there was no significant heavy industry. In May 1880 the municipal *Situation industrielle* listed the largest employer as the railway workshops, with 150 men, the next biggest being Goupil, the fine art print and photography business, whose factory had about a hundred staff. The other firms were often in the luxury goods trade; Louis Vuitton had manufactured luggage in Asnières since 1860, and there were two perfumeries and a printer, as well as establishments making glue and candles.[22] This contrasted starkly with the opposite bank: Clichy with its gas, chemical and glass works, Levallois-Perret with its established zinc oxide factory.[23]

In the *Bathers* Seurat not only summarised the Asnières area, its topographical constituents both natural and man-made, but he also gave his gloss on the suburban population. By the 1880s areas such as Courbevoie and Asnières, where land was more expensive because of the railway link with Paris, were havens for the middle and lower middle classes.

140. Jean-François Raffaëlli, *Street Scene*, c.1880–5
Oil on wood, 56.2 x 73.6 cm
Boston, Museum of Fine Arts

141. Alfred Roll, *Labour: Building Site at Suresnes (Seine)*, 1885
Oil on canvas, 440 x 600 cm
Cognac, Musée Municipal

These were often people who worked in, or had elected to retreat from, the city. Périer's 1890 account listed 'landlords, retired people, Parisian businessmen, employees of the railway companies, banks, civil servants from ministries and important institutions. There are also many artists, journalists, and workers of all kinds of trade . . . [and] some poor people'.[24] This is a snapshot that corresponds nearly enough to the one of local industry. Together they show an Asnières with its shops and service businesses, its offices, workshops and small factories, all run by a busy *petite bourgeoisie* with a limited local proletarian workforce. Alongside this were commuters and the rentiers who had settled there, both middle-class strata for whom, scoffed the astute social commentator Jules Claretie, such an area was 'countryside' (*campagne*), 'the realisation of their dream: a bargain basement eclogue'.[25] But Asnières or Courbevoie were not stable bourgeois havens. The lines between the classes, especially the *petite bourgeoisie* and the proletariat, were indistinct, with shopkeepers, craftsmen and their like forming blurred intermediate groupings.[26] Indeed, the cosy prosperity of the area was in question. Republican Socialists were arguing that the suburbs were where cheap salubrious housing should be provided for workers, and taking steps to facilitate this by passing a law in 1883 reducing commuter train fares, dropping the Asnières–Paris ticket from

4.20 francs to 1 franc on selected trains used by workers.[27] Add to this the progress made by socialist candidates in the 1886 by-election in the industrial areas to the north and west of Paris – Saint-Denis, Saint-Ouen, Puteaux [28] – and the ambiguous identity of Asnières becomes clearer.

Seurat was far from being the only painter who tried to find ways of representing the suburban populations during the 1880s. His choices included a number of typologies. Raffaëlli, who had settled in Asnières in 1878, had made a speciality out of images depicting the local impoverished and the *petit bourgeois* as hard-pressed, scruffy and melancholy, a characterisation taken up in the prose of his friend Huysmans (Plate 140). Roll's giant canvas *Labour* (Plate 141), from the Salon of 1885, was at once a naturalistic depiction of a construction site at Suresnes with its industrious, collaborative workforce and an implicit allegory of the Republic, the foundations of the future being fraternally laid. In 1890 Alphonse Cornet exhibited *Wedding at Asnières* (Plate 142). Representing almost the same spot as the *Bathers*, the trees of the Grande Jatte lining the background, its good-humoured, heterogeneous procession, scattered with anecdotal incident such as the fallen toddler or the roistering drunk, could hardly be more at variance with Seurat's still, silent citizens. Nor did Seurat show any interest in the commonplace subjects,

142. Alphonse Cornet, *Wedding at Asnières*, 1890
Oil on canvas, 127 x 200 cm
Riom, Musée Mandat

143. Emile Friant, *Monday's Work*, 1884
Oil on canvas, 44.5 x 43.0 cm
Nancy, Musée des Beaux-Arts

descendants of those mid-century prints that showed comfortably off groups, sleek and flirtatious, of the kind in Renoir's *Luncheon of the Boating Party* (Washington, Phillips Collection) or Roger Jourdain's *Sunday* (location unknown). Shown at the Salon of 1878, Jourdain's canvas, as John House was the first to show, was paired with *Monday*, an image of workers drinking rather than going to work.[29] The idea of Saint Lundi, the illicit Monday off, was also taken up by Emile Friant in a small painting of 1884 (Plate 143). A former pupil of Cabanel at the Ecole des Beaux-Arts, Friant hardly used the 'triangular' seated pose to convey the classical harmony of the body; rather, by having the spectator look down on these casual, furtive types, we are given a moral superiority over them. The *Bathers* fits none of these templates. Unlike the Friant, we face Seurat's figures as equals, although they do not return our gaze. Whereas Cornet's painting registers a hierarchy within the suburban populations, the *Bathers* apparently involves no deprecation or exclusion. It has none of the bonhomie of Renoir or Jourdain's festivities. Above all, unlike any of the paintings with which it has here been contrasted, the *Bathers* establishes no relations – by gesture, look or narrative – between its figures. Whereas others painted cohesive fragments of a complex society, Seurat painted society fragmented into disparate individuals.

1. Sotheby's, 23 June 1981, no. 64.
2. Thomson 1994; London 1995.
3. Lebon and Pelet 1888, p. 34; Baedeker 1881, p. xxiv.
4. Sutter 1964, p. 12.
5. Pinkney 1958, p. 165; Evenson 1979, p. 220.
6. Lebon and Pelet 1888, p. 34.
7. 'The Paris Ouvrier' 1879.
8. Haussonville 1881.
9. Tucker 1982; Clark 1985, 147–204; Herbert 1988, pp. 195–263, Thomson 1994, pp. 27–37.
10. Bigot 1877, p. 1046; Lafenestre 1879, p. 481.
11. Rosenthal 1911, p. 66.
12. Moffett et al. 1986, p. 269, nos. 139, 153, 158.
13. Wildenstein 1974, nos. 456–7.
14. Paris, Grand Palais, 1974, no. 112.
15. Signac 1964, p. 29.
16. Thomson 1994, pp. 20–1.
17. Hégo 1991; Zimmermann 1991, p. 136.
18. Gutwirth 1983, no. 72.
19. Labédollière 1861, p. 135; Périer 1890, p. 9.
20. Barron 1886, pp. 98–9; Périer 1890, p. 61.
21. Vuagneux 1906, pp. 128–9; Tombs 1981, p. 127; Boime 1995, pp. 173–5.
22. Asnières, Hôtel de Ville, Archives, liasse no. 24, pièce no. 51; Périer 1890, pp. 11–12; Petit 1939, p. 70; Flohic et al. 1994, p. 58.
23. Barron 1886, p. 40.
24. Périer 1890, p. 11.
25. Claretie 1883, p. 148.
26. Haupt 1984, p. 105.
27. Faure 1993, pp. 231–2.
28. Berlanstein 1984, p. 159.
29. House 1980, p. 348, figs. 54, 55.

1884: Rejection and Response

In the spring of 1884 Seurat submitted the *Bathers* to the jury of the Salon. Founded in 1699, the Salon was France's major art exhibition. During the nineteenth century it had passed through and survived many vicissitudes. At times annual, at others biennial, control of the Salon had been disputed by the different regimes and the Academy, and by the mid-nineteenth century the authority of its often conservative jury, devoted to *la grande peinture*, had been undermined by the eventual triumph of painters such as Théodore Rousseau, whom it had regularly rejected. Under the Third Republic the Salon was held annually, but the government increasingly favoured Charles Blanc's proposal that a triennial exhibition should be staged, on the grounds that great works took time to gestate and that work of sufficient status could not be produced on a yearly cycle. The first *Exposition nationale triennale* was held in 1883; it was not a success and, as Seurat worked on the *Bathers*, its (doomed) future was under discussion: artists and public wanted an annual exhibition; for painters, sculptors and their colleagues it was still the prime opportunity to put their works on view, attract critical response, and make sales to institutional and private purchasers; for senior artists it remained a sphere of authority and influence; and for a broad public it remained a talking point, a cultural yardstick. In recent decades the easel painting had become a prestigious unit in consumer culture, a capital investment, sign of class status and cultural calibre. To meet this demand from the prosperous classes not only had the number of art dealers in Paris burgeoned, but also the number of independent exhibitions – the Société des Aquarellistes, the Société des Pastellistes, the Cercle Volney, and others – at which successful artists sold more casual work than at the Salon. The Salon then, independent of the government and run by artists elected by their peers since 1881, continued as the pivot of the French art world, but its position was no longer as firm as in mid-century.[1]

As the son of a hierarchy-conscious family and an ex-pupil of the Ecole des Beaux-Arts, Seurat would have expected to exhibit at the establishment Salon; in 1883 and 1884, when he made his first submissions to the jury, he had no alternative. It seems that he originally planned to show a drawing of his mother sewing, *Broderie* (New York, Metropolitan Museum), at the Salon of 1883, but eventually submitted his portrait of Aman-Jean (Plate 20), whose *Saint Julian* (Carcassonne, Musée des Beaux-Arts) won a third-class medal that year.[2]

He probably entered the portrait not only because it was a grander and more visible drawing, but also because it was more traditional, being a variant on the Louvre's portrait of Erasmus by Holbein, an artist Seurat admired. Furthermore, it was in the 'new' tenebrist drawing style he had recently forged with Laurent and others. Showing a large item intended to make an impact and reworking a major work from the Louvre was a doubly ambitious step for a Salon debut, even if the work was in the 'lesser' medium of drawing. The portrait of Aman-Jean was briefly praised in a review by Roger Marx,[3] encouraging the artist and alerting Marx to look out for Seurat's submissions the following year.

The Salon of 1884 was typical of the Salons of the early eighties, at which reviewers detected a bewildering plurality of styles and subjects, something variously interpreted as perhaps dangerous eclecticism in the absence of specific schools of painting or as indicative of the vitality of French art evident in its individualism.[4] Critics characterised the exhibition according to their *partis-pris*. The reactionary Houssaye rejoiced that 'painters are going back to elevated subjects, to history, to heroic or religious figures . . . Impressionism is losing ground . . . The vulgar or banal scenes of contemporary life, which proliferated yesterday on canvases of fifty superficial metres, are more modest and remain within the small formats from which they should never have strayed'.[5] But the 'traditions of the Ecole [are] manifestly overtaken and defeated', countered the more liberal Fourcaud, although he flinched at the 'infinite number of plebeian pictures, often mediocre, sometimes detestable'.[6] In the broad terms of the complex and continuing struggle between *la grande peinture* and naturalism, the forces of the former retained their institutional rank at the 1884 Salon. Elected by fellow exhibitors and listed in numbers of votes won, the ten leading jurors comprised Jean-Jacques Henner, Henri-Joseph Harpignies, Léon Bonnat, François-Louis Français, Antoine Vollon, Jean-Paul Laurens, Tony Robert-Fleury, Puvis de Chavannes, Jules Lefèbvre and Bouguereau.[7] Not all were Academicians, but history painters easily predominated. Although no painter received enough votes to win the medal of honour, in the election Bouguereau came first, followed by Fernand Cormon, Henner and Puvis – *la grande peinture* once again predominant.[8] The Prix du Salon, given by the Minister of Public Instruction and the Fine Arts, went to a painting that pleased few by a pupil of Cabanel, Paul Leroy.[9]

A sample of works exhibited in 1884 gives something of the
Salon's character, of the options Seurat had rejected, of the
Bathers' potential competition. Bouguereau's enormous
Childhood of Bacchus (Plate 144), measuring over six metres in
length, was his most ambitious painting for many years. Its
combination of male and female nudes in active poses was a
display of his virtuoso draughtsmanship, the painting itself a
statement about his pre-eminence as a practitioner of *la grande
peinture* . Properly for such a work, classical sculpture was
quoted, the shoulder-high Bacchus and his carrier a citation of
the *Faun and Kid,* a plaster cast of which Seurat had copied
three times as a student.[10] Costume pieces were still popular,
and Adrien Moreau's *The Ferry* (Plate 145) was intended to
show 'a cross-section of all the social classes of the seventeenth
century', the artist explained in a letter to his dealer.[11] Themes
from daily life were plentiful. Octave Gallian exhibited *A
Buoy in Toulon Harbour* (Plate 146), an animated sunlit scene
of urchins swimming, the spontaneous poses of the stretching
and clambering figures offset by that of the boy on the left,
clasping his knee like Flandrin's Polytes (Plate 108), Victor
Gilbert's *Meat Porters* and Ernest Delahaye's *Gasworks at
Courcelles* (Plates 148 and 147) both represented the Parisian
proletariat at work, the one an image of collaborative muscular
effort, the other of labour under unpleasant industrial
conditions. Scenes from naturalist literature were on show,
including Paul-Emile Boutigny's depiction of the final scene

144. Adolphe-William Bouguereau, *The Childhood of Bacchus,*
1883–4. Oil on canvas, 331 x 610 cm. Private Collection

145. Adrien Moreau, *The Ferry*, 1884
Oil on canvas, 129.5 x 200.7 cm
Location unknown

146. Octave Gallien, *A Buoy in Toulon Harbour*, 1884
Oil on canvas, 145 x 250 cm
Cannes, Musée de la Castre

147. Ernest Delahaye, *Gasworks at Courcelles*, 1884
Oil on canvas, 136 x 184 cm
Paris, Musée du Petit Palais

148. Victor Gilbert, *Meat Porters*, 1884
Oil on canvas, 201 x 159 cm
Bordeaux, Musée des Beaux-Arts

from Guy de Maupassant's story *Boule de Suif* (Plate 149), in which the good-hearted prostitute, humiliated by the German officer, is repudiated by the compatriots she has self-sacrificingly aided. Finally, Louis-Henri Deschamps's *Seen One Spring Day* (Plate 150) applied an ironic title to a scene of searing social realism, with three ragged children left numbed in a cottage, a crucifix beside the empty pallet suggesting the death of their parent, possibly a motif inspired by the caring Catholicism promoted by the likes of Otherin d'Haussonville. Of the paintings in this sample, the Bouguereau remained unsold because of the price the artist demanded; the Moreau was exported to the United States, where it swiftly found a buyer; the Gallian and the Gilbert were purchased from the Salon by the State for the museums of Cannes and Bordeaux respectively, and the Delahaye for the municipal collections of Paris; and finally both the Boutigny and the Deschamps were bought for the museum in Carcassonne with funds from a private donation.[12]

Meeting in late April, the jury at the Salon of 1884 apparently rejected the *Bathers*. We do not know why. Hundreds of works were passed in quick succession before the jurors and decisions were made verbally and rapidly. The process was always a lottery, especially for an unknown young artist without a patron on the jury, as was Seurat's case. Habitually there were grievances about partiality and unfairness, and the art critic of *Gil Blas* reported that his newspaper had received many complaints from artists which compromised the jury's performance.[13] The art world gossip, retailed in *L'Intransigeant*, insisted that the jury of 1884 had

149. Paul-Emile Boutigny, *Boule de Suif*, 1884
Oil on canvas, 145 x 200 cm
Carcassonne, Musée des Beaux-Arts

150. Louis-Henri Deschamps, *Seen One Spring Day*, 1884
Oil on canvas, 150 x 200 cm
Carcassonne, Musée des Beaux-Arts

been more severe than that of 1883. The paper's critic Edmond Jacques had heard it alleged that so harsh had been its judgements on submissions by artists whose names began with letters early in the alphabet, that by the time the jury reached R or S it seemed that it would not select enough paintings to fill the exhibition and so it accepted 'everything it saw'.[14] Jacques did not trust this tale, and certainly Seurat was not a beneficiary. The reviewer of the *Journal des Arts* claimed that limitations of space had restricted the number of canvases accepted, forcing good works to be hung high and increasing the number of the disaffected whose pictures had been refused.[15] If space was at a premium, this might have been a reason for the rejection of the *Bathers*, a canvas of two metres by three. The entrenched prejudices of supporters of *la grande peinture* against scenes of everyday life trespassing on the grand scale reserved for history painting were not confined to the Establishment; when Pissarro argued that the *Grande Jatte* should be exhibited at the 1886 Impressionist exhibition because it was most interesting, Degas countered, 'Oh! I can see that very well, Pissarro, it's just that it's *big*!'[16] However, on the evidence of a drawing in *Paris illustré* showing stacks of canvases rejected from the Salon of 1885, more small and medium-sized canvases were refused than large ones, possibly because they were more plentiful and were reckoned to have a better chance on the art market.[17] By the 1880s size alone prevented neither the modern subject's acceptance at the Salon nor its purchase by the State or institutional collections. Of the sample from the Salon of 1884 just considered, all had a major dimension in the region of two metres, and photographs of the

works bought that year by the State reveal a large proportion of similarly scaled or larger canvases.[18] Seurat would have chosen substantial dimensions for the *Bathers* for several reasons – to attract attention, to prove his mastery of a large surface and possibly his fitness for decorative commissions – and they seem unlikely to have been the cause for its rejection.

The painting's subject would not necessarily have counted against it. The 1884 sample reveals that 'banal' subjects – and indeed images of labour, industry and poverty far more stark and tactile than Seurat's balmy suburban riverbank – passed the jury and won sales. The figures in the *Bathers* are lower-class types; Seurat used a centuries-old convention of codifying common figures from the everyday urban world by their physiognomy and costume.[19] This was standard practice among contemporaries; all the modern scenes in the sample employed it, and the jury would have taken no exception. Alfred Roll exhibited two paintings of Parisian types at the Salon of 1884, *Roubey, Cement Mixer* and *Marianne Offrey, Herb Seller* (Geneva, Musée d'Art et d'Histoire; Pau, Musée des Beaux-Arts). By representing them life-size and giving their names as well as the occupations they typified, the Republican Roll drew critical attention and made an egalitarian point.[20] Roll's figures face the viewer, confronting us with ragged clothing, hardened hands, and careworn stares. These were no doubt among the 'plebeian pictures' that Fourcaud found 'detestable', and in 1884 they presented the middle-class Salon visitor with the image of the lower classes far more forcefully than the *Bathers* would have done. Indeed, Boutigny's *Boule de Suif*, with its juxtaposition of hypocritical bourgeoisie and alienated prostitute, or even Moreau's *The Ferry*, albeit in historical costume, deliberately set up class relations in their narratives. Seurat's painting can hardly have offended on class grounds, if paintings such as these were accepted.

Perhaps the *Bathers* failed to pass muster on stylistic grounds. All the paintings illustrated in this sample from the Salon of 1884, of whatever 'style' or subject, whether by Bouguereau, Moreau or Gallian, have legible relationships between their figures. By contrast, in the *Bathers* the figures form no groups related by action, gesture or anecdote; rather they exist in the unlinked isolation that in 1877 Véron had found reprehensible in the compositions of Ecole-trained painters (see p. 90). This depiction of the figures as individual units was, at one level at least, the result of Seurat's studio practice, for the models had been drawn individually rather than as groups and made their way on to canvas so. Again, it may be that some members of the jury found in the *Bathers* too evident echoes of the work of Puvis de Chavannes. Art critics in the early 1880s were certainly aware of Puvis's influence on young painters. At the Salon of 1883, for example, Henri Daras's *Sufficient unto the Day is the Evil thereof* (Plate 151) was accused of imitating Puvis,[21] and indeed its flat, dry surface, high horizon and reductive, slightly clumsy drawing is reminiscent of recent canvases by Puvis, such as the *Prodigal Son* (Zurich, Bührle Collection) shown at the Salon of 1879. It is possible that the *Bathers* was seen as the latest of a whole crop of Puvis clones and rejected by academic members of the jury attempting to restrict Puvis's influence on young artists.

Finally, it might be suggested that one reason for the *Bathers'* rejection was that it perplexed the jury, that it was such a stylistic hybrid that it was not easily understood. The balance of its design, its disposition of figures and other structural elements within the landscape composition were reminiscent of Poussinesque prototypes and echoed recent work by Puvis. The general stasis of the poses, and in particular the harmonious triangles and arcs of the straw-hatted youth, evoked the order and equilibrium of the classical ideal in which Seurat had been trained and which still dominated teaching at the Ecole des Beaux-Arts. But at the Salon things were different. Senior proponents of *la grande peinture* might remain in positions of authority on the jury, but other forces impinged upon the Salon. Here the photographic record of paintings bought by the State is useful evidence. The Republican regime purchased many landscapes and scenes of everyday life from the Salon of 1884. The historical subjects it selected were chiefly naturalistically rendered narratives from the Middle Ages or the French Revolution; only Edouard-Louis-Paul Fournier's overplayed *Orestes taking refuge at the Altar of Apollo at Delphi* and Hector Leroux's stately *Vestal Virgins fleeing Rome* (locations unknown) represented the

ancient world. Léon de Winter's *Sheep Shearer* (location unknown) worthily adapted the pose of the Antique *Arrotino*, but into a mundane if muscular pastoral.[22] The *Bathers'* implicit vaunting of classical credentials did not necessarily guarantee success at a Salon subject to public and Republican pressures for pictures easily legible in style and subject. If the *Bathers'* classicism could have seemed rather out-dated, its chromatics might have appeared too adventurous to the Salon jury, established history painters to whom a high-key tonality, play of complementary colours and textured, albeit quite systematic, brushwork smacked of *impressionnisme* and the alarmingly modern. For the Salon jury, then, the *Bathers* may have held too many paradoxes. Well-schooled in balanced design, but lacking cohesion in the figures; the models gracefully correct in pose but inappropriately abrupt in modelling; borrowing from Puvis's serene simplifications but repudiating his timeless subjects; representing the suburbs, that quintessentially modern setting, and yet with a poise undeserved by their pullulating populations, it could be argued that to the establishment judges in 1884 the *Bathers* failed to 'add up'.

There was no such difficulty with a jury at the Groupe des Artistes Indépendants. This organisation was set up in the wake of the mass rejections from the Salon of 1884. It was one of an increasing number of exhibitions established, often on an ad hoc basis, to put on public display work the Salon declined to accommodate; the Salon des Refusés of 1863 and the 1874 show which came to be known as the first Impressionist exhibition were celebrated predecessors. It seems that on 11 April a group of rejected artists met to discuss their position, and on the 16th a hundred or so held a meeting which argued for liberty of artistic expression and formed a committee with the intention of winning support from either the State or the municipality of Paris.[23] This in itself was a political act typical of the early 1880s, in the climate of a Republic ostensibly opposed to hierarchies and committed to egalitarian reform. In the event the city of Paris, aware of its radical traditions, was prepared to sponsor an independent exhibition, loaning the Group a temporary building, erected to house a provisional post office, in the Cour des Tuileries, a central site adjacent to the Louvre. The show opened on 15 May, a fortnight after the Salon, ran to 1 July, and 402 artists showed work here,. On the first day it was visited by President Grévy, the Director of Fine Arts, the Prefect of the Seine and the President of the Conseil Municipal of Paris, the Republic thus demonstrating its neutrality and the city its tolerance in artistic matters.[24] They would have seen the *Bathers*, which Seurat had sent to the new jury-less exhibition. He must have calculated that he had no other choice. To resubmit the painting to the Salon in 1885 would be to court another rejection. Besides, he had lavished much effort on it and wanted it shown; to hide it away would not launch his career as a painter while Laurent, Séon, Aman-Jean and other colleagues were furthering theirs. And for a young painter with no name, no dealer's gallery or established artist's club would be likely to display a large canvas. To get the *Bathers* on show in the spring of 1884, it had to be with the Indépendants.

Reaction to the exhibition of the Groupe des Artistes Indépendants was mixed. Several newspapers, including the radical *L'Intransigeant*, balked at its title on the grounds that the eclecticism on view echoed the Salon and that it was scarcely 'independent'. 'Mediocre' was a common description, and the Salon jury seemed vindicated.[25] Nevertheless, experienced critics argued that there was work of quality on show, both by respected painters the jury should not have refused – in *Le Temps* Jules Claretie identified Van Beers and Poirson – and by young artists. Picking out two who 'perhaps will be famous one day' Claretie named Monsieur Le Natur and Mademoiselle Denyse Carrère, both of whose work has remained *terra incognita* to the history of art. More perceptively he also mentioned Odilon Redon, because his work was at least independent, and, among those 'preoccupied with *plein air*', Seurat.[26] Claretie was not alone in drawing attention to the *Bathers*. Roger Marx, reminding the readers of *Le Voltaire* that he had noticed Seurat's drawing at the 1883 Salon (Plate 20), recognised individuality in 'his impressionist painting'.[27] In *L'Intransigeant* Edmond Jacques was not unsympathetic, enlarging on Claretie's appreciation of the painting's atmospheric character by writing that 'behind and under some prismatic eccentricities [Seurat] conceals the most distinguished qualities of draughtsmanship and envelops his bathing men, his ripples, his horizons in warm tones'.[28] Under the pseudonym of 'Trublot', Paul Alexis, naturalist writer and friend of Zola and Cézanne, published a column on cultural matters in the left-wing *Cri du Peuple*. Inclined to support the new, his response to the *Bathers* showed him rather stumped: 'it's a fake Puvis de Chavannes. What funny bathing men and women! But it's so committed [*convaincu*] that it's almost touching and I don't dare joke any more.'[29] Sloppy in observing the sex of the figures, Alexis at least recognised a serious work and suggested its slightly uncomfortable relationship with Puvis's painting: a more attentive response than that of Paul de Katow in *Gil Blas*, who merely listed the painting by 'Sieurat' [sic] among the 'curiosities'.[30]

The critical reaction to the *Bathers* on the only occasion it was exhibited in Paris during Seurat's lifetime was hardly disappointing, given the general tenor of responses to the Indépendants' show and perhaps also the fact that the painting was poorly hung, apparently in the bar.[31] In 1884 it was cast either as a brightly painted landscape in a 'modern' style or as

151. Henry Daras, *Sufficient unto the Day is the Evil thereof*, 1883
Oil on canvas, 180 x 140 cm
Private Collection

a well-crafted figure painting in the Puvis vein. This was adequate praise and not ridicule. It justified Seurat's decision to exhibit with the Groupe des Artistes Indépendants just as repudiation by the Salon seems to have encouraged him to take his chances with the emergent avant garde. At one of the meetings winding up the rather ramshackle organisation of the Groupe, which was replaced by the Société des Artistes Indépendants, Seurat sat next to Paul Signac.[32] This meeting was followed by others with fellow exhibitors at the Groupe; Charles Angrand, Henri-Edmond Cross and Albert Dubois-Pillet formed the kernel of the group which, during the next couple of years, would coalesce around Seurat and use the exhibitions of the Société des Indépendants as their public platform. Refused by the Salon, poorly hung at the Groupe, handled briefly and oversimply by those critics who noticed it, the *Bathers* nevertheless achieved what Seurat had intended it to do; it launched his career as a painter of serious ambition.

Characterising the *Bathers*

Faced with a large painting by an unknown artist that had been refused by the Salon, the critics at the Indépendants in the spring of 1884 could do no more than snatch at its meanings and significance. Over a century later, with a knowledge of Seurat's later work and his established reputation as one of the most important innovators in late nineteenth-century French art, there is a substantial body of critical opinion on the *Bathers* and it is a challenge to the art historian to attempt to characterise this great painting for our generation without diminishing its visual poetry. To do so one should set aside – difficult as this artifice may be – Seurat's later work and reputation, the better to understand the choices Seurat made as he executed and pondered the *Bathers* and to unravel the complexities of his masterpiece with the critical and cultural mechanisms current in 1884.

From Seurat's training and by his own account of his reading as a student we have established that the tuition at the Ecole des Beaux-Arts and the aesthetic of Charles Blanc especially instilled in the young artist an idealising aesthetic. How then did this find form in the *Bathers*? What was the nature of Seurat's processes of idealisation? Surprisingly perhaps, the painting does not look like an Ecole product. It does not have the smoothly worked brushstrokes of a Bouguereau or a Merson, stereotyped *têtes d'expression* (heads representing different emotions), quotations from Antique sculpture, skilfully drawn figurative groupings and the other trappings of Ecole and Salon accreditation. On the other hand Seurat's repertoire of graceful and compact poses carries the lingering stamp of the ideal: the bow to Ingres in the boy seen from the back; the seated figure whose pleasing curves and triangles derive from the *académies* (nude studies from life) of Flandrin and his ilk; the lad hallooing, bonneted like a wingless Mercury. Paul Smith has suggested that the influence of Blanc's *Grammaire des arts du dessin*, which argued that artists transform nature into essential, eternal forms, is particularly apparent in the simplification of Seurat's drawing of the figures, which renounces detail for a synthetic unity.[33] Yet even within this indubitable idealism there is resistance. None of the figures has facial features with which the spectator can engage. Not only do they look resolutely away, but the figures have schematic, even non-existent eyes or mouths. The central bather, his hair pressed into a sweaty rimmed helmet by the now discarded straw hat, once had clearer features; reworked, his face appears purplish and pustular. According to an 1885 volume on physiognomy, the pseudo-science which held that physical appearance provides the clue to character, livid complexion was a sign of alcohol abuse, frizzy hair of 'physical vigour' but 'not of intellectual superiority', and hair combed low over the forehead of a stupid appearance.[34] By this account, the features of the central youth quite contradict the elevated serenity of his fellows' poses. The subversion of the ideal of the human figure central to *la grande peinture* by naturalistically rendered types was of pressing anxiety at the Ecole; in his 1885 lecture Boulanger, sniping at Cazin's recent work (Plate 152), damned 'representing a hero from Homer in the guise of a back-street prowler'.[35] Such fears, such contradictions within the picture, may have been a cause for the *Bathers'* rejection from the Salon.

When one looks not at individual figures but at the painting as a whole its idealising nature becomes clearer. The *Bathers* has a stillness, a monumentality, a unity of atmosphere, light and moment that set it apart from many of the paintings with which we have drawn parallels. It does not equate exactly with a contemporary canvas such as Cazin's *Judith* (Plate 113); while both artists ennobled the ordinary, Cazin's efforts to elide opposites – here the Biblical and the naturalistic – were more overt than Seurat's. The *Bathers'* enveloping luminosity and ordered disposition of forms make it distinct from the very different kinds of naturalism represented by Loir's *Quai national* or Renoir's *Boating on the Seine* (Plates 133 and 129), both of which use handling of paint to animate the scene and the spectator's perception of it. By contrast, the discipline of touch employed by Seurat steadies and slows the eye's pace over the canvas, a process which enhances the *Bathers'* aura of serenity and evokes, for all the image's contemporaneity, a sense of timelessness. Coupled with that quality, Seurat's controlled brushwork is also the vehicle for the distribution of tones and colours that spread a warm clear light throughout his painting, the greens and blues of grass and water enlivened by the tonal contrasts of shadow and sunlight and the aerial perspective which melds the distant bridges and factories into a mollifying summer haze. The artist's manipulation of light and colour in the artifice of his canvas, his transformation of the raw material of nature into a cohesive picture, was itself an idealising process brought off with remarkable confidence by the young painter.

That textural, chromatic and atmospheric harmony was built on a compositional framework rooted in one of the most

152. Jean-Charles Cazin, *Ulysses after the Shipwreck*, c.1880–4
Oil on canvas, 73.3 x 59.7 cm
London, Tate Gallery, on loan to the National Gallery

emphatically idealistic currents within *la grande peinture*. Seurat was uninterested in the dramatic, dynamic traditions of history painting, in Michelangelo or Rubens; he spurned the emphatic gestures in the work of his professor, Lehmann. Among contemporaries he was drawn to the work of Puvis de Chavannes, who in the early 1880s stood for an art of classicising order so starkly reductive that at least two critics at the Salon of 1884, while praising his contribution, warned against this 'dangerous master' and 'the abuse of his methods that others commit'.[36] In his stately disposition of figurative groups within finely calibrated landscapes Puvis democratised the noble, marrying an idealising aesthetic to the ideology of the Third Republic. In the *Bathers* Seurat, flouting the warnings of those critics, adapted many of Puvis's pictorial procedures, but to a different purpose, at the same time as he transgressed the example of Puvis, more candidly striving for an egalitarian ideal by using pictorial means to dignify the ordinary.

Both the *Bathers* and *Doux Pays*, the painting which was probably in Alexis's mind when he compared Seurat and Puvis, are rooted in Poussin's work, in particular those Poussins which, like the 1638 *Finding of Moses* (Plate 103), achieve their authority as works of art by compacting gravity of figures, stability of landscape and intensity of subject. We have seen how Seurat's mentor Blanc picked out this specific Poussin as a prime example of the artist's transformation of observation of nature into elevated artistic expression. For French painters in the 1880s, Seurat among them, Poussin was not just a salient figure of the national school from whose achievements the ambitious should learn. Poussin's work exemplified the elision of pictorial order and moral order. By Seurat's adherence to vital aspects of that tradition – to balance of forms, grandeur of figures, unity of design and moment – the *Bathers* subscribed to an idealistic aesthetic.

What separates the *Bathers* from, say, the paintings of Puvis or Merson, what signals its discontent with the idealism which to an extent it honoured, is its insistently modern motif: a 'banal' scene of male bathers at unprepossessing Asnières. Something of the picture's resolution of the struggling pressures of idealism and modernity comes in its negotiation of the suburban subject. By 1884 the Parisian suburbs had been a controversial theme in French culture for two decades. The year 1864 might be taken to typify the frictions. That year Hippolyte Collard, a specialist in recording modern structures,

produced an album of six photographs of the docks at Saint-Ouen, an heroicisation of up-to-the-minute construction and commerce.[37] But suburbs such as Asnières and Puteaux were treated more ambivalently in the Goncourt brothers' novel *Renée Mauperin*, published the same year, and described as 'foul yet radiant, wretched yet gay, popular and full of life, where Nature peeps out here and there between the buildings, the work and the business, like a blade of grass held between a man's fingers'.[38] Twenty years on the motifs both Collard and the Goncourts itemised as 'suburban' – quaysides and lifting bridges, fishermen and barges, trains and factories – were shared by Seurat in the drawings he made as he worked gradually towards the *Bathers*. By the early 1880s industry had become so dominant in the Parisian suburbs that it was demonised in some quarters, condemned as 'an abscess working on the social body', destroying the 'ideal world of religion, philosophy . . . morality and art'.[39] This was a conservative position, of course, and against its ideals could be posited the ideal of the modern, the nineteenth century's vaunting of technological and industrial progress. Seurat's own stance on this is nicely poised in the *Bathers*. On the one hand his riverbank represents the man-made and the natural in a more equal balance than that of the Goncourt's simile, and pushes bridges and factories into the hazy distance. On the other, Seurat places those very elements centrally; their regular shapes define the horizon and the frontier of his figures' world. And by titling his painting 'Asnières' he introduced the uncertainties people felt towards the suburbs. Why did Seurat choose Asnières as the site of his masterpiece? Perhaps it was to do with Blanc's idealising aesthetic, the site found by Seurat/Poussin walking by the Seine/Tiber transformed into art. Perhaps it was motivated by emulation – of the suburban passages in naturalist novels and suburban sites he had seen tackled in Salon paintings or those Monet exhibited in 1879 – and the need of a youthful artist to follow a lead. Did Seurat also subscribe to the ideal of the modern? Was he sophisticated enough at twenty-four to perceive the ambiguities and temporariness of the suburbs?

To answer such questions we need to clarify the nature of the *Bathers'* modernity, and can usefully focus on the painting's figures. In the imagery of the period suburban scenes were commonly peopled with specific types, whose presence was a means of codifying the character of a locale, giving the fluctuating, 'modern' identity of the suburb some legibility. The most frequent of these were the middle classes promenading, as in Manet's *Banks of the Seine*, or boating, as represented by Morlon and Renoir, and the lower classes, either at work – in, for instance, Delahaye's *Gasworks* or Monet's *Men unloading Coal* – or struggling for an existence in the scruffy new growth that surrounded the city, frequently depicted by Raffaëlli (Plate 140). In his drawings of the early 1880s Seurat worked through much of this typology, especially at the proletarian end of the class spectrum. As he planned the staffage of the *Bathers* he would have called upon his experience of these types, but how categorisable his figures would have been in contemporary terms is a matter of contention among art historians today. The men on the bank and the lads bathing have been identified as working class, most consistently by left-wing writers; to stress their disadvantaged status T. J. Clark has even suggested that they are swimming opposite the mouth of the great collector pipe which poured the sewage of all Paris into the Seine.[40] Although the river beyond the sewer-pipe was intensely foul for at least a kilometre, belching bubbles of fetid gas and necessitating regular dredging because the watercourse became clogged with ordure, the sewer actually debouched just downstream from the Pont d'Asnières, beyond the bridges in the distance of the *Bathers*. A recent report by the Préfecture boasted that, by contrast, the river upstream of the sewer outlet, flowing through the south-western suburbs from Sèvres to the Asnières bridges, was 'almost free of sewer water'.[41] The cleanliness of the suburban Seine, in other words, echoed the class status of the localities through which it flowed. The stretch at Courbevoie and Asnières which Seurat painted was not to be compared to that at industrial Clichy and Saint-Ouen, downstream from the sewer pipe and beyond his horizon. As Alain Corbin has pointed out, cleanliness and class went hand-in-hand in the contemporary social imagination, with the bourgeoisie fearful of contagion from the proletariat.[42] The bodies of Seurat's bathers are not dirty, their linen is clean, and they sport bowlers, straw-hats and elastic-sided boots rather than the blue overalls, caps, and hob-nailed boots of the industrial working classes. These appear in some of Seurat's preliminary oil sketches for the *Bathers* (for example Plate 54), in which the industrialised horizon plays a more dominant rôle than in the final canvas and horses, perhaps haulage nags, are being washed in the river. It may be that Seurat originally saw the motif as working class, but gradually

changed his staffage to the more *petit bourgeois* figures in the finished work. Such a shift may have been due to a deepening understanding of the population of the Asnières–Courbevoie riverbank as he painted there during the summer of 1883, or to a desire to moderate his picture's personnel for the Salon, to avoid being categorised as a peddler of proletarian images. But Asnières was a mixed neighbourhood, and while the figures of the *Bathers* may well represent the clerical staff and skilled workers of the *petite bourgeoisie*, we do well to remember that the boundaries between this social group and the working classes were in constant fluctuation. Modern uncertainy about the social status of these people perhaps echoes Seurat's subliminal uncertainties as he brushed in his figures.[43] The types on Seurat's fictive riverbank are neither emphatically of a single class, like Monet's oppressed proletarian coal heavers, nor obviously contrasted, like those in Béraud's canvas (Plates 132 and 134). They do not easily correspond to the conventional typologies of the Parisian suburbs, their uncomfortable relationship to the established pictorial codes something of a parallel to the friable status of the *petite bourgeoisie* in the class hierarchy.

What else might Seurat tell about the figures basking in the sunshine? It has been suggested that they are 'celebrating' Saint Lundi, the French workers' illicit skiving-off work on a Monday.[44] But there is no pictorial evidence for this, and nor does the title prompt such an interpretation. When a middle-class painter represented this kind of behaviour, the image was typically condemnatory (Plate 143). It is unlikely that bourgeois, industrious Seurat would have adopted another tone, and the figures in the *Bathers* are far from furtive or down-at-heel. Hollis Clayson and Robert Herbert have both commented on the absence of women in the *Bathers*, with the exception of the anonymous figure behind the parasol on the ferry crossing to the island of the Grande Jatte.[45] It is indeed a bachelor picture, painted by an unmarried and as far as we know unattached young man of twenty-four. Women had hitherto played a minor rôle in Seurat's work. Most of the life models he had drawn at the Ecole had been men; female figures appear schematically in his small paintings of rural life; and only in his conté crayon drawings do women feature regularly, usually as faceless creatures reduced to types and distanced by the play of the medium. In contemporary representations of Paris woman was a problematic totem for the male artist, her class and moral status as fascinating and ambiguous as the flux of the city, her modishness and desirability symptomatic of the pacy precariousness of urban life: the very emblem of modernity. There is none of this in the *Bathers*; in age-group and sex it represents a world very close to what Seurat knew from his immediate existence. Here, limited personal experience and limited grasp of the mechanisms of modernity go hand-in-hand.

Charles Meissonier's *Summer* (Plate 122) also represents young men swimming in the Seine, but with the figures linked by gesture and gaze in narrative relationships. That kind of collective coherence was expected in the pictures of the 1880s, especially ones representing the modern world and so calling on the visual skills people apply in their everyday lives. Praising Raffaëlli's representations of the suburban populations Gustave Geffroy pointed out how 'the rag-picker, the road mender and the bourgeois have all the gestures and movements of their occupations'.[46] Seurat chose not to pursue this kind of descriptive naturalism. The figures of the *Bathers* form no groups, do not touch or look at each other, and their resting or swimming is an individual rather than a collective activity. Perhaps this sense of fragmentation is not just the result of Seurat's studio practice; the way he put the picture together. It may be indicative of his taciturn temperament, the intrusion of his character into his work. Perhaps one should not seek to separate this from the way he saw the world, perceiving the modern as a pattern of isolated existences, so that the *Bathers* depicts uniformity of pleasure in relaxation but individual experience of it. With hindsight one can find a similar view of the world in Seurat's later and very different paintings, such as *Circus* (1890–1; Paris, Musée d'Orsay), in which the audience watch the spectacle in rigid isolation.

Interpreting the *Bathers* forces us to ask how it looks, and why it might look like that, and it is part of the richness of Seurat's mesmerising masterpiece that we have to admit that these questions defy pat answers. The painting seems to resonate with paradoxes. The ensemble is harmonised by the warm joyous light which radiates from the canvas, and yet the figures appear isolated, unconvivial, even sullen. There is something truculent about its muteness, uncomfortable about its serenity. The picture was crafted out of apparently antithetical traditions and materials: a stately design siting forms in ordered planar space descended from Poussin; poses, some derived from the academic canon, rendered as essential forms as Charles Blanc prescribed; the reductive drawing and

chalky, textured brushwork proffered by Puvis de Chavannes; the riverside motif conventional in nineteenth-century French landscape; the Third Republic's ideological tolerance for the democratic and the modern; and the experimental chromatics that young painters were beginning to prise from textbooks, the example of the Impressionists, and hard looking at nature. Setting himself the task of painting his masterpiece as a grand composition of a suburban subject, Seurat's solution emerged not only from the choice of those complex and contradictory ingredients, but also from his denials. With the dogged exclusiveness of the young, Seurat made a picture which is not Puvis, not Monet, not Raffaëlli.

Along with other painters of his generation – Laurent or Lerolle – he was reaching for a new ideal, a new chapter in the tradition of *la grande peinture*: the fusion of the modern and the monumental. Motivated by his Ecole training, his reading of Blanc, and perhaps the programme to decorate the *mairies* of Paris, the *Bathers* might have been, at one level at least, a public statement that he was worthy of such a public commission. Its grand scale, lucid forms, apparent combination of human dignity and the modern industrial landscape, and even the inclusion of a somewhat *de trop* tricolour all suggest that it was. And yet there are crucial slippages between Seurat's conception and the Republican norm. Laurent's scheme for Saint-Maur (Plate 117) dutifully featured the family, society's fundamental unit, but the *Bathers* transgresses this social ideal. There are no families, no bonding, no real communication. Denying exchange between its figures, it refuses to comply with the institutional requirement for legibility. The societies of the western suburbs of Paris which Seurat sought to synthesise – Asnières, Courbevoie and Clichy – presented a fluctuating complex of growth and prosperity, dereliction and instability. Seurat chose to represent the bank on which, by and large, the population was burgeoning, housing was congenial and light industry provided employment. With the *Bathers* Seurat kept his distance from the big factories and slum conditions of the far bank, where crime and insurrectionary politics festered among the *mauvaises populations*. If the local town-hall decorations were intended to promote Republican moral order in these edgy localities, if a painting such as Cornet's *Wedding at Asnières* (Plate 142) presents an immediately decipherable construction of communal bonhomie, Seurat's silent, static image seems to offer contradictory readings, appearing simultaneously stable and socially fissured. The figures dominate the canvas with the scale of heroes, and yet their pasty, unmuscular bodies and invisible or unappealing physiognomies make them teasingly unheroic. The whole picture seems to be made up of such paradoxes. It represents an uncommunicative gathering, immobile exercise. Its silent theatre fails to communicate with the viewer in the institutional terms of Salon popularity or Republican didacticism. Yet by judicious use of colour and texture Seurat coalesced nature and industry, suburb and sunlight, in this manufactured idyll, prising grandeur out of these apparent disjunctions. In the soft, embracing light of the riverbank, Seurat's bathers seem perfect formal units, and yet in social terms they are isolated and thus imperfect. That tension in what we see, that jarring of the harmony, that imperfection in perfection, is what gives the *Bathers* its aura of mystery.

1. Mainardi 1993.
2. H. 582; Christophe 1890.
3. Marx 1883.
4. Chennevières 1880, p. 402; Buisson 1881, p. 475; Jacques 1 May 1884.
5. Houssaye 1884, p. 560.
6. Fourcaud 1884, pp. 378, 390.
7. 'Concours et Expositions' 22 March 1884, p. 94.
8. 'Recompenses du Salon' 31 May 1884, p. 174.
9. Lafenestre 1884, pp. 1–2; Houssaye 1884, p. 569.
10. Haskell and Penny, 1981, no. 37; H. 299–301.
11. Atlanta 1983, no. 55.
12. Paris, Petit Palais, 1984–5, no. 100 (Bouguereau); Atlanta 1983, no. 55 (Moreau); Toulon 1988–9, p. 202 (Gallian); Cleveland 1980–2, no. 191 (Gilbert); Laffon, i, 1981, no. 311 (Delahaye); Mozziconacci 1990, nos. 26, 71 (Boutigny, Deschamps).
13. Katow 21 April 1884.
14. 'Beaux-Arts' 7 April 1884; Jacques 1 May 1884.
15. Dalligny 6 May 1884.
16. Bailly-Herzberg (ed.) 1986, p. 45 (letter of 8 May 1886).
17. Becker 1995, p. 143, pl. 11.
18. Musée d'Orsay, Documentation.
19. Herbert 1962, pp. 65–70; Thomson 1985, pp. 64–74.
20. Dalligny 13 May 1884; Gautier 10 May 1884; Fouquier 1884.
21. Veron 1883, p. 118 (from Angoulême 1986–7, p. 66).
22. Haskell and Penny 1981, no.11; London 1991–2, p. 118.
23. Angrand 1965, pp. 29–30.
24. Mainardi 1993, p. 122; Rewald 1948, p. 45.
25. Jacques 24 May 1884; Katow 17 May 1884.
26. Claretie 16 May 1884.
27. Marx 16 May 1884.
28. Jacques 24 May 1884.
29. 'Trublot' 17 May 1884.
30. Katow 17 May 1884.
31. Rewald 1948, p. 46.
32. Letter of 12 Nov. 1919 (Malibu, J. Paul Getty Center Library).
33. Smith 1990, p. 384; Paris, Grand Palais, 1991, p. 148.
34. Mouton 1885, pp. 65,69–70.
35. Boulanger 1885, p. 7.
36. Fouquier 1 May 1884; Fourcaud 1884, p. 466.
37. McCaulay 1994, pp. 215–16.
38. Goncourt 1864 (1902, p. 11.).
39. Mouton 1885, pp. 296–7.
40. House 1980, p. 346; Boime 1995, p. 173; Clark 1985, p. 163.
41. *Préfecture* 1875, pp. 41,44; Neuville 1880, pp. 37–9.
42. Corbin 1994, p. 227.
43. Thomson 1985, p. 125; Thomson 1989, pp. 182–3; Clayson 1989, p. 162; Zimmermann 1991, p. 140; Paris, Grand Palais, 1991, pp. 150–1; Smith 1997
44. House 1980, p. 348; Clayson 1989, p. 162.
45. Clayson 1989, p. 162; Paris, Grand Palais, 1991, p. 151.
46. Geffroy 1894, p. 208.

The Echo of the *Bathers*

Representing the Suburbs after 1884

Writing to the critic Félix Fénéon in June 1890 Seurat recalled that he had begun work on his next major canvas on Ascension Day 1884. This fell on 22 May, scarcely more than a week after the opening of the Groupe des Artistes Indépendants exhibition at which the *Bathers* was on view.[1] A resolved study for the new painting was hung at the first show of the Société des Artistes Indépendants in December 1884, and the completed picture was apparently ready to be submitted to its second exhibition in March 1885, which was cancelled. Seurat's second large painting, partially retouched, was finally put on show in May 1886 at the eighth and last Impressionist

exhibition, entitled *A Sunday on the Grande Jatte (1884)*, the artist publicly signalling his picture's genesis in the year the *Bathers* was finished and displayed (Plate 153). Reviewing the 1886 Impressionist show, most critics concurred that the *Grande Jatte* was a calculated pitch for leading status in the Parisian avant garde.[2] Critical reaction was largely favourable. This was because most of the reviewers were not establishment critics, such as Houssaye and Fourcaud, but young writers, some of them poets and novelists rather than professional art critics, who had emerged during the last couple of years. Of the same generation as Seurat, they were forcing the

153. *A Sunday on the Grande Jatte (1884)*, 1884–6
Oil on canvas, 207 x 308 cm
The Art Institute of Chicago

boundaries of naturalism in literature and developing a Symbolist aesthetic, which stressed the evocation of mood and underlying reality rather than the precise rendition of nature. Introduced to such writers by Signac, whom he had met at the public meetings of the Indépendants in the spring of 1884, Seurat found a degree of common cause with Fénéon, Jean Ajalbert or Paul Adam.[3] Whether with words or paint, these young men sought to recast the modern as something stylish and allusive rather than merely descriptive, and the informal creative cadre they formed made Seurat part of a more deliberately innovative circle than his former Ecole friends.

Seurat made the *Grande Jatte* at a period of transition not only between styles but also between artistic communities and their aesthetics. To what extent Seurat envisaged the *Grande Jatte* as a combative break from the more conservative *Bathers*, rather than a logical development of it, needs to be gauged.

There are links between the two canvases. As the *Bathers* was completed and the *Grande Jatte* begun, certain techniques remained constant. Chief among these was Seurat's use of the *balayé* (criss-cross, literally 'swept') brushstroke to block in the basic chromatic structure, though this was not as densely textured as in the *Bathers*. Seurat also chose to paint his image

154. *Study for the 'Grande Jatte', c.*1884–5
Oil on wood, 15.2 x 24.8 cm
London, National Gallery (CAT. 80)

155. *Study for the 'Grande Jatte', c.*1884–5
Oil on wood, 16 x 25 cm
London, National Gallery (CAT. 79)

of the Grande Jatte on a canvas the same size as the *Bathers*, two metres by three, a decision that registered no diminution of his ambition, at least. It may also have been connected to Seurat's choice of site for his second picture, for the northern tip of the island of the Grande Jatte appears in the upper right-hand corner of the *Bathers*; thus in broad, if not topographically exact, terms his two images 'face' each other. These similarities have led some commentators to suggest that the two form a pair, polarised not only by their physical placement on facing banks of the Seine but by the classes they have been claimed to represent, the proletariat in the *Bathers* and the *bourgeoisie* in the *Grande Jatte*.[4]

Here the differences between the two come into play. We have already seen that the figures in the *Bathers* probably represent the *petit-bourgeois* or artisanal population of Asnières, not simply the proletariat, while the *Grande Jatte* seems to show a quite wide social spectrum, not just the middle classes. Nor do the paintings function as a pair.

Their horizons are pitched at different levels; they represent very different numbers of figures, drawn and modelled somewhat differently; and the retouched surface of the *Grande Jatte* is busier and more animated. The *Grande Jatte* had a more convoluted genesis than the *Bathers*. It involved more preliminary drawings and *croquetons* (Plates 154 and 155), and the drawings in particular served new functions. One sheet was used to plot the whole landscape, laying it out like an empty stage set on which Seurat would parade his figures (Plate 158). Another acted as a cartoon for the right-hand side of the composition, placing figures, shadows and tree-trunks in resolved relation to each other (Plate 156). Drawings had not been used in this way for the *Bathers*, neither had substantial paintings on canvas – the one Seurat painted of the landscape 'stage' he exhibited in December 1884 as a work in its own right.[5] A second canvas was squared up to follow the proportions of the drawing for the composition's right half, and was used to explore that area's chromatic structure (Plate 157).

156. *The Couple: Study for the 'Grande Jatte'*, *c.*1884–5
Conté crayon on paper, 31.4 x 23.6 cm
London, British Museum (CAT. 82)

157. *Couple walking: Study for the 'Grande Jatte'*, *c.*1884–5
Oil on canvas, 81.3 x 61.5 cm
Cambridge, Fitzwilliam Museum (CAT. 83)

158. *Landscape with Dog:*
Study for the 'Grande Jatte', *c.*1884–5
Conté crayon on paper, 42.5 x 62.8 cm
London, British Museum (CAT. 81)

159. *Study for the 'Grande Jatte', c.*1884–5
Oil on canvas, 70.5 x 104.1 cm
New York, Metropolitan Museum of Art (CAT. 84)

A third served as an advanced study of the whole composition and contains almost all the elements that found their way into the completed painting (Plate 159). However, this large study, although close to the final design of the *Grande Jatte*, reveals how, even at such an ostensibly developed stage, the picture's constituents were still in a state of some flux. The figures in the background have been added as afterthoughts over the original surface, and the profiles of other figures adjusted. Indeed, the *Grande Jatte* itself was retouched in places after its initial completion in the spring of 1885.[6] Thus, in the project as a whole there was both more deliberation over a longer term and more changes and additions than in the *Bathers*, as was probably inevitable for a canvas incorporating a greater number of figures. The *Grande Jatte* necessitated a more complex developmental process to create an image more complex in surface and colour, staffage and meanings, though perhaps lacking both the luminous unity and poetic serenity of the *Bathers*.

Although not a pair to the *Bathers*, the *Grande Jatte* was of course a second representation of the reach of the Seine between Courbevoie and Asnières. The vicinity, its populations and the kind of diagonal composition it suggested evidently satisfied Seurat, and his second pictorial meditation on these western suburbs of Paris is a double development from the *Bathers*. On the one hand reconsideration of similar site and composition served as a convenient base for the stylistic progress just outlined, and on the other it encouraged a denser interpretation of the suburban locale. Following on from critics' reactions in 1886, art historians have interpreted the austerely drawn profiles, processional gravity and quirky details of this sun-drenched scene in various ways. The *Grande Jatte* has been seen both as a parody of middle-class pomposity and as a harmonious bourgeois utopia; it has been cast as a society in which the family fails to function, or in which prostitution lurks beneath its stately surface.[7] However we choose to read the *Grande Jatte*, it is clear that Seurat's introduction of women, his grouping and juxtaposition of widely various types, and the artful use of accessories add up to a more conscious modernity than had been within his ambit when he painted the *Bathers*. Another significant difference is not just the number of figures but what they are doing. Because nothing happens between the figures in the *Bathers*, the painting gains in serenity but fails quite to register either as a moralising modern 'history' painting, as its scale would seem to classify it, or as a narrative 'genre' picture, which its subject suits. In the *Grande Jatte* Seurat seems to have tried to remedy this. His personages do not merely sit: they act — fishing, reading, strolling — and interact — playing music, caressing the baby, running back to Mummy. In this sense the *Grande Jatte* does not only remedy the 'deficiencies' of the *Bathers*, it is also a step towards a more intricate and animated conception of representing modern life. Ironically, as Seurat seems to have striven to add vitality to his figure compositions, he also increased the rigidity of the figures, a contradiction, perhaps inadvertent, which set style and subject in powerful, disturbing conjunction. This momentum in Seurat's creative temperament pushed him further towards the experimental avant garde, leaving his masterpiece the *Bathers*, for all its figures' simplifications and distractedness, as the most humanist of his great paintings.

We have seen how, in broad terms, the *Bathers* had emerged from two main currents: the classical figurative tradition and the nineteenth-century's dedication to landscape painting. In conclusion it is worth considering how, over the next few years, both these had a residual effect in the work of Seurat, as well as how some of the artists in his orbit responded to his initiatives as a painter of the north-western suburbs. Just as the *Grande Jatte* had developed from the *Bathers*, so a body of landscape painting by Seurat and others followed from the experience of the *Grande Jatte* in 1886. The *Bathers* itself slipped into the background, eclipsed by the 'tableau manifeste', as one critic called the *Grande Jatte*, which had caused such a stir at the last Impressionist exhibition.[8] Known only to those who remembered it from the Indépendants in 1884 and the few who may have seen it in Seurat's studio, Jules Christophe had to inform the readers of his 1890 profile

160. *Study for 'The Seine at Courbevoie', c.*1885
Oil on wood, 24.9 x 15.7 cm
London, National Gallery (CAT. 77)

of Seurat that the *Bathers* had been the artist's first major painting, while it is clear from Jules Antoine's obituary the following year that he did not know the picture.[9] Nevertheless, the site of both Seurat's first large paintings, the reach of the Seine at Asnières, became for the next few years a key setting for essays in experimental landscape painting.

Seurat himself still occaisonally worked in the north-western suburbs after the exhibition of the *Grande Jatte*, producing canvases of standard landscape size, the figurative element much reduced (Plate 160). The most evocative of these is the *Bridge at Courbevoie*, made in late 1886 (Plate 161). Set towards the southern end of the Grande Jatte, facing north-west, it repeats the compositional counterpoint of the

two exhibition pictures, setting diagonal bank against hard-edged horizon. But this is no grand painting, the scale of its figures causing the spectator to match up to them, to ponder a relationship with them as exemplars or equals. Its modest format and close-toned play of secondary greens and violets, its regular play of the right-angles and ellipses of masts and jetties, arch and chimney, its subordination of the effects of nature – leafy bough or mist-veiled waterway – to the will of the artist's pointillist surface all register a shift in Seurat's aesthetic. The *Bridge at Courbevoie* is a poetic picture, inviting meditation, in which the viewer's response is stirred more by colour and form than by subject or resemblance. In this sense,

it is a Symbolist painting, adhering to the new aesthetic Seurat shared with his recently made literary friends. Nevertheless, although reduced in rôle, the human figure still has a part to play here, and these ciphers silhouetted against the Seine, isolated and silent, are offspring of the same creative temperament that crafted the mute youths of the *Bathers*.

A similar shift in aesthetic priorities is also apparent in the work of other painters at this period, all aware of Seurat's initiatives. Between 1885 and 1888, but with a period of particular intensity in 1887, Signac and Charles Angrand, close friends of Seurat, as well as Vincent van Gogh and Emile Bernard, all painted on the stretch of the Seine between

Asnières and Courbevoie. There were a number of motives for this. For Signac and Bernard, whose parents lived in Asnières, it was home turf, while for Montmartre-based Angrand and Van Gogh, as for Seurat, this suburban vicinity was conveniently reached by train or omnibus. The prevalence of suburban motifs in the literature they read, both by writers of the previous generation such as the Goncourts and Huysmans and of their own, notably Ajalbert, gave the outskirts of Paris a modern, cross-disciplinary status as a subject. But surely the example of Seurat, who in two successive exhibition pictures had used this area for compositions that demonstrated distinctly progressive development in his painting, confirmed this choice, having validated Asnières as the key site for forging a modern pictorial style. In November 1885 Signac painted the *Seine at Asnières* (Plate 163), which was shown the following year at the Impressionist exhibition in the same room as the *Grande Jatte*. Although not as systematic in surface as Seurat's big picture, Signac's canvas, in contrast to his painting of the previous year (Plate 136), shows greater concern to unify touch and chromatics. Eighteen months later, in the spring of 1887, he had pushed his painting further along. In *The Clipper, Asnières* (Plate 164) broad blocks of colour representing the river's ripples and reflections are

paired with vibrant dots which register the dance of sunlight upon the ordered perspectives. A year later still and the unifying device of pointillism was inherent in Signac's style. In *the Bridge at Asnières (The Stern of the Tub in the Sun)* (Plate 165) a flecked and dotted touch is used variously to stand in for the glare on the sun on paintwork or its mellow glow in the sky. This trio of paintings does more than mark out Signac's painterly progress over two-and-a-half years. It measures out his commitment to Asnières as a site. All three were painted on the Asnières bank (see Plate 162). For the 1885 painting, Signac stood with his back to the railway bridge, facing south-west to where the trees on the Grande Jatte can be seen as a grey mass just right of centre. *The Clipper* takes the view between the road and railway bridges, looking south-east to the Clichy bank, while the 1888 canvas points north-east, downstream towards the two bridges, through the centre of which can be seen the gantry he had painted in 1884. Spread over three years, as they are, this trio of paintings represent motifs within a few hundred metres of each other. Signac's loyalty to the site is equalled by the consistency with which he represented it. All three pictures render industry and leisure in some kind of balance, setting off sailing boats and riverside bistros against the gasworks, factories and busy bridges of these

161. *The Bridge at Courbevoie*, 1886–7,
Oil on canvas, 46.4 x 55.3 cm
London, Courtauld Institute Galleries (CAT. 78)

162. Schematic map of the Asnières/Clichy area of the north-west suburbs of Paris, with key indicating views illustrated in this book.

A Seurat, *Bathers at Asnières*
    (PLATE 178)

B Monet, *Men unloading Coal*
    (PLATE 132)

C Monet, *Ile de la Grande Jatte*
    (PLATE 130)

D Signac, *Coal Crane, Clichy*
    (PLATE 136)

E Seurat, *A Sunday on the Grande Jatte*
    (1884) (PLATE 153)

F Signac, *The Seine at Asnières*
    (PLATE 163)

G Van Gogh, *The Bridges, Asnières*
    (PLATE 166)

H Bernard, *Iron Bridges, Asnières*
    (PLATE 167)

I Signac, *The Clipper, Asnières*
    (PLATE 164)

J Signac, *Bridges at Asnières*
    (The Stern of the Tub in the Sun)
    (PLATE 165)

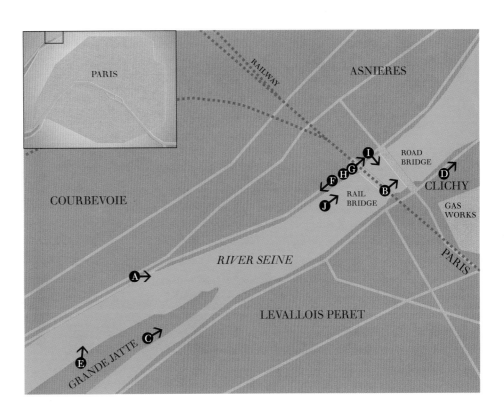

suburbs. In essence, this is a polarity similar to that employed by Seurat in the *Bathers*.

Vincent van Gogh concentrated his representations of Asnières into the spring and summer months of 1887.[10] During this period his work made a rapid stylistic transition, aided by a certain degree of tutelage he received from Signac. The atmospheric *Fishing in Spring* (Plate 168), animated by graphic brushwork, still owes something to the example of Monet's naturalism, whereas *The Bridges, Asnières* (Plate 166), executed in the summer, makes more of surface marks and the play of complementaries, replacing the bucolic verdancy of the earlier painting with a focus on the starkly engineered structures of the Asnières reach. Emile Bernard, who had experimented with a pointillist touch in 1886, had rejected it by the following year, when he worked with van Gogh at Asnières. Now painting in an almost ruthlessly reductive style, Bernard's *Iron Bridges, Asnières* (Plate 167) represented the riverbank in stark synthesis, the silhouettes of his figures hunched in the autumnal chill. The extent to which Bernard sinned against exactitude is apparent from the way in which the curving quayside by the railway bridge, represented both

163. Paul Signac, *The Seine at Asnières*, 1885
Oil on canvas, 60 x 89 cm
Private collection (CAT. 85)

164. Paul Signac, *The Clipper, Asnières*, 1887
Oil on canvas, 46 x 55 cm
Private Collection (CAT. 90)

165. Paul Signac, *Bridge at Asnières*
(The Stern of the Tub in the Sun), 1888
Oil on canvas, 46 x 65 cm
Private Collection (CAT. 91)

166. Vincent van Gogh, *The Bridges, Asnières*, 1887
Oil on canvas, 52.5 x 65.0 cm
Zurich, Foundation E.G. Bührle Collection (CAT. 88)

in Van Gogh's *Bridges* and Signac's 1885 canvas (Plates 166 and 163), is wrenched straight to form a diagonal against which the geometry of the bridges is pitched. Austere shapes, inanimate surfaces and steely tones mark Bernard's canvas as offering a very different reading of the suburb to the sunlit stillness of Seurat's two large canvases or the lively touch and colour of Signac and Van Gogh's riverbank scenes. Finally, Angrand's evolution as a painter of the suburbs should be taken into account. His *Western Railway Line leaving Paris: View from the Fortifications* (Plate 169), made in 1886, has a

specificity akin to Seurat's titles. Showing the track that a couple of kilometres further on crosses the bridge at Asnières, Angrand's diagonal composition bears a passing resemblance to that of the *Bathers*, with the Seine swapped for marshalling yards, while a figure in proletarian blue overalls who would not have been out of place in Seurat's *croquetons* looks on from the left. Three years on, another of Angrand's canvases of the Seine registered not only the shift in his own aesthetic but also the end of this avant garde's intense phase of interest in the suburbs as spur for pictorial innovation. He referred to *Dawn*

167. Emile Bernard, *Iron Bridges, Asnières*, 1887
Oil on canvas, 45.9 x 54.2 cm
New York, Museum of Modern Art (CAT. 89)

on the Seine (Plate 170), a subtle medley of blues, greens and violets whose pointillist haze reduces the far factories to mysterious tessellations, as a 'Symphony in grey', insisting on a frankly Symbolist interpretation.[11]

Accounting for this group of paintings does more than indicate the extent to which, in the wake of the *Bathers* and the *Grande Jatte*, a tightly defined suburban locality to the north-west of Paris served as a laboratory for pictorial innovation and stylistic exchange. Between the artists involved there were differences as well as similarities. Angrand,

Bernard and Van Gogh had not submitted to such an intense academic training as Seurat, while Signac was essentially self-taught. For them, independent painting centred not on the figure but on landscape, following the example of the previous generation of Monet and his comrades. However, alongside the consensus that the Asnières area was the place to paint grew up another, about how to paint it. Most of these pictorial explorations of the north-western suburbs do not shy from representing it as a man-made locale. Van Gogh's *Fishing in Spring* may set up a fiction of 'rural' suburb, but other

representations made different choices, defining 'suburb' in different ways. The *Bathers*, among the earliest of this generation's suburban motifs and the one most closely tied to an idealising tradition, placed figures at rest in verdant nature against a backdrop of the modern and industrial, enveloping the whole in mellowing light. By 1887 more options were opening. Canvases such as Signac or Van Gogh's *Bridges* (Plates 165 and 166) represented industrial reality – gasworks, chimneys, trains – in some kind of balance with leisure: sailing dinghy, riverbank café and pink parasol. This was, after all, the polarity of commerce and consumerism that provided the force-field which energised the nineteenth-century capitalist culture on which the Parisian bourgeoisie thrived. Another option threw that contented equation out of kilter. Bernard's

Iron Bridges or Signac's *Clipper* tip the balance, so that the human and the recreational seem clutched in a rigidly engineered armature of metal and stone. The motivation for such a harsh, unidealised representation of the suburbs is the result not merely of stylistic evolution but also of the pessimism and social radicalism that characterised the end of the 1880s far more than it had the earlier years. In the end, however, all these canvases are pictorial enquiries about the place of humanity in an emphatically man-made environment.[12] This was an issue increasingly and consciously faced by people in the 1880s, and it troubles us today. It is part of the greatness of paintings such as the *Bathers* that through pictorial means they continue to give resonance to such essential concerns.

168. Vincent van Gogh, *Fishing in Spring*, 1887
Oil on canvas, 50.5 x 60.0 cm
Art Institute of Chicago (CAT. 87)

169. Charles Angrand, *The Western Railway Line leaving Paris: View from the Fortifications*, 1886
Oil on canvas, 73 x 92 cm
Private Collection (CAT. 86)

170. Charles Angrand, *Dawn on the Seine*, 1889
Oil on canvas, 65 x 81 cm
Geneva, Musée du Petit Palais

The Continuity of the Classical

The *Bathers* was not Seurat's only exhibition painting with discernible links to the figurative tradition taught at the Ecole. While the *Grande Jatte* was its immediate successor, once again deploying figures in frieze-like profile and dignified poses in an (albeit somewhat ersatz and ironic) idyllic pastoral, Seurat perhaps approached the innate classicism of the *Bathers* most closely in the *Models* (Plate 171). The *Models* was

Seurat's third major canvas, slightly shorter than its predecessors at two by two-and-a-half metres. He seems to have begun the project in 1886, perhaps in reaction to criticism of the *Grande Jatte*, but it was not ready for the Salon des Indépendants in the spring of 1887, at which he exhibited a small but refined panel of the central figure. Perhaps to resolve difficulties, he produced a complete study for the

171. *The Models*, 1886–8. Oil on canvas, 200 x 250 cm. Merion, Barnes Foundation

composition, significantly more detailed although smaller than the canvas he had painted for the ensemble of the *Grande Jatte* (Plates 172 and 159). The *Models* was finally exhibited with the Indépendants in 1888, alongside the smaller and more pictorially radical *Parade du Cirque* (Circus Sideshow; 1887–8, New York, Metropolitan Museum).[13] As a project, the *Models* can be seen at one level as another large-scale meditation on the classicising figurative tradition, at the time when Seurat's other work, for instance the *Bridge at Courbevoie* (Plate 161), was pulling in another direction, that of Symbolism. As such, the *Models* seems to a certain extent to be at odds with Seurat's main momentum as an artist; for all its satisfying pictorial qualities, it gives something of a retrospective identity to this stage of his career.

172. *The Models: Small Version, c.*1887–8. Oil on canvas, 39.5 x 49.0 cm. Berggruen Collection (CAT. 60)

Seurat's contemporaries found that the *Models* called the classical and academic to mind, Christophe's 1890 profile comparing Seurat's central figure to Ingres's celebrated *La Source* (The Spring; 1820s/1855–6, Paris, Musée d'Orsay).[14] In his composition Seurat set three models in various stages of undress against a corner of his studio. The two seated figures flanking the standing woman create an informal but harmonious pyramidal symmetry, like relief sculptures on a classical pediment. The left-hand model, seen from behind, has been compared to the back of a pose that Ingres reused in several compositions (Plate 173). The posture of the right-hand woman, casually pulling on a stocking, seems to be an approximate but artful quotation of the Antique, the *Spinario*, casually extracting a thorn (Plate 174). Praised by Sutter for its 'perfect harmony' and laid down by the sculptor Eugène Guillaume, director of the Ecole in Seurat's last year there, as a

paradigm to which modern artists should aspire, it was a commonplace pose for Seurat to cite.[15] The suggestion that the central figure quotes another Antique sculpture, the *Venus Pudica*, is less easy to sustain. This statue covers her groin with only one hand, as do other Antique Venus types who raise the other to shield their breasts. A closer parallel to Seurat's central model might be the figure of Hope in Hippolyte Flandrin's murals for Saint-Germain-des-Prés, who is posed with similar frontality and both of whose hands are clasped before her, a posture commonly used by nineteenth-century artists to convey graceful modesty (Plate 175). With his Parisian models, Seurat contrived a modern variant of the classical Three Graces.

Imaginatively eliding the observed and the contemporary into the classical was a game nineteenth-century artists liked to play. Ingres's late *Venus of Paphos* (c.1858; Paris, Musée

173. Jean-August-Dominique Ingres, *The Small Bather*, 1826,
Oil on canvas, 32.7 x 25.0 cm
Washington, DC, Phillips Collection (CAT. 61)

174. Anonymous Italian, *The Spinario*,
First quarter of the sixteenth century. Bronze, 14.7 cm high
Washington, DC, National Gallery of Art

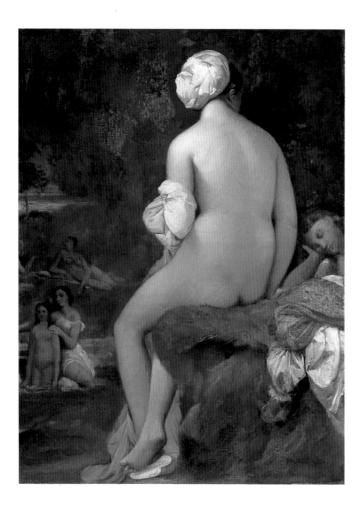

d'Orsay), for instance, was the transformation of a clothed portrait drawing by Paul Flandrin into a painted fantasy of a nude Venus.[16] It was conventional too in its return to the nude, on which Seurat's Ecole training had been founded, both in copies after Antique sculptures such as the Borghese *Ares* (Plate 2) and drawings from the life (Plate 3).[17] Seurat remained proud of his student work from the life model, and Gustave Kahn remembered that he kept one of his life studies made in Lehmann's atelier on his studio wall.[18] A powerfully realised life drawing such as the *Standing Man, Hands Outstretched* (Plate 3) fuses naturalistic observation with the balance of its symmetrical pose, a combination repeated in the central figure of the *Models.*

In painting the *Models* Seurat seems to have been rising to a challenge laid down by critics in 1886, to apply his new technique of division of tone and *pointillé* touch to the painting of flesh.[19] This was the kind of work done so well by the seductively emollient brush of the nineteenth-century academics – Ingres, Flandrin or Lehmann himself (Plate 176) – and it could be that Seurat might have reckoned the case for his innovations unproven until his new methods had matched their old. While the figures themselves embody the tension between the conventional and the contemporary, in its background the *Grande Jatte* manifests the latter, tipping the balance towards the modern. Thus, the nude of classical art translates into the naked of the everyday studio; the ideal figure of mythology becomes the primped and bustled ideal of contemporary fashion, as represented in Seurat's image of the island, or, in his representation of the studio, the bony figure of the impoverished model.[20] Like the male cast of the *Bathers* Seurat's models are silent and isolated each from the other, despite their shared space and activity. This has led some to the rather robotic interpretation that Seurat schematically represented the same model three times. It may be better to see the painting as a representation of three models – undressing, decorously posing and dressing again – in the hope of being hired to pose.[21] In his 1890 *Hommes d'aujourd'hui* essay Christophe had no trouble seeing the figures anecdotally, referring to them putting their clothes back on.[22] In that case, it is the closest to a genre scene, with a narrative being played out, that Seurat ever came, and again shows how the *Models* is almost at odds with other currents in Seurat's work, notably the stark, sinister evocation of the city in the *Parade du Cirque.* A subtle and contradictory work, the *Models* shows how, almost a decade after leaving the Ecole and four years after completing the *Bathers*, the lure of classicism and tradition still had a significant presence in the complex creative temperament of the innovative Seurat.

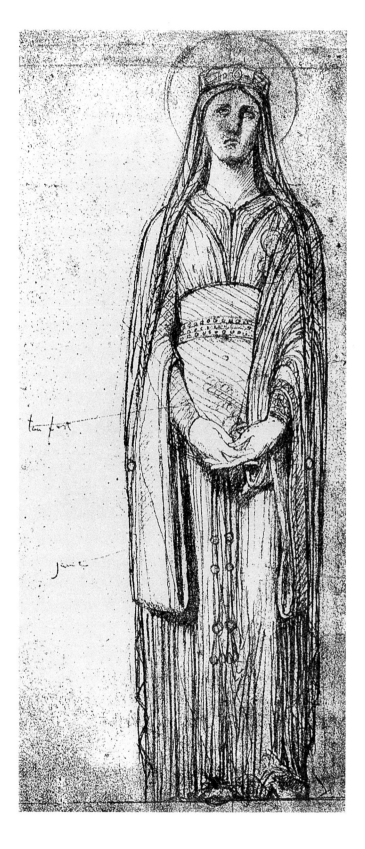

175. Hippolyte Flandrin, *Hope: Study for the mural decorations for the church of Saint-German-des-Près*, c.1840–6
Pencil, dimensions and location unknown

Looking at a reproduction of the *Bathers* during his last interview before he died in 1947, Pierre Bonnard remarked, 'It's magnificent, like the *Models*'.[23] A photograph of his studio at Le Cannet, taken by Brassaï the year before, shows a postcard of the *Bathers*, then in the Tate Gallery, juxtaposed with another of a classical sculpture (Plate 177). This modest record gives us, literally, a snapshot of how the *Bathers* might count for a painter in the twentieth century. Pinned on the wall alongside an oil sketch of a seated nude by Renoir, displayed above the practical paraphernalia of daily studio activity, the image of the *Bathers* acted as one of the touchstones of Bonnard's creative life. It took its place in Bonnard's *musée imaginaire* with Vermeer's *Little Street* (Amsterdam, Rijksmuseum), works by Seurat's great contemporaries Monet, Cézanne and Gauguin, and by another restless transformer of styles, Picasso. For Bonnard, as for so many other artists and admirers among us who have stood before the big canvas, so commanding and light-filled, or admired its poise, calm and wit in reproduction, the *Bathers* has a secure place in the western pictorial pantheon, an unforgettable icon of the modern and monumental, the experimental and the eternal.

176. Henri Lehmann, *Nude: Study for 'The Bathers'*, c.1840
Oil on canvas, 35.0 x 22.3 cm
Private Collection (CAT. 64)

1. Dorra and Rewald 1959, p. xxvii, n. 34; Thomson 1985, p. 97.
2. Thomson 1985, pp. 114-16; Ward 1986, pp. 434-9.
3. Coquiot 1924, p. 38.
4. Medlyn 1975, pp. 54-8; House 1980, pp. 346-7.
5. H. 131.
6. Thomson 1985, pp. 97-114; Zimmermann 1991, pp. 171-95, 213-22; Paris, Grand Palais, 1991, pp. 172-4, 210-11.
7. Clark 1985, pp. 261-7; Thomson 1985, pp. 115-25; House 1989; Nochlin, 1989; Clayson 1989; Zimmermann 1991, pp. 135-48; Paris, Grand Palais, 1991, pp. 174-8.
8. Hemel 1886.
9. Christophe 1890; Antoine 1891, p. 93.
10. Thomson 1987; Welsh-Ovcharov 1988, p. 122-33.
11. Charles Angrand in a letter to Charles Frechon, early April 1889 (Angrand 1988, p. 32).
12. Thomson 1994, pp. 27-37.
13. Zimmermann 1991, pp. 332-44; Françoise Cachin, in Paris, Grand Palais, 1991, pp. 273-94.
14. Christophe 1890.
15. Sutter 1865, p. 84; Guillaume 1879, p. 211.
16. Toussaint 1985, pp. 129-37.
17. Holloway 1963, p. 284.
18. Kahn 1891, p. 107.
19. Fénéon, 'Les Impressionnistes en 1886', Paris 1886 (Fénéon, i, 1970, p. 37).
20. Geffroy 1888; House 1980, p. 350; Smith 1991, p. 23.
21. Dorra and Rewald 1959, p. xci; Prak 1971, p. 377; Richardson 1978, p. 67; Thomson 1985, pp. 145-7; Françoise Cachin, in Paris, Grand Palais, 1991, pp. 273-80.
22. Christophe 1890.
23. Joëts 1953, p. 9.

177. Brassaï, *Bonnard's studio at Le Cannet*, 1946. Photograph

Chronology

Compiled by Sarah Herring

1859

Georges-Pierre Seurat born 2 December, 60 rue de Bondy (now rue René Boulanger), Paris.

1870

Lives at Fontainebleau with his family during the Franco-Prussian War and the Commune.

1876

Follows drawing lessons at the Ecole Municipale de Sculpture et de Dessin of the 10th arrondissement, Paris, of which the head is the sculptor Justin Lequien *fils* (1826–82).

Draws from antique casts and makes copies after Ingres, Raphael, Poussin and Holbein.

Makes friends with fellow student, Amand-Edmond Jean, later known as Aman-Jean.

1878

2 February: submits works for admission to the Ecole des Beaux-Arts.

19 March: enters the atelier of Henri Lehmann, a former student of Ingres. Aman-Jean enters on 13 August 1878, and Ernest Laurent on 12 August 1879.

19 March: placed 67 out of 80 in the competition for places.

13 August: placed 77 out of 80 in the competition.

Reads Charles Blanc's *Grammaire des arts du dessin*, published in 1867.

Draws in the Louvre.

1879

18 March: placed 47 out of 70 in the competition for places.

April–May: with Aman-Jean and Ernest Laurent probably visits the 4th Impressionist Exhibition, which includes works by Caillebotte, Cassatt, Degas, Lebourg, Monet and Pissarro.

8 November: begins his military service in Brest, Brittany.

1880

Finishes military service, and returns to Paris.

1881

24 February: attends a sale of paintings at the Hôtel Drouot and makes notes on three paintings by Delacroix.

May–June: Puvis de Chavannes exhibits at the Salon *The Poor Fisherman*, of which Seurat makes a free copy.

Reads Ogden Rood's *Modern Chromatics*, published in French in 1881.

1882

Rents a studio at 16 rue de Chabrol in the 10th arrondissement.

1883

May–June: exhibits for the first time at the Salon. In the catalogue the drawing is called *Broderie*, but according to Roger Marx it was the portrait of Aman-Jean (Plate 20).

Spring: starts work on *Bathers at Asnières* (Plate 178).

1884

Bathers at Asnières is rejected from the Salon.

May–June exhibits *Bathers at Asnières* with the Groupe des Artistes Indépendants, a group of artists, many of whom had been refused by the Salon jury of that year. The exhibition takes place in a temporary building in the place du Carrousel, near the site whether the Tuileries had stood.

June: the Société des Artistes Indépendants is set up.

Meets Paul Signac.

Starts work on *A Sunday on the Grande Jatte (1884)* (Plate 153).

December: exhibits a group of pictures, including studies for *A Sunday on the Grande Jatte* and the portrait of Aman-Jean, with the Société des Artistes Indépendants.

1885

A Sunday on the Grande Jatte is ready to be exhibited at the second exhibition of the Sociéte des Artistes Indépendants, but the show is cancelled.

Spends the summer at Grandcamp on the Normandy coast.

Meets Camille Pissarro.

August: Charles Henry's *Introduction à une ésthétique scientifique* published in the *Revue contemporaine*, then in a brochure. Seurat annotates his copy.

October: reworks *A Sunday on the Grande Jatte*.

1886

April–May: his works are included in the exhibition, *Works in Oil and Pastel by the Impressionists of Paris*, New York. *Bathers at Asnières* and a study for *A Sunday on the Grande Jatte* are among the works shown.

May–June: exhibits works at the 8th and last Impressionist exhibition at 11 rue Lafitte, including *A Sunday on the Grande Jatte*, *Le Bec du Hoc*, *Grandcamp* and other Grandcamp views.

By this date has a studio at 128bis boulevard de Clichy, Montmartre.

June–August: stays at Honfleur, Normandy, and paints seven canvases.

August–September: exhibits works at the 2nd exhibition of the Société des Artistes Indépendants, including *A Sunday on the Grande Jatte*, *Le Bec du Hoc*, *Grandcamp* and *Corner of a Dock (Honfleur)*.

September: Félix Fénéon employs for the first time the term 'méthode néo-impressionniste', in an article published in *L'Art Moderne*.

Autumn: begins work on the *Models* (Plate 171).

23 October: the Belgian poet Emile Verhaeren visits Seurat and buys *Corner of a Dock (Honfleur)*. Seurat invited to exhibit with Les Vingt, Brussels.

1887

January sends seven paintings to Les Vingt for their 4th annual exhibition in February, including *A Sunday on the Grande Jatte*, *Le Bec du Hoc, Grandcamp* and views painted at Honfleur.

March–May: exhibits paintings at the 3rd exhibition of the Société des Artistes Indépendants, including views painted at Honfleur, and a study for the *Models*.

Autumn: begins work on *Parade du Cirque*.

November: meets Vincent van Gogh.

December–January: exhibits with Signac and Van Gogh at Antoine's Théâtre Libre, 96 rue Blanche.

Begins work on the small version of the *Models* (Plate 172).

1888

Publication of Charles Henry's *Cercle Chromatique*.

January–February: exhibits in rooms at *La Revue Indépendante*.

March–May: exhibits works at the 4th exhibition of the Société des Artistes Indépendants, including the large version of the *Models* and *Parade du Cirque*.

Spring: works at La Grande Jatte with Charles Angrand, producing *Landscape, Island of the Grande Jatte*.

July: works at Port-en-Bessin, north of Bayeux on the Normandy coast, producing six canvases.

1889

Paints the Eiffel Tower before construction is completed.

February: exhibits works with Les Vingt in Brussels, including *Landscape: Island of the Grande Jatte*, and the large version of the *Models*.

Summer: visits Le Crotoy on the Picardy coast, producing two canvases.

Begins work on *Chahut*.

September–October: exhibits at the 5th exhibition of the Société des Artistes Indépendants, including the two views of Le Crotoy and *Port-en-Bessin*.

Moves studio from the boulevard de Clichy to the passage de l'Elysée des Beaux-Arts, also in Montmartre.

1890

16 February: birth of Seurat and Madeleine Knoblock's son, Pierre-Georges.

March–April: exhibits paintings at the 6th exhibition of the Société des Artistes Indépendants, including five Port-en-Bessin marines, *Chahut* and *Young Woman powdering herself*, which is a portrait of Madeleine Knoblock.

April: Jules Christophe publishes article on Seurat in *Les Hommes d'aujourd'hui*.

June: works at Gravelines, near Calais, producing four canvases.

Autumn: begins work on his last painting, *Circus*.

1891

February: exhibits paintings with Les Vingt in Brussels, including *Chahut*, the two views of Le Crotoy and the works painted at Gravelines.

March–April: exhibits works at the 7th exhibition of the Société des Artistes Indépendants, including *Circus* and the four Gravelines canvases.

26 March: falls ill.

29 March: dies.

31 March: buried at Père-Lachaise cemetery, Paris.

3 May: under the direction of Félix Fénéon the works from Seurat's studio are divided between Madeleine Knoblock and Seurat's brother, Emile.

1892

February: Les Vingt organise a homage to Seurat.

March–April: the Société des Artistes Indépendants organise a homage.

December: the first Neo-Impressionist exhibition is organised, and includes works by Seurat.

1899

Publication of Signac's *De Delacroix au néo-impressionisme* by *La Revue Blanche*.

1900

Seurat retrospective at *La Revue Blanche*. Fénéon buys *Bathers at Asnières*, Signac buys *Circus*, and M. Brû buys *A Sunday on the Grande Jatte*.

1905

Bathers at Asnières exhibited at Seurat retrospective, Salon des Artistes Indépendants.

1924

Bathers at Asnières purchased for the Tate Gallery by the Trustees of the Courtauld Fund through the Independent Gallery; Lucien Pissarro acts as the intermediary with Fénéon.

1961

Bathers at Asnières transferred from Tate Gallery to National Gallery.

Lenders to the Exhibition

The Visitors of the Ashmolean Museum: CAT. 35

Baltimore Museum of Art: CAT. 30

Berggruen Collection: CATS. 20, 27, 60

Fondation Beyeler, Riehen/Basel: CAT. 22

Bristol Museums and Art Gallery: CAT. 40

Trustees of the British Museum: CATS. 36, 81, 82

The Brooklyn Museum: CAT. 69

Foundation E.G. Bührle Collection, Zurich: CAT. 88

The Art Institute of Chicago: CATS. 9, 87

Sterling and Francine Clark Art Institute,
   Williamstown, Mass.: CAT. 58

The Cleveland Museum of Art: CAT. 10

Collection EWK, Bern: CAT. 31

The Courtauld Institute Galleries, London
   (Samuel Courtauld Trust): CATS. 42, 78

Syndics of the Fitzwilliam Museum Cambridge: CAT. 34

Glasgow Museums: Art Gallery and Museum, Kelvingrove:
   CATS. 2, 47, 49, 76

Glasgow Museums: The Burrell Collection: CAT. 51

Hamburger Kunsthalle: CAT. 55

Harvard University Art Museums,
   Fogg Art Museum: CAT. 15

Provost and Fellows of King's College,
   Cambridge: CAT. 83

The Metropolitan Museum of Art, New York: CATS. 33, 84

Musée d'Art Moderne de Saint-Etienne: CAT. 57

Musée des Beaux-Arts de Nantes: CAT. 65

Musée des Beaux-Arts, Nice: CAT. 67

Musée Carnavalet, Paris: CAT. 68

Musée de L'Ile de France, Château de Sceaux: CAT. 52

Musée du Louvre, Paris: CATS. 21, 38, 56

Musée Marmottan, Paris: CAT. 54

Musée d'Orsay, Paris: CATS. 8, 71

Museum of Fine Arts, Boston: CATS. 39, 66

The Museum of Modern Art, New York: CAT. 89

Nasjonalgalleriet Oslo: CAT. 72

National Gallery of Art, Washington, DC: CAT. 53

The National Gallery of Scotland: CATS. 7, 17

Trustees of the National Museums and Galleries of
   Merseyside: CAT. 48

The Nelson-Atkins Museum of Art, Kansas City,
   Missouri: CAT. 12

Ordrupgaard, Copenhagen: CAT. 75

The Phillips Collection, Washington, DC: CATS. 46, 61

Private Collection: CATS. 3, 4, 5, 14, 16, 18, 26, 28, 29, 37, 41, 43,
   44, 59, 63, 64, 70, 74, 85, 86, 90, 91

Robert and Lisa Sainsbury Collection,
   University of East Anglia: CAT. 24

Tate Gallery, London: CAT. 13

University of Manchester, Whitworth Art Gallery: CATS. 25, 50

Collection of Margo and Irwin Winkler: CAT. 62

The Woodner Collections, New York: CAT. 32

Yale University Art Gallery: CATS. 19, 23

Works in the Exhibition

1 PLATE 178
Bathers at Asnières, 1884
Oil on canvas, 201 x 300 cm
London, National Gallery

2 PLATE 48
*The Riverbanks: Study for
'Bathers at Asnières'*, 1882–3
Oil on wood, 15.9 x 25.1 cm
Glasgow Museums: Art Gallery and
Museum, Kelvingrove

3 PLATE 52
*Horses in the Water: Study for
'Bathers at Asnières'*, 1883–4
Oil on wood, 15.2 x 24.8 cm
Private Collection on extended loan to
the Courtauld Institute Galleries,
London

4 PLATE 50
*Bathers: Study for
'Bathers at Asnières'*, 1883–4
Oil on wood, 15.5 x 25.0 cm
Private Collection

5 PLATE 51
*Horse and Boats:
Study for 'Bathers at Asnières'*, 1883–4
Oil on wood, 15.2 x 24.5 cm
Private Collection

6 PLATE 53
*The Rainbow:
Study for 'Bathers at Asnières'*, 1883–4
Oil on wood, 15.5 x 24.5 cm
London, National Gallery

7 PLATE 54
*The Black Horse:
Study for 'Bathers at Asnières'*, 1883–4
Oil on wood, 15.9 x 25.0 cm
Edinburgh, National Gallery of Scotland

8 PLATE 55
*Bathers in the Water:
Study for 'Bathers at Asnières'*, 1883–4
Oil on wood, 15.5 x 25.0 cm
Paris, Musée d'Orsay. Donation de la
Baronne Eva Gebhard-Gourgaud, 1963

9 PLATE 60
Final Study for 'Bathers at Asnières',
1883–4
Oil on wood, 15.8 x 25.1 cm
The Art Institute of Chicago,
Gift of the Adele R. Levy Fund

10 PLATE 57
Study for 'Bathers at Asnières', 1883–4
Oil on wood, 15.7 x 25.0 cm
The Cleveland Museum of Art, Bequest
of Leonard C. Hanna, Jr, 1958.51

11 PLATE 56
Study for 'Bathers at Asnières', 1883–4
Oil on wood, 16 x 25 cm
London, National Gallery

12 PLATE 59
*Two Seated Figures:
Study for 'Bathers at Asnières'*, 1883–4
Oil on wood, 17.5 x 26.3 cm
Kansas City, Missouri, The Nelson-Atkins
Museum of Art (Purchase: Nelson Trust)
33-15/3

13 PLATE 58
*Clothes on the Grass:
Study for 'Bathers at Asnières'*, 1883–4
Oil on wood, 16.2 x 24.8 cm
London, Tate Gallery, on loan to the
National Gallery. Presented by Alex Reid
and Lefevre 1926

14 PLATE 61
*The Seine with Clothing on the Bank:
Study for 'Bathers at Asnières'*, 1883–4
Oil on wood, 17.1 x 26.4 cm
Private Collection

15 PLATE 62
*Hat, Shoes and Undergarments:
Study for 'Bathers at Asnières'*, 1883–4
Conté crayon on paper, 23.6 x 30.9 cm
Fogg Art Museum, Harvard University
Art Museums, Gift of Lois Orswell

16 PLATE 63
*Boy viewed from behind:
Study for 'Bathers at Asnières'*, 1883–4
Conté crayon on paper, 32.0 x 24.5 cm
Private Collection

17 PLATE 64
*Seated Nude Boy:
Study for 'Bathers at Asnières'*, 1883–4
Conté crayon on paper, 31.7 x 24.7 cm
Edinburgh, National Gallery of Scotland

18 PLATE 66
Study for 'Bathers at Asnières', 1883–4
Conté crayon on paper, 32.4 x 24.1 cm
Private Collection

19 PLATE 67
The Echo: Study for 'Bathers at Asnières',
1883–4
Conté crayon on paper, 31.2 x 24.0 cm
Yale University Art Gallery, Bequest of
Edith Malvina K. Wetmore

20 PLATE 73
*Man in a Bowler Hat: Study for 'Bathers
at Asnières'*, 1883–4
Conté crayon on paper, 24 x 30 cm
Berggruen Collection

21 PLATE 74
*Reclining Man: Study for 'Bathers at
Asnières'*, 1883–4
Conté crayon on paper, 24 x 31 cm
Paris, Musée du Louvre, Département
des Arts Graphiques

22 PLATE 75
*Reclining Man: Study for 'Bathers at
Asnières'*, 1883–4
Conté crayon on paper, 24.5 x 31.5 cm
Riehen/Basel, Fondation Beyeler

23 PLATE 82
*Seated Boy with Straw Hat: Study for
'Bathers at Asnières'*, 1883–4
Conté crayon on paper, 24.1 x 31.2 cm
Yale University Art Gallery, Everett V.
Meeks, BA 1901, Fund

24 PLATE 6
Woman seated on a Bench, c.1880–1
Pencil on paper, 16.0 x 10.5 cm
Robert and Lisa Sainsbury Collection,
University of East Anglia

25 PLATE 7
The Seamstress: A Painting on the Wall,
c.1881–2
Charcoal on paper, 23.1 x 18.1 cm
University of Manchester,
The Whitworth Art Gallery

26 PLATE 12
Crouching Boy, c.1882
Conté crayon on paper, 32 x 25 cm
Private Collection

27 PLATE 9
Sleeping Man, c.1881–2
Conté crayon on paper, 24.0 x 31.5 cm
Berggruen Collection

28 PLATE 1
Woman reading, c.1883
Conté crayon on paper, 30.7 x 23.3 cm
Private Collection, California

29 PLATE 8
The Nanny, c.1882
Conté crayon on paper, 32 x 25 cm
Private Collection

30 PLATE 5
Two Men walking in a Field, c.1882–4
Conté crayon on paper, 31.8 x 24.3 cm
The Baltimore Museum of Art:
The Cone Collection, formed by
Dr Claribel Cone and Miss Etta Cone of
Baltimore, Maryland (BMA 1950.12.664)

31 PLATE 13
Locomotive, c.1882–4
Conté crayon on paper, 24.5 x 31.8 cm
Bern, Collection EWK

32 PLATE 14
The Drawbridge, c.1882–4
Conté crayon on paper, 24.3 x 30.5 cm
New York, The Woodner Collections

33 PLATE 20
Portrait of Aman-Jean, 1883
Conté crayon on paper, 62.2 x 47.5 cm
Lent by The Metropolitan Museum of Art.
Bequest of Stephen C. Clark, 1960

34 PLATE 15
Jean-François Millet, *The Tired
Haymaker*, c.1850
Black chalk on paper, 27.0 x 20.6 cm
Lent by the Syndics of the Fitzwilliam
Museum, Cambridge

35 PLATE 17
Henri Fantin-Latour, *A Woman sewing
(Mademoiselle Nathalie Fantin-Latour)*,
1857
Charcoal touched with white chalk on
paper, 30.0 x 29.6 cm
The Visitors of the Ashmolean Museum

36 PLATE 18
Albert Lebourg, *Reading (Evening)*,
c.1879
Black chalk heightened with white on
paper, 43.2 x 28.1 cm
London, Trustees of the British Museum

37 PLATE 19
Léon-Augustin Lhermitte, *Bathers at
Mont-Saint-Père*, 1884
Charcoal on paper, 30.7 x 47.5 cm
New York, Private Collection

38 PLATE 4
Ernest-Joseph Laurent, *Georges Seurat:
Study for 'Scene at the Brook'*, 1883
Black chalk on paper, 39 x 29 cm
Paris, Musée du Louvre, Département
des Arts Graphiques

39 PLATE 16
Jean-François Millet, *Watering Horses,
Sunset*, 1866
Pastel and conté crayon on paper,
38.1 x 48.3 cm
Boston, Museum of Fine Arts.
Gift of Quincy Adams Shaw through
Quincy A. Shaw, Jr, and Mrs Marian
Shaw Haughton

40 PLATE 30
Sunset, c.1881
Oil on wood, 15.2 x 24.8 cm
Bristol Museums and Art Gallery

41 PLATE 22
Fisherman in a Moored Boat, c.1882
Oil on wood, 16.5 x 24.8 cm
Private Collection on extended loan to
the Courtauld Institute Galleries,
London

42 PLATE 33
Man painting a Boat, c.1883
Oil on wood, 15.9 x 25.0 cm
London, Courtauld Institute Galleries
(The Samuel Courtauld Trust)

43 PLATE 31
Man in a Boat, c.1884
Oil on wood, 17.6 x 26.8 cm
Private Collection on extended loan to
the Courtauld Institute Galleries,
London

44 PLATE 32
A Boat near the Riverbank, Asnières,
c.1883
Oil on wood, 15 x 24 cm
Private Collection

45 PLATE 23
The Seine at Asnières, c.1883
Oil on wood, 15.8 x 24.7 cm
London, National Gallery

46 PLATE 21
The Stone Breaker, c.1882–3
Oil on wood, 15.4 x 24.9 cm
Washington, DC, The Phillips Collection

47 PLATE 24
Houses among Trees, c.1883
Oil on wood, 16 x 25 cm
Glasgow Museums: Art Gallery and
Museum, Kelvingrove

48 PLATE 35
Ville-d'Avray, White Houses, c.1883
Oil on canvas, 33.5 x 46.0 cm
Board of Trustees of the National
Museums and Galleries on Merseyside
(Walker Art Gallery, Liverpool)

49 PLATE 41
Seated Boy in a Meadow, c.1882–3
Oil on canvas, 63.5 x 79.6 cm
Glasgow Museums: Art Gallery and
Museum, Kelvingrove

50 PLATE 109
Pierre-Cécile Puvis de Chavannes,
Solitude, c.1879–82
Pastel on paper mounted on canvas,
32.0 x 41.3 cm
University of Manchester,
The Whitworth Art Gallery

51 PLATE 27
Honoré-Victorin Daumier, *The Bathers*,
c.1846–8
Oil on wood, 25.4 x 32.1 cm
Glasgow Museums: The Burrell
Collection

52 PLATE 26
Paul Huet, *L'Ile Séguin, Watering Place*,
1820
Oil on canvas, 12.5 x 34.5 cm
Sceaux, Musée de L'Ile de France

53 PLATE 28
Jean-Baptiste-Camille Corot,
River Scene with a Bridge, 1834
Oil on paper mounted on canvas,
25 x 33 cm
Washington, DC, National Gallery of Art,
Ailsa Mellon Bruce Collection 1970.17.22

54 PLATE 29
Oscar-Claude Monet, *The Railway
Bridge, Argenteuil*, 1874
Oil on canvas, 14 x 23 cm
Paris, Musée Marmottan

55 PLATE 34
Stanislas-Victor-Edmond Lépine, *The
Seine at La Garenne Saint-Denis*, 1874–8
Oil on canvas, 34.5 x 54.5 cm
Hamburger Kunsthalle

56 PLATE 103
Nicolas Poussin, *The Finding of Moses*,
1638
Oil on canvas, 93.5 x 121.0 cm
Paris, Musée du Louvre, Département
des Peintures

57 PLATE 108
Hippolyte Flandrin, *Priam's Son, Polytes,
observing the Greeks approaching Troy*,
1834
Oil on canvas, 205 x 148 cm
Musée d'Art Moderne de Saint-Etienne

58 PLATE 107
Adolphe-William Bouguereau, *Seated
Nude*, 1884
Oil on canvas, 116.5 x 89.8 cm
Williamstown, Mass., Sterling and
Francine Clark Art Institute

59 PLATE 111
Jean-Francis Auburtin after Puvis de
Chavannes, *Doux Pays*, c.1885–90
Oil on paper pasted on canvas,
50.5 x 99.0 cm
Private Collection. The Artist's Family.
Exhibited in 1990, *Auburtin le
Symboliste de la mer*, Paris

60 PLATE 172
The Models: Small Version, c.1887–8
Oil on canvas, 39.5 x 49.0 cm
Berggruen Collection

61 PLATE 173
Jean-August-Dominique Ingres,
The Small Bather, 1826
Oil on canvas, 32.7 x 25.0 cm
Washington, DC, The Phillips Collection

62 PLATE 2
*Warrior with a Helmet: Copy after the
Borghese 'Ares'*, c.1877–8
Conté crayon on paper, 64.5 x 49.0 cm
Collection of Margo and Irwin Winkler

63 PLATE 3
Standing Man, Hands Outstretched,
c.1877–8
Charcoal on paper, 73.7 x 48.3 cm
New York, Private Collection

64 PLATE 176
Henri Lehmann, *Nude: Study for
'The Bathers'*, c.1840
Oil on canvas, 35.0 x 22.3 cm
New York, Private Collection

65 PLATE 105
Luc-Olivier Merson, *Saint Antony of
Padua preaching to the Fishes*, 1880
Oil on canvas, 88.5 x 152.0 cm
Musée des Beaux-Arts de Nantes

66 PLATE 124
Jean-Charles Cazin, *Riverbank with
Bathers*, 1881
Oil on canvas, 131.2 x 147.0 cm
Boston, Museum of Fine Arts. Peter
Chardon Brooks Memorial Collection,
Gift of Mrs Richard M. Saltonstall
20.593

67 PLATE 133
Luigi Loir, *Quai national at Puteaux*,
1878
Oil on canvas, 85 x 164 cm
Nice, Musée des Beaux-Arts

68 PLATE 134
Jean Béraud, *The Banks of the Seine*,
c.1880
Oil on canvas, 46 x 56 cm
Paris, Musée Carnavalet

69 PLATE 127
Charles-François Daubigny, *The Seine at Mantes*, 1856
Oil on canvas, 48.8 x 75.6 cm
The Brooklyn Museum, Gift of Cornelia E. and Jennie A. Donnellon (33.271)

70 PLATE 128
Edouard Manet, *The Seine at Argenteuil*, 1874
Oil on canvas, 62.3 x 103.0 cm
Private Collection on extended loan to the Courtauld Institute Galleries, London

71 PLATE 132
Oscar-Claude Monet, *Men unloading Coal*, 1875
Oil on canvas, 54 x 66 cm
Paris, Musée d'Orsay

72 PLATE 130
Oscar-Claude Monet, *Ile de la Grande Jatte*, 1878
Oil on canvas, 50 x 61 cm
Oslo, Nasjonalgalleriet

73 PLATE 129
Pierre-Auguste Renoir, *Boating on the Seine*, c.1876
Oil on canvas, 71 x 92 cm
London, National Gallery

74 PLATE 137
Gustave Caillebotte, *Bridge at Argenteuil and the Seine*, c.1880–5
Oil on canvas, 65 x 82 cm
Private Collection

75 PLATE 135
Jean-Baptiste-Armand Guillaumin, *Quai de Bercy, Paris*, c.1885
Oil on canvas, 60 x 92 cm
Copenhagen, Ordrupgaard

76 PLATE 136
Paul Signac, *Coal Crane, Clichy*, 1884
Oil on canvas, 59.0 x 91.4 cm
Glasgow Museums: Art Gallery and Museum, Kelvingrove

77 PLATE 160
Study for 'The Seine at Courbevoie', c.1885
Oil on wood, 24.9 x 15.7 cm
London, National Gallery

78 PLATE 161
The Bridge at Courbevoie, 1886–7
Oil on canvas, 46.4 x 55.3 cm
London, Courtauld Institute Galleries (The Samuel Courtauld Trust)

79 PLATE 155
Study for the 'Grande Jatte', c.1884–5
Oil on wood, 16 x 25 cm
London, National Gallery

80 PLATE 154
Study for the 'Grande Jatte', c.1884–5
Oil on wood, 15.2 x 24.8 cm
London, National Gallery

81 PLATE 158
Landscape with Dog: Study for the 'Grande Jatte', c.1884–5
Conté crayon on paper, 42.5 x 62.8 cm
London, Trustees of the British Museum

82 PLATE 156
The Couple: Study for the 'Grande Jatte', c.1884–5
Conté crayon on paper, 31.4 x 23.6 cm
London, Trustees of the British Museum

83 PLATE 157
Couple walking: Study for the 'Grande Jatte', c.1884–5
Oil on canvas, 81.3 x 61.5 cm
Lent by the Provost and Fellows of King's College, Cambridge (Keynes Collection), on loan to the Fitzwilliam Museum, Cambridge

84 PLATE 159
Study for the 'Grande Jatte', c.1884–5
Oil on canvas, 70.5 x 104.1 cm
Lent by the Metropolitan Museum of Art. Bequest of Sam A. Lewisohn, 1951

85 PLATE 163
Paul Signac, *The Seine at Asnières*, 1885
Oil on canvas, 60 x 89 cm
Private Collection

86 PLATE 169
Charles Angrand, *The Western Railway Line leaving Paris: View from the Fortifications*, 1886
Oil on canvas, 73 x 92 cm
Private Collection

87 PLATE 168
Vincent van Gogh, *Fishing in Spring*, 1887
Oil on canvas, 50.5 x 60.0 cm
The Art Institute of Chicago, gift of Messrs Charles Deering McCormick, Brooks McCormick and Roger McCormick

88 PLATE 166
Vincent van Gogh, *The Bridges, Asnières*, 1887
Oil on canvas, 52.5 x 65.0 cm
Zurich, Foundation E.G. Bührle Collection

89 PLATE 167
Emile Bernard, *Iron Bridges, Asnières*, 1887
Oil on canvas, 45.9 x 54.2 cm
New York, The Museum of Modern Art, Grace Rainey Rogers Fund, 1962

90 PLATE 164
Paul Signac, *The Clipper, Asnières*, 1887
Oil on canvas, 46 x 55 cm
Private Collection – Courtesy of Alex Reid & Lefevre Ltd

91 PLATE 165
Paul Signac, *Bridge at Asnières (The Stern of the Tub in the Sun)*, 1888
Oil on canvas, 46 x 65 cm
Private Collection – Courtesy of Alex Reid & Lefevre Ltd

Bibliography

Amsterdam, Van Gogh Museum, *Pierre Puvis de Chavannes*, 1994

Angoulême, Musée des Beaux-Arts, *Henry Daras (1850–1928)*, 1986–7

Charles Angrand, *Correspondances, 1883–1926*, ed. Françoise Lespinasse, Rouen, 1988

Pierre Angrand, *Naissance des Artistes Indépendants, 1884*, Paris, 1965

Jules Antoine, 'Georges Seurat', *Revue Indépendente*, XIX, April 1891, pp. 89–93

Marie Jeannine Aquilino, 'Painted Promises: The Politics of Public Art in Late Nineteenth-Century France', *Art Bulletin*, LXXV, no. 4, Dec. 1993, pp. 697–712

Art Institute of Chicago Museum Studies, XIV, no. 2, 1989 [Special Issue, 'The Grande Jatte at 100']

Atlanta, High Museum of Art; Norfolk, Chrysler Museum; Raleigh, North Carolina Museum of Art; Sarasota, Ringling Museum of Art: *French Paintings from Southern Collections*, 1983

Marie-Madeleine Aubrun, *Henri Lehmann, 1814–1882: catalogue raisonné de l'oeuvre*, 2 vols., Paris, 1984

Marie-Madeleine Aubrun, *Jules Bastien-Lepage, 1848–1884: catalogue raisonné de l'oeuvre*, Paris, 1985

Michael Ayrton, 'Seurat's *Une Baignade, Asnières*', *The Listener*, 14 April 1960, pp. 660–2

Karl Baedeker, *Paris and its Environs*, London, 1881

Janine Bailly-Herzberg (ed.), *Correspondance de Camille Pissarro, I: 1865–1885*, Paris, 1980; *II: 1886–1890*, Paris, 1986

Louis Barron, *Les Environs de Paris*, Paris, 1886

Paul Baudoüin, 'Mes Souvenirs', *Gazette des Beaux-Arts*, pér. 6, XIII, May 1935, pp. 295–314

'Beaux-Arts', *L'Intransigeant*, 7 April 1884

Edwin Becker, 'Felicien Freiherr von Myrbach: painter, illustrator, reformer', *The Van Gogh Museum Journal*, 1995, pp. 134–47

L. Bénédite, *Albert Lebourg*, Paris, 1923

G. Berger, 'Le Poussin: cours donné à l'Ecole nationale des beaux-arts', *L'Art*, XI, 1877, pp. 73–80

L. R. Berlanstein, *The Working People of Paris, 1871–1914*, Baltimore, 1984

Charles Bigot, 'L'Exposition des Intransigeants', *La Revue Politique et Littéraire*, 2me. sér., 28 April 1877, pp. 1045–8

Charles Bigot, 'Le Salon de 1883, I', *Gazette des Beaux-Arts*, pér. 2, XXVII, June 1883, pp. 457–76; 'Le Salon de 1883, II', XXVIII, July 1883, pp. 5–23

Charles Blanc, 'Eugène Delacroix', *Gazette des Beaux-Arts*, 16, 1864, pp. 5–27, 97–129

Charles Blanc, *Grammaire des arts du dessin*, Paris, 1867

Albert Boime, 'Seurat and Piero della Francesca', *Art Bulletin*, XLVIII, June 1965, pp. 265–71

Albert Boime, *The Academy and French Painting in the Nineteenth Century*, London, 1971

Albert Boime, 'The Teaching Reforms of 1863 and the Origins of Modernism', *Art Quarterly*, n.s.1, 1977, pp. 1–39

Albert Boime, 'The Teaching of Fine Arts and the Avant-Garde in France during the Second Half of the Nineteenth Century', *Magazine of Arts*, Dec. 1985

Albert Boime, *Art and the French Commune: Imagining Paris after War and Revolution*, Princeton, 1995

Marie-Christine Boucher, *Palais des Beaux-Arts de la Ville de Paris. Musée du Petit Palais: catalogue des dessins et peintures de Puvis de Chavannes*, Paris, 1979

Gustave Boulanger, *A nos Elèves*, Paris, 1885

Elaine Brody, *Paris: The Musical Kaleidoscope, 1870–1925*, New York, 1987

Jules Buisson, 'Le Salon de 1881, I', *Gazette des Beaux-Arts*, pér. 2, XXIII, June 1881, pp. 473–513

Chansons: les environs de Paris par des membres du Caveau, Paris, 1880

Julia M. Cartwright, *Jean-François Millet: His Life and Letters*, London, 1896

Blandine Chavanne and Bruno Gaudichon, *Catalogue raisonné des peintures des XIX et XX siècles … dans les collections du Musée de la Ville de Poitiers et de la Société des Antiquaires de l'Ouest*, Poitiers, 1988

Philippe de Chennevières, 'Le Salon de 1880, I', *Gazette des Beaux-Arts*, pér. 2, XXI, May 1880, pp. 393–407

Philippe de Chennevières, *Souvenirs d'un Directeur des Beaux-Arts*, Paris, 1979 (first ed. 1883–9)

Jules Christophe, 'Georges Seurat', *Les Hommes d'aujourd'hui*, no. 368, 1890, n.p.

Jules Claretie, *La Vie à Paris, 1883*, Paris, n.d. [1884]

Jules Claretie 'La Vie à Paris', *Le Temps*, 16 May 1884

Kenneth Clark, *Looking at Pictures*, London, 1960

T. J. Clark, *The Painting of Modern Life: Paris in the Art of Manet and his Followers*, London, 1985

Hollis Clayson, 'The Family and the Father: The *Grande-Jatte* and its Absences', *Art Institute of Chicago Museum Studies*, XIV, no. 2, 1989, pp. 155–64

Cleveland Museum of Art; Brooklyn Museum; St Louis Art Museum; Glasgow Art Gallery: *The Realist Tradition: French Painting and Drawing, 1830–1900*, 1980–2

'Concours et Expositions', *Chronique des Arts et de la Curiosité*, no. 7, 17 Feb. 1883, p. 49

'Concours et Expositions. Salon de 1884. Le Jury de Peinture', *Chronique des Arts et de la Curiosité*, no. 12, 22 March 1884, pp. 94–5

'Concours et Expositions', *Chronique des Arts et de la Curiosité*, no. 16, 21 April 1883

'Concours et Expositions', *Chronique des Arts et de la Curiosité*, no. 31, 4 Oct. 1884, p. 429

Douglas Cooper, *'Une Baignade, Asnières'*, London, n.d. [1946]

Gustave Coquiot, *Seurat*, Paris, 1924

Alain Corbin, *The Foul and the Fragrant: Odour and the French Social Imagination*, London, 1994

A. Dalligny, 'Le Salon de 1884: La Peinture', *Le Journal des Arts*, 6 and 13 May, 3 and 5 June 1884

Département de la Seine: état des communes à la fin du XIX siècle. Asnières: notice historique et renseignements administratifs, Montevrain, 1902

Lois Dinnerstein, 'Beyond Revisionism: Henry Lerolle's *The Organ*', *Arts Magazine*, LIV, no. 5, Jan. 1980, pp. 172–6

Henry Dorra and John Rewald, *Seurat: l'oeuvre peint. Biographie et catalogue critique*, Paris, 1959

N. Evenson, *Paris: A Century of Change, 1878–1978*, New Haven and London, 1979

A. Faure, 'A l'Aube des transports de masse: l'exemple des "trains ouvriers" de la banlieue de Paris (1883–1914)', *Revue d'histoire moderne et contemporaine*, 40–2, April–June 1993, pp. 228–55

Félix Fénéon, *Oeuvres plus que complètes*, ed. Joan U. Halperin, 2 vols., Geneva, 1970

I. Fiedler, 'A Technical Evaluation of the *Grande Jatte*', *Art Institute of Chicago Museum Studies*, XIV, no. 2, 1989, pp. 173–9

I. Fiedler, 'Materials used in Seurat's *La Grande* Jatte, including Colour Changes and Notes on the Evolution of the Artist's Palette', *Preprints of the Twelfth Annual Meeting of the American Institute for Conservation*, Los Angeles, 1984

Neil M. Flax, 'Charles Blanc: le modernité malgré lui', in *La Critique d'art en France, 1850–1900*, ed. Jean-Paul Bouillon, Saint-Etienne, 1989, pp. 95–104

Jean-Luc Flohic et al., *Le Patrimoine des communes des Hauts-de-Seine*, Charenton-le-Pont, 1994

Henri Fouquier, 'Le Salon de 1884', *Gil Blas*, 1 May 1884

Louis de Fourcaud, 'Le Salon de 1884, I', *Gazette des Beaux-Arts*, pér. 2, XXIX, May 1884, pp. 377–90; 'Le Salon de 1884, II', June 1884, pp. 465–92; 'Le Salon de 1884, III', XXX, July 1884, pp. 50–63

Erich Franz and Bernd Growe, *Seurat Drawings*, Boston, 1984

C. Frémine, 'Les Artistes indépendants au Pavillon de la Ville de Paris', *Le Rappel*, 11 Dec. 1884

Roger Fry, *Transformations*, London, 1926

John Gage, 'The Technique of Seurat: A Reappraisal', *Art Bulletin*, LXIX, Sept. 1987, pp. 448–54

John Gage, *Colour and Culture*, London 1993

J.-G. Gassies, *Le Vieux Barbizon: souvenirs de jeunesse d'un paysagiste*, Paris, 1907

Judith Gautier, 'Le Salon', *Le Rappel*, 10 May 1884

Judith Gautier, 'Exposition des artistes indépendants', *Le Rappel*, 16 May 1884

Gustave Geffroy, *La Vie artistique: histoire de l'impressionnisme*, Paris, 1894

Gustave Geffroy, 'Pointillé-Cloisonnisme', *La Justice*, 11 April 1888

Alphonse Germain, 'A travers les Jurys des Salons', *Entretiens politiques et littéraires*, no. 15, June 1891, pp. 206–9

Robert Goldwater, 'Puvis de Chavannes: Some Reasons for a Reputation', *Art Bulletin*, XXVIII, March 1946, pp. 33–43

Edmond de Goncourt, *Renée Mauperin*, Paris, 1864 (trans. J. Fitzmaurice-Kelly, London, 1902)

Granville, Hôtel des Ventes, *Atelier Ernest Laurent, 1859–1929*, 1993

Eugène Guillaume, 'Le Salon de 1879: la peinture, II', *Revue des Deux Mondes*, pér. 3, XLIX, 1 July 1879, pp. 185–211

Suzanne Gutwirth, 'Jean-Charles-Joseph Rémond (1795–1875): premier Grand Prix de Rome du paysage historique', *Bulletin de la Société de l'Histoire de l'Art Français*, année 1981, Paris, 1983, pp. 189–218

Joan U. Halperin, *Félix Fénéon: Aesthete and Anarchist in Fin-de-Siècle Paris*, New Haven and London, 1988

Francis Haskell and Nicolas Penny, *Taste and the Antique: The Lure of Classical Sculpture, 1500–1900*, New Haven and London, 1981

César Mange de Hauke, *Seurat et son Oeuvre*, 2 vols., New York, 1961

Otherin d'Haussonville, 'La Misère à Paris, I: la population indigente et les quartiers pauvres', *Revue des Deux Mondes*, pér. 3, XLV, 15 June 1881, pp. 812–49

H.-G. Haupt, 'The Petite Bourgeoisie in France, 1850–1914: In Search of the Juste Milieu?', in *Shopkeepers and Master Artisans in Nineteenth-Century Europe*, ed. G. Crossick and H.-G. Haupt, London, 1984, pp. 95–119

Mark Haworth-Booth, *Camille Silvy: 'River Scene, France'*, Malibu, 1992

Jean-Marie Hégo, 'Où situer exactement *Une Baignade, Asnières?*', unpublished typescript, Courbevoie, 1991

H. von Helmholtz, 'L'Optique et la peinture', in E. Brücke, *Principes scientifiques des beaux-arts*, Paris, 1878

H. von Helmholtz, *Physiological Optics*, English trans. of 3rd German edn. (Hamburg 1911), New York, 1924 (first pub. 1866)

C. Heintz, 'Huysmans et les dîners de banlieue', *Bulletin de la Société J.-K. Huysmans*, no. 43, 1962, pp. 361–4

Frédéric Henriet, *Le Paysagiste au champs*, 2nd enlarged edn., Paris, 1876

Maurice Hermel, 'L'Exposition de peinture de la rue Lafitte', *La France libre*, 27 May 1886

Robert L. Herbert, 'Seurat and Puvis de Chavannes', *Yale University Art Gallery Bulletin*, XXV, Oct. 1959, pp. 22–9

Robert L. Herbert, 'A Rediscovered Drawing for Seurat's Baignade', *Burlington Magazine*, CII, no. 689, August 1960, pp. 368, 370

Robert L. Herbert, *Seurat's Drawings*, New York, 1962

Robert L. Herbert, *Impressionism: Art, Leisure and Parisian Society*, New Haven and London, 1988

R. Herz-Fischler, 'An Examination of Claims concerning Seurat and the Golden Number', *Gazette des Beaux-Arts*, 101, March 1983, pp. 109–12

R. Ross Holloway, 'Seurat's Copies after Antique Sculpture', *Burlington Magazine*, CV, no. 723, June 1963, p. 284

W. I. Homer, *Seurat and the Science of Painting*, Cambridge, Mass., 1964

John House, 'Meaning in Seurat's Figure Paintings', *Art History*, III, no. 3, Sept. 1980, pp. 345–56

John House, 'Reading the *Grande-Jatte*', *Art Institute of Chicago Museum Studies*, XIV, no. 2, 1989, pp. 115–31

Henry Houssaye, 'Le Salon de 1882, I: la grande peinture et les grands tableaux', *Revue des Deux Mondes*, pér. 3, LI, 1 June 1882, pp. 561–86

Henry Houssaye, 'Le Salon de 1884', *Revue des Deux Mondes*, pér. 3, LXIII, 1 June 1884, pp. 560–95

Joris-Karl Huysmans, *Oeuvres complètes de J.-K. Huysmans, VI: l'art moderne*, Paris, 1929

Joris-Karl Huysmans, *Les Soeurs Vatard*, Paris, 1879 (1880 edn.)

E. Jacques, 'Beaux-Arts', *L'Intransigeant*, 16 April 1884

E. Jacques, 'Le Salon de 1884', *L'Intransigeant*, 1 May 1884

E. Jacques, 'Beaux-Arts: Salon des Indépendants', *L'Intransigeant*, 24 May 1884

Paul Jamot, 'Artistes Contemporains: Ernest Laurent', *Gazette des Beaux-Arts*, pér. 4, L, March 1911, pp. 173–203

Thea Jirat-Wasiutynski, 'Tonal Drawing and the Use of Charcoal in Nineteenth-Century France', *Drawing*, XI, no. 6, 1990 pp. 121–4

Vojtech and Thea Jirat-Wasiutynski, 'The Uses of Charcoal in Drawing', *Arts Magazine*, 1980, pp. 128–35

Jules Joëts, 'Deux Grands Peintres au Cannet: le dernier entretien de Pierre Bonnard', *Arts-Documents*, no. 29, Feb. 1953, pp. 8–9

L. Johnson, *The Paintings of Eugène Delacroix: A Critical Catalogue*, III, IV, 1832–63, Oxford, 1986; V, VI, Oxford, 1989

J.-S.-.E. Julia de Fontenelle and P. Poisson, *Manuel complet du marchand papetier et du régleur*, Paris, 1828

Gustave Kahn, 'Georges Seurat', *L'Art moderne*, no. 14, 5 April 1891, pp. 107–10

G. Kahn, *The Drawings of Georges Seurat*, New York, 1971

P. de Katow, 'Les Refusés', *Gil Blas*, 21 April 1884

P. de Katow, 'Le Salon des Artistes Indépendants', *Gil Blas*, 17 May 1884

M. Kemp, *The Science of Art: Optical Themes in Western Art from Brunelleschi to Seurat*, New Haven and London, 1990

H. Kühn and M. Curran, 'Chrome Yellow and other Chromate Pigments: B. Zinc Yellow', in R. Feller (ed.) *Artists' Pigments: A Handbook of their History and Characteristics*, I, Cambridge and Washington, 1986, pp. 187–204

Emile de Labédollière, *Histoire des environs du nouveau Paris*, Paris, 1861

Georges Lafenestre, 'Les Expositions d'Art: les Indépendants et les Aquarellistes', *Revue des Deux Mondes*, pér. 3, XX, 15 May 1879, pp. 478–85

Georges Lafenestre (ed.), *Exposition des Beaux-Arts: le Livre d'Or du Salon de Peinture et de Sculpture*, Paris, 1884

Georges Lafenestre, 'Le Salon de 1886, I: la peinture', *Revue des Deux Mondes*, pér. 3, LXXV, 1 June 1886, pp. 580–609

Georges Lafenestre, 'Le Salon de 1888, I: la peinture', *Revue des Deux Mondes*, pér. 3, no. LXXXVII, 1 June 1888, pp. 640–73

Juliette Laffon, *Palais des Beaux-Arts de la Ville de Paris: catalogue sommaire illustré des peintures*, 2 vols., Paris, 1981

Jules Laforgue, 'Peintures décoratives de M. Henry Daras à Saint-François de Sales', *Chronique des Arts et de la Curiosité*, 12 Nov. 1881, pp. 278–9

Maxime Lalanne, *Le Fusain*, Paris, 1869

André Lebon and Paul Pelet, *France as it is*, London, 1988

A. Lee, 'Seurat and Science', *Art History*, 10, 1987, pp. 203–26

Paul Lefort, 'Charles Blanc', *Gazette des Beaux-Arts*, pér. 2, XXV, Feb. 1882, pp. 121–4

Miriam Levin, *Republican Art and Ideology in Late Ninetenth Century France*, Ann Arbor, 1986

A. Lemaistre, *L'Ecole des Beaux-Arts dessinée et raconté par un élève*, Paris, 1889

London, Courtauld Institute Galleries, *Impressionism for England. Samuel Courtauld as Patron and Collector*, 1994

London, Hayward Gallery; Paris, Grand Palais: *Toulouse-Lautrec*, 1991–2

London, National Gallery, *Seurat's 'Bathers, Asnières' and the Crisis of Impressionism: Painting in Focus 6*, 1976

London, National Gallery, *Art in the Making: Impressionism*, 1990

London, South Bank Centre, *Landscapes of France: Impressionism and its Rivals*, 1995

Wiepke Loos, *The Fodor Collection: Nineteenth-Century French Drawings and Watercolours from Amsterdam's Historisch Museum*, Amsterdam, 1985

Elizabeth A. McCauley, *Industrial Madness: Commercial Photography in Paris, 1848–1871*, New Haven and London, 1994

K. McLaren, *The Colour Science of Dyes and Pigments*, Bristol, 1983

Patricia Mainardi, *The End of the Salon: Art and the State in the Early Third Republic*, Cambridge, 1993

K. E. Maison, *Honoré Daumier: Catalogue Raisonné, I (Paintings)*, London, 1968

Azar du Marest, *A Travers l'Idéal: fragments du journal d'un peintre*, Paris, 1901

Michael Marlais, 'Seurat et ses amis de l'Ecole des Beaux-Arts', *Gazette des Beaux-Arts*, pér. 6, Oct. 1989, pp. 153–68

Roger Marx, 'Le Salon, VI (fin)', *Le Progrès artistique*, 15 June 1883

Roger Marx, 'L'Exposition des Artistes Indépendants', *Le Voltaire*, 16 May 1884

Roger Marx, 'La Décoration de la Mairie de Courbevoie', *Le Voltaire*, 8 Dec. 1884

Roger Marx, 'Exposition des Indépandants', *Le Voltaire*, 10 Dec. 1884

Roger Marx, 'Albert Lebourt', *Gazette des Beaux-Arts*, II, 1903

Timothy Mathews, 'Sex and the Occult in Symbolist Art and Literature', in *Artistic Relations: Literature and the Visual Arts in Nineteenth-Century France*, ed. P. Collier and R. Lethbridge, New Haven and London, 1994, pp. 264–77

J. C. Maxwell, *The Scientific Papers of James Clerk Maxwell*, ed. W. D. Niven, 2 vols., Cambridge, 1890

J. Meder, *The Mastery of Drawing*, rev. ed., New York, 1978

Sally Medlyn, 'The Development of Georges Seurat's Art, with Special Reference to the Influence of Contemporary Anarchist Philosophy', MA thesis, University of Manchester, 1975

André Michel, 'Le Salon de 1885, I', *Gazette des Beaux-Arts*, pér. 2, XXXI, May 1885, pp. 395–403; 'Le Salon de 1885, II', June 1885, pp. 473–96

P. Michel (ed.), *Jean-François Raffaëlli, Octave Mirbeau: correspondance*, Tusson, 1993

Minneapolis Institute of Arts, *James Tissot: Catalogue Raisonné of the Prints*, 1978

Eugène Montrosier, *Peintres modernes: Ingres, H. Flandrin, Robert-Fleury*, Paris, 1882

Eugène Mouton, *La Physionomie comparée: traité de l'expression dans l'homme, dans la nature et dans l'art*, Paris, 1885

Jean-François Mozziconacci, *Collections du Musée des Beaux-Arts de Carcassonne, V: répertoire des peintures du XIXe siècle*, Carcassonne, 1990

Alexandra R. Murphy, *Jean-François Millet*, Boston, 1984

G. Neuville, *Des Eaux de Paris: essai d'analyse micrographique comparée. Ses Rapports avec l'hygiène et la pathologie*, Paris, 1880

New York, Shepherd Gallery, *French Nineteenth-Century Drawings, Pastels, Watercolours*, 1977–8

Benedict Nicolson, 'Seurat's La Baignade', *Burlington Magazine*, LXXIX, no. 464, Nov. 1941, pp. 138–46

Linda Nochlin, 'Seurat's Grande Jatte: An Anti-Utopian Allegory', *Art Institute of Chicago Museum Studies*, XIV, no. 2, 1989, pp. 133–53

Gustave Ollendorff, 'La Peinture au Salon de 1885', *Revue des Deux Mondes*, pér. 3, LXIX, 15 June 1885, pp. 909–32

Georges Olmer et Saint-Juirs, *Salon de 1886*, Paris, 1886

'The Paris Ouvrière', *The Boulevard*, no. 25, 15 Oct. 1879

C.A. Padgham and J.E. Saunders, *The Perception of Light and Colour*, London, 1975

J.-N. Paillot de Montabert, *Traité complet de la peinture*, 10 vols. Paris, 1829

Paris, Grand Palais, *Le Musée du Luxembourg en 1874*, 1974

Paris, Grand Palais; Ottawa, National Gallery of Canada; San Francisco, Californian Palace of the Legion of Honor: *Fantin-Latour*, 1983

Paris, Grand Palais; New York, Metropolitan Museum: *Georges Seurat, 1859–1891*, 1991–2

Paris, Musée des Arts Décoratifs, *Souvenir d'Aman-Jean (1859–1936)*, 1970

Paris, Musée d'Orsay, *Van Gogh à Paris*, 1988

Paris, Musée d'Orsay, *Arts incohérents: académie du dérisoire*, 1992

Paris, Petit Palais; Montreal, Musée des Beaux-Arts; Hartford, Conn., Wadsworth Atheneum: *William Bouguereau, 1825–1905*, 1984–5

Paris, Petit Palais, *Le Triomphe des Mairies: grands décors républicains à Paris*, 1986–7

Edmé Périer, *Notes sur la ville d'Asnières*, Asnières, 1890

Patrick-Gilles Persin, *Aman-Jean: peintre de la femme*, Paris, 1993

Joseph Petit, *Asnières*, Nanterre, 1939

'Pierre', 'L'Exposition des Artistes Indépendants', *Le Journal des Arts*, 27 May 1884

'Pierre', 'Concours pour la décoration de la salle des mariages de la Mairie de Courbevoie', *Le Journal des Arts*, 9 Dec. 1884

David Pinkney, *Napoleon III and the Rebuilding of Paris*, Princeton, 1958

Poissy, Musée de Poissy, *Charles Meissonier, 1844–1917: l'héritier*, 1988

R. Piot, *Les Palettes de Delacroix*, Paris 1931

A. Piron, *Eugène Delacroix: sa vie et ses oeuvres*, Paris 1865, repr. as E. Delacroix, *Oeuvres littéraires*, 2 vols., Paris 1923

Griselda Pollock, *Avant-Garde Gambits, 1888–1893: Gender and the Colour of Art History*, London, 1992

Niels Luning Prak, 'Seurat's Surface Pattern and Subject Matter', *Art Bulletin*, LIII, no. 3, Sept. 1971, pp. 367–78

Préfecture du Département de la Seine, Direction des Eaux et des Egouts: renseignements généraux sur les eaux et les egouts de la Ville de Paris, Paris, 1875

Antonin Proust, 'Le Salon de 1882, I', *Gazette des Beaux-Arts*, pér. 2, XXV, June 1882, pp. 533–54

Jean-François Raffaëlli, 'Une Lettre de J.-F. Raffaëlli à Huysmans', *Bulletin de la Société J.-K. Huysmans*, no. 14, May 1936, pp. 232–3

'Récompenses du Salon', *Chronique des Arts et de la Curiosité*, no. 22, 31 May 1884, pp. 174–5

John Rewald, *Georges Seurat*, Paris, 1948; 2nd edn. 1990

John Rewald (ed.), 'Extraits du journal inédit de Paul Signac, I, 1894–1895', *Gazette des Beaux-Arts*, 6th period, XXXVI, 1949, p. 114

John Richardson, *Seurat: Paintings and Drawings*, London, Artemis S.A., 1976

Riom, Musée Mandet, *Alphonse Cornet, 1839–1898*, 1981

K. Robert [pseud. of G. Meusnier], *Traité pratique de peinture à l'huile: paysage*, Paris, 1878

Georges Rivière, *Renoir et ses Amis*, Paris, 1921

O. N. Rood, *Modern Chromatics*, New York, 1879, French edn. 1881

Léon Rosenthal, 'Ernest Laurent', *Art et Décoration*, 3, 1911, pp. 6–76

H. Rossotti, *Colour*, Harmondsworth, 1983

John Russell, *Seurat*, London, 1965

Héléne Seyrès (ed.), *Corresondances, témoignages, notes inédites, critiques*, Paris, 1991

P. D. Sherman, *Colour Vision in the Nineteenth Century: The Young–Helmholtz–Maxwell Theory*, Bristol, 1981

Paul Signac, *D'Eugène Delacroix au néo-impressionnisme*, Paris, 1899 (ed. Françoise Cachin, Paris, 1964)

Armand Silvestre, 'Le Monde des Arts: le Salon de 1881', *La Vie Moderne*, no. 21, 21 May 1881, pp. 324–5

Paul Smith, 'Seurat: The Natural Scientist?', *Apollo*, CXXXII, no. 346, Dec. 1990, pp. 381–5

Paul Smith, 'Was Seurat's Art Wagnerian? And What If It Was?', *Apollo*, CXXXII, no. 353, July 1991, pp. 21–8

Paul Smith, *Seurat and the Avant-Garde*, New Haven and London, 1997

Harriet K. Stratis, 'Beneath the Surface: Redon's Methods and Materials', in *Odilon Redon: Prince of Dreams*, exhibition catalaogue, Art Institute of Chicago; Amsterdam, Van Gogh Museum; London, Royal Academy: 1994–5

David Sutter, *Esthétique générale et appliquée contenant les règles de la composition dans les arts plastiques*, Paris, 1865

David Sutter, 'Les Phénomènes de la vision;, *L'Art*, VI, 1, Feb.–March 1880

Jean Sutter, 'Recherches sur la vie de Georges Seurat (1859–1891)', unpublished typescript, Paris, 1964

Richard Thomson, *Seurat*, Oxford, 1985

Richard Thomson, 'Van Gogh in Paris: The Fortifications Drawings of 1887', *Jong Holland*, III, no. 3, Sept. 1987, pp. 14–25

Richard Thomson, *Degas: The Nudes*, London, 1988

Richard Thomson, 'The Grande Jatte: Notes on Drawing and Meaning', *The Art Institute of Chicago Museum Studies*, XIV, no. 2, 1989, pp. 181–97

Richard Thomson, *Monet to Matisse: Landscape Painting in France, 1874–1914*, Edinburgh, 1994

Richard Tilston, *Seurat*, London, 1991

Robert Tombs, *The War against Paris, 1871*, Cambridge, 1981

Musée de Toulon, *Le Musée à cent ans*, 1988–9

Hélène Toussaint, *Les Portraits d'Ingres: peintures des musées nationaux*, Paris, 1985

'Trublot' [Paul Alexis], 'A Minuit: les Indépendants', *Le Cri du Peuple*, 17 May 1884

Paul Tucker, *Monet at Argenteuil*, New Haven and London, 1982

L. Venturi, 'Piero della Francesca – Seurat – Gris', *Diogenes*, II, Spring 1953, pp. 19–23

Richard Verdi, 'Poussin's Life in Nineteenth-Century Pictures', *Burlington Magazine*, CXI, no. 801, Dec. 1969, pp. 741–50

Emile Verhaeren, 'Georges Seurat', *Société Nouvelle*, April 1891, repr. in *Sensations*, Paris, 1927, p. 198

Eugène Veron, 'L'Ecole française de peinture en 1877: notes et réflexions', *L'Art*, XI, 1877, pp. 176–9

Théodore Véron, *9e Annuaire: Dictionnaire Véron ou Organe de l'Institut Universel des Sciences, des Lettres et des Arts du XIXe Siècle (Section des Beaux-Arts), Salon de 1883*, Paris and Poitiers, 1883

H. Vuagneux, *Courbevoie et ses environs*, Poissy, 1906

Martha Ward, 'The Eighth Exhibition: The Rhetoric of Independence and Innovation', in, Washington 1986, pp. 421–39

Washington, DC, National Gallery of Art; San Francisco, Fine Arts Museums, *The New Painting: Impressionism, 1874–1886*, 1986

J. Watrous, *The Craft of Old Master Drawings*, Madison, 1957

Dorothy Weir Young, *The Life and Letters of J. Alden Weir*, New Haven, 1960

Daniel Wildenstein, *Claude Monet: biographie et catalogue raisonné*, I, Lausanne and Paris, 1974

Michael L. Zimmermann, 'Seurat, Charles Blanc, and Naturalist Art Criticism', *The Art Institute of Chicago Museum Studies*, XIV, no. 2, 1989, pp. 199–209

Michael L. Zimmermann, *Seurat and the Art Theory of his Time*, Antwerp, 1991

Index

Photographic Credits

© ADAGP, Paris and DACS, London 1997: Plates 36, 39, 134, 163, 164, 165, 169

© DACS 1997: Plate 19

Bordeaux, Photograph © Musée des Beaux-Arts de Bordeaux: Plate 148

Boston, Mass., © 1997 Museum of Fine Arts, Boston, all rights reserved: Plates 16, 124

Cambridge, by kind permission of the Provost and Fellows of King's College, Cambridge; Plate 157

Carcassonne, Photograph Patrice Cartier: Plates 149, 150

Chicago, Photograph © 1997, The Art Institute of Chicago, all rights reserved: Plates 60, 153, 168

Cleveland, Ohio, © The Cleveland Museum of Art: Plate 57

Cognac, Phototype Ch. Collas & Cie, Cognac, Plate 141

Courbevoie, Photograph Jean-Pierre Copitet: Plate 118

Edinburgh, Photograph Joe Rock: Plates 126, 131

Hamburg, Photograph Elka Walford, Hamburg: Plate 34

Göteborg, Photograph Silvio Plehan: Plate 121

London, By permission of the British Library: Plates 38 (8708.cc.17), 47 (786.1.35)

London, © British Museum: Plates 18, 156, 158

London, Photograph Courtauld Institute of Art: Plates 102, 111

London, © Tate Gallery, London 1997: Plates 58, 152 (Presented by Arthur R. Anderson, 1927)

Merion, Pa., Photograph © 1997 by the Barnes Foundation, all rights reserved: Plate 171

Nantes, Photograph Ville de Nantes: Plate 105

New York, Christie's Images: Plate 125

New York, Copyright © 1997 By The Metropolitan Museum of Art, all rights reserved: Plates 20, 115, 159

New York, Photograph © 1997 The Museum of Modern Art, New York; Plate 167

Nice, Photograph Lorenzo, Artephot: Plate 133

Norwich, Photograph James Austin: Plate 24

Oslo, Photograph J. Lathion, © Nasjonalgalleriet 1997: Plate 130

Oxford, © Ashmolean Museum, University of Oxford: Plate 17

Paris, Photograph Giraudon: Plate 29

Paris, Photograph © Arch. Phot. Paris/CNMHS: Plate 110

Paris, Photographie Brassaï, © Copyright Gilberte Brassaï, all rights reserved: Plate 177

Paris, Photograph © RMN: Plates 4, 55 (photograph Hervé Lewandowski), 74, 103 (photograph Arnaudet) 114; 132

Paris, Photograph © Photothèque des Musées de la Ville de Paris: Plates 116, 134, 147

Poitiers, Service photographique, Musée de Poitiers, photograph Christian Vignaud: Plate 151

Sceaux, Photograph Pascal Lemaitre: Plates 26, 138

Stockholm, Photograph Bildarkivet Nationalmuseum: Plate 65

Troyes, Donation Pierre et Denise Lévy: Plate 36

Washington, DC, © 1997 Board of Trustees, National Gallery of Art: Plates 28, 174

Washington, DC, © The Phillips Collection: Plates 21, 173

Williamstown, Mass., © Sterling and Francine Clark Art Institute: Plate 107

178. *Bathers at Asnières*, 1884
Oil on canvas, 201 x 300 cm
London, National Gallery (CAT. 1)